Born Entrepreneurs, Born Leaders

Born Entrepreneurs, Born Leaders

How Your Genes Affect Your Work Life

SCOTT SHANE

OXFORD
UNIVERSITY PRESS

2010

OXFORD
UNIVERSITY PRESS

Oxford University Press, Inc., publishes works that further
Oxford University's objective of excellence
in research, scholarship, and education.

Oxford   New York
Auckland   Cape Town   Dar es Salaam   Hong Kong   Karachi
Kuala Lumpur   Madrid   Melbourne   Mexico City   Nairobi
New Delhi   Shanghai   Taipei   Toronto

With offices in
Argentina   Austria   Brazil   Chile   Czech Republic   France   Greece
Guatemala   Hungary   Italy   Japan   Poland   Portugal   Singapore
South Korea   Switzerland   Thailand   Turkey   Ukraine   Vietnam

Published by Oxford University Press, Inc.
198 Madison Avenue, New York, NY 10016

www.oup.com

Oxford is a registered trademark of Oxford University Press

Library of Congress Cataloging-in-Publication Data
Shane, Scott.
Born entrepreneurs, born leaders : how your
genes affect your work life / Scott Shane.
p. cm.
Includes index.
ISBN   978-0-19-537342-4
1. Behavior genetics.   2. Psychology, Industrial.   I. Title.
QH457.S53 2010
158.7—dc22   2009011648

1 3 5 7 9 8 6 4 2

Printed in the United States of America
on acid-free paper

To Lynne, Ryan, and Hannah

Contents

Acknowledgments

I decided to write this book after spending several years researching the effects of genetics on entrepreneurial activity. Ever since my colleague Nicos Nicolaou first came to me with the idea of examining the genetic basis of entrepreneurship, I have been fascinated with how genes influence work-related behavior. It seems that the colloquial phrase "born entrepreneur" is true; some people have an innate predisposition to start businesses.

While I enjoy authoring scholarly articles, carefully outlining my research for my peers, I also like writing for a broader audience. I believe that good research can be explained to thoughtful readers in a clear and entertaining way. I have written books on a number of topics that have followed this model of translating academic research into something that nonacademic readers could follow and enjoy. But I had not done that for my work on genetics and business.

At first I wasn't sure that I should write such a book. I'm not a genetics expert. I got interested in the topic from the perspective of a business school researcher seeking to explain business, not from the point of view of a geneticist seeking to examine genetics. But when I began to post some blogs about my research on genetics and entrepreneurship, I was emboldened. There was tremendous interest in this line of research (dare I say, much more than the other topics I have looked at). I realized that most people weren't interested in the science behind what I was doing, or even the way that researchers need to design their studies to get their answers. While those things are important, most readers wanted to know what I and other researchers had found, and the implications of those findings.

Originally, I thought I would write a book about genetics and entrepreneurship. But I quickly realized that topic would be too narrow. Not only is there insufficient research to support a book-length manuscript, but also most prospective readers were interested in more than just how genetics influences business formation. They were interested in genetic effects on entrepreneurship as part of the wider effect of DNA on work-related behavior. So I broadened my scope to include that topic.

No book like this is ever really written by one author. While I discuss some of my own work in chapter 9, most of what I have done is to translate the research of other academics into language that most people can understand, and to highlight the implications of those studies for your work life. Therefore, this book would have been impossible without many researchers' scholarly efforts. I hope that my footnotes to their work will provide sufficient acknowledgment of my debt of gratitude for their tireless efforts to make the discoveries discussed in this book.

Several people helped me immensely in writing the book. First, and foremost, I must thank Nicos Nicolaou, who brought the idea of genetic influences on business activity to my attention and has been my co-author on a number of scholarly articles in this area. I would also like to thank Tim Spector and Lynn Cherkas of the Department of Twin Research & Genetic Epidemiology at St. Thomas Hospital and King's College London. It is in concert with Tim and Lynn, and from data that they collected, that Nicos and I have written most of our scholarly articles on genetics and entrepreneurship.

Four people read drafts of this book and provided very valuable comments on it: Peter Little, Jay Narayanan, Nicos Nicolaou, and Barbara Oakley. This book would not have been possible without your help.

Lastly, I would like to thank my wife, Lynne; daughter, Hannah; and son, Ryan. Each of you helped me in your own ways. Hannah and Ryan assisted me by being excellent playmates when I needed breaks from writing. Lynne aided by encouraging and supporting my efforts to write this book.

Born Entrepreneurs, Born Leaders

1

Introduction

If you are like most people, you probably recognize intuitively that your genes—the DNA that makes you who you are—affect your work life. At the most basic level, you probably believe that being tall is important to becoming a professional basketball player, and you might even blame your height for the fact that you don't currently play for the New York Knicks. Since you probably remember enough high school biology to recognize that your genes affect how tall you are, you probably have a gut sense that your DNA is at least partially responsible for your failure to get drafted into the NBA.

If you thought about it a little bit more, you'd probably realize that your genes affect other things about your work life, too. If you are among the large number of people who wear glasses or contact lenses because your eyesight is worse than 20/70, you don't have good enough vision to be a military pilot.[1] So the variants of the genes that affect eyesight influence your job choice, too. And unless you are among the small number of supermodels reading this book, you might have even cursed your parents for the genes that kept you from that modeling career. In fact, you might even think that genetics has something to do with the business success of your annoying brother-in-law—the one all the relatives refer to as a "born entrepreneur."

But even though you probably recognize at some level that your genes affect your work life, you probably haven't thought about the myriad of influences that your genes have on your job choice, work performance, work values, career, job satisfaction, and a variety of

1

other aspects of life at the office. Moreover, you are unlikely to have considered the wide-ranging implications that genetic effects have for you, your employer, and for policy makers.

Genes Affect Nearly Everything

For decades now, researchers have been systematically studying the effect of genes on human activity. The results of these efforts might seem astonishing to those of you unaccustomed to thinking about genetics. Our DNA affects pretty much *all aspects of behavior*, from educational performance to job satisfaction to entrepreneurship to voting preferences, and so on.

For example, numerous studies have shown that genes account for a big portion of the difference between people in both intelligence and personality. More than half of the variance between people in scores on both IQ assessments and tests of the OCEAN model of personality are genetic. (The OCEAN model is also known as the big five model of personality. It is made up of the dimensions of openness to experience, conscientiousness, extraversion, agreeableness, and neuroticism, which spell OCEAN if the first letter of each personality characteristic is used as its abbreviation.)

But our genes affect much more than our level of intelligence or our personality; they also affect whether we generally view the world positively or negatively, whether we have high or low activity levels, whether we are better at math or writing, whether we are rich or poor, whether we are satisfied with or hate our jobs, whether we want to start our own businesses or work for someone else, whether we are charismatic leaders (getting others to follow our direction by dint of our personality) or transactional leaders (motivating others to do what we ask by offering them rewards); and a host of other things. In fact, our genes even influence much of the difference between us in the quality of our first impressions;[2] and the odds that we will vote in an election.[3]

In recent years, researchers have gone beyond studies that calculate the share of behavior that is explained by genetic factors to identify the variants of specific genes that account for behavioral differences. For instance, researchers have found that two serotonin system genes (the serotonin system influences our level of social interaction and trust in others) account for about 10 percent of the variance among people in their odds of voting in an election.[4]

But the specific genes that influence behavior aren't limited to just these two serotonin system genes, and their effects aren't confined to voting. Studies have now shown that a number of different genes, particularly those that influence the production of the neurotransmitters dopamine and serotonin (chemicals that control brain function) affect risk taking, responsiveness to stress, impulsivity, novelty seeking, and a host of other human attributes that influence work life.[5]

Take, for example, how people choose between alternatives with uncertain outcomes, such as financial investments in two projects. Some people select the option that has a greater chance of succeeding, while other people pick the one with the higher expected value (the odds of succeeding multiplied by the payoff from success or failure). It turns out that a difference in the DNA sequence for a serotonin gene influences whether people focus on the odds of winning, or overall expected value, when choosing between uncertain alternatives.[6]

The Business World Ignores Genetics

The effect of our genes on our work life isn't discussed very much in business publications. Despite the large body of research showing that genes influence a wide range of human behaviors, including many that are found in the workplace, the role of genetics gets a couple of paragraphs of mention, at most, in management textbooks. And in more popular business books, the role of genetics is pretty much ignored.

Most writers don't look carefully at genetic effects on work-related behavior because they start with the assumption that we are all born as blank slates. Whatever happens to us, and whatever work-related behaviors we develop, they contend, is a function of the choices we make. Free will and self-made behavior are the dominant philosophical concepts underpinning business writing, and no one wants to spend much time on things that don't fit neatly into that package.

But just because research on genetics lies outside most writers' preconceived notions doesn't mean genes are irrelevant. Even though people are complex, and what we do in organizations is influenced by a wide variety of factors, genetics research can help us to understand how we act in the workplace. And even if you don't like the idea of genetic influences on job-related behavior, you can't make these effects go away by ignoring them. Whatever your view on genetics, you need to consider how they influence activity in the work world. *Because* genes matter, understanding *how* they affect behavior is important to employers, employees, and policy makers.

That's where this book comes in. Its goal is to summarize the vast body of research on genetics and different aspects of your work life and to reveal its implications. This book discusses how your genes influence your work interests, work values, decision making, risk taking, management style, approach to leadership, creativity, entrepreneurship, and work performance, among other aspects of your work life. More important, this book outlines the implications of these genetic effects for you, your employer, and policy makers.

What Does "Genetic" Mean?

This book is serious about discussing the influence of genetics on work-related behavior. So, rather than casually saying some people are "born entrepreneurs" or that "leadership must be in their genes," I look at what research shows about how your genes *actually influence* your behavior in the workplace. To do that, I need to offer up a few definitions about matters genetic before getting into the substance of the discussion.

Genes are the basic unit of heredity. They are composed of deoxyribonucleic acid (DNA), which carries instructions for how to make molecules called proteins.[7] Genes come in different versions (called alleles) that provide alternative instructions for making the proteins that they are tasked with producing. Which protein-making plans you get depends on the variants that your parents have to pass on to you. When this book discusses "genetic differences," it is referring to the differences in the instructions for the production of proteins that are transferred from parents to their children through their DNA. When this book discusses "genetic influences on work-related behavior" it is referring to the effect that differences in the DNA codes for protein production have on how people act in the work world.

The next chapter will get into how variations in codes for the production of proteins can influence behaviors and attitudes, such as the type of leader that a person becomes or whether the individual is willing to make risky investments. But before we get there, we need to deal with three important issues: the fear people have when they think about genetics and human behavior, what researchers are saying, and not saying, when they talk about genetic effects on behavior, and why you should care about how your genes influence your actions and attitudes at work. Let's start with the fear.

The Fear Problem

Discussions about genetic effects on human behavior upset a lot of people. While few object to the idea that genes impact attributes like hair color, many believe that evidence of a genetic influence on behavior cheapens human volition. They think that if genetics affects how human beings act, then people are no longer making choices, becoming characters programmed at birth, in ways reminiscent of a B-grade science fiction movie. One author summed up this perspective quite clearly when he said,

> If we are only living out our lives like actors reading our lines, then the nobility of life is cheapened. Our accomplishments are not really earned, they are simply arrived at. Our failures are just as expectable. We are like genetic rockets, programmed to travel in a set direction with a given amount of fuel. Barring some accident of fate, our trajectory is predetermined—we are just along for the ride.[8]

Many people also dislike genetic studies because they believe that the information gathered by researchers will be used for evil purposes— to categorize human beings before they are born, to justify maltreatment of certain individuals, to "prove" racist theories, or to selectively create men and women that fit desired goals.[9] In fact, a survey by Johns Hopkins University's Genetics and Public Policy Center found that 92 percent of Americans were concerned that others would use their genetic information adversely.[10]

There is no denying the fact that genetics has been used for some terrible purposes in the past. Members of the eugenics movement of the early twentieth century, which sought to "improve" human traits by selective breeding, gave genetics a negative reputation by using it to justify not only discrimination but the forced sterilization—even killing—of certain groups of people.[11] Josef Mengele, a German scientist and SS officer, further contributed to genetics' bad name for his horrific experiments on twins in Nazi concentration camps, conducted in the name of research on heredity.

However, these fears reflect a misunderstanding of what knowledge of the influence of genetics on workplace behavior really means. Just because our genes affect behavior does *not* mean that people can no longer make their own choices about what to think or how to act. Genes are not destiny; they are merely one more factor that affects the odds that something will occur. Just like learning that the opposing team's quarterback has an injured finger on his throwing hand might increase the chances that you will beat the line on your bet on this Sunday's football game, knowing that you have version A of a gene rather than version B might affect the probability that you will have high job satisfaction. (Non-U.S. readers: substitute "the opposing team's striker has an injured toe on one of his feet" for the description of the quarterback in the previous sentence and you'll get the picture.) Knowing that you have the favorable version of a gene no more guarantees that you will be satisfied in your job than knowing about the player's injury ensures that you will win your bet.

Ironically, it's the failure to acknowledge that your genes influence your work-related behavior that *increases* the chance that biology will become destiny, not the other way around. As noted author Louann Brizendine wrote in *The Female Brain,*

> If you're aware of the fact that a biological brain state is guiding your impulses, you can choose not to act or to act differently than you might feel compelled. But first we have to learn to recognize how the ... brain is genetically structured. ... Without that recognition, biology becomes destiny and we will be helpless in the face of it. ... If in the name of free will—and political correctness—we try to deny the influence of biology on the brain, we are fighting our own nature. ... Biology powerfully affects but does not lock in our reality. ... Understanding our innate biology empowers us to better plan our future.[12]

Sadly, it is those who are unwilling to acknowledge the effect that their genes have on their behavior who are most likely to become prisoners of their biology.

Knowledge of how genetics affects work-related behavior doesn't mean that such information will be used for evil. Genetic information, like all data, can be used for good and bad purposes. An understanding of genetic effects on behavior can be employed to justify eugenics, but it can also be used to improve people's lives through targeted interventions that help those with a genetic predisposition perform better.

Failure to gather valuable genetic information in the name of avoiding potentially bad uses will keep us from realizing the benefits of genetics.

Moreover, the potential for misuse of genetic information is no reason to avoid understanding the impact of genes on behavior. Pretending that DNA doesn't affect how people act on the job isn't going to make genetic influences go away. It's just going to make people ignorant of those effects. Everyone, that is, except those who want to misuse the information.

If we think that people will employ genetic data in undesirable ways, then we need to put proper safeguards in place. That's what we do with other types of information. Take, for example, inside knowledge of companies' unannounced decisions. People misuse this type of information all the time. Does that mean we should pretend that people can't make money trading stocks on the basis of inside tips? No. It means that we need to understand how this type of knowledge can be used and misused and, to the extent that it can be employed improperly, put the right controls in place to minimize its misuse. The same is true for genetic information. We need to understand how genetics influences workplace behavior and then figure out the proper controls to institute to minimize the misuse of this information.

Caveats and Limitations

Because genetics is such a hot-button topic, I want to clarify a few things about what this book is arguing and not arguing. Very simply, my thesis is that it is *very* unlikely that what people do in organizations is *solely* the result of environmental forces. Genetic factors influence the tendency of people to engage in workplace behaviors in a myriad of ways, and these effects have implications that you should be aware of.

So, what am I *not* arguing? First, I am definitely, certainly, unequivocally not arguing that your genes *determine* anything about your work-related activity. Genes don't *cause* people to engage in any behaviors or hold any attitudes.[13] They merely influence the odds that someone will engage in those behaviors or hold those attitudes. Moreover, even if a person has a gene variant that increases the chances that she will engage in a certain behavior, she can act counter to that genetic propensity. Just as people with the blond version of the hair-color genes can dye their hair brown, people with the pro-novelty version of the novelty-seeking genes can follow familiar routines.[14]

Second, I am definitely, certainly, unequivocally *not* saying that the environment has zero effect on your workplace behavior. Just because this book focuses on the ways that your genes impact how you act at work doesn't mean that the environment lacks influence. The reality is that, for most things about us, genetic and environmental factors both matter. Consider height, for example. Some of us have variants of genes that make us shorter, while others have versions that make us taller. But the height genes' effects don't negate environmental influences on how tall we are. In fact, studies have shown that improved diet and other contextual factors have led the average height of people in different countries to go up, even among people who have the "short" versions of the "height" genes.[15]

The same is true for the workplace behaviors discussed in this book. For instance, some people have variants of genes that increase their odds of starting businesses. This genetic endowment means that these people have a greater chance of becoming entrepreneurs than other people. But environmental factors, such as access to capital, still affect the odds that people will go into business for themselves.[16] So if you suddenly received some money from winning the lottery, your probability of starting a company would go up. In this case, the environmental factor, how much capital you have, and your genes both influence your odds of becoming an entrepreneur.

In fact, this book doesn't even argue that genetic factors are more important determinants of your work-related behavior than environmental forces. For many aspects of workplace behavior, genes influence a minority of the difference among people, with most of that variation being a function of people's experiences and the situations they are in. All this book is saying is that your genetic endowment affects a sizable chunk of your work-related attitudes and behaviors, a big enough portion that genetic effects aren't trivial, and shouldn't be ignored.

Third, I am not arguing that a single gene for leadership, job satisfaction, or entrepreneurship exists in the way that one gene explains why people are afflicted with certain disorders, like Huntington's disease. Work-related behaviors, like leadership and job satisfaction, are complex and varied, and the causal chain from encoding a particular protein to engaging in the behaviors is pretty long, making it *very* unlikely that a particular version of a *single* gene accounts for the differences between people in their tendency to take part in these things. To date, there is little evidence of a single gene accounting for any aspect of human behavior—from intelligence to personality.

It's true that a mutation in a single gene causes Huntington's disease, a disorder in which those afflicted develop antisocial personality traits. And a variant of a single gene related to the neurotransmitter monoamine oxidase A (MAOA), which I'll call the "antisocial" gene, can predispose a person to hostile or disruptive behavior. However, for most behaviors, tens, if not hundreds, of genes are probably involved, with each gene influencing only a small portion of our behavior. For instance, if genetics accounts for 40 percent of the difference between people in whether they take charge of a group, and 40 genes affect this process, each gene would, on average, be responsible for only 1 percent of the variance in the tendency to become a leader. Moreover, some genes respond to environmental stimuli, influencing behavior only if a person has certain experiences and not others. Therefore, typically, the link between genes and behavior is far more complex than a straightforward one gene-one behavior relationship.

(Although the connection between genes and behavior is rarely one-to-one, throughout this book I give all of the genes descriptive names, as I did with MAOA, which I called the "antisocial" gene in the previous paragraph. I am sure that many geneticists will be bothered by this approach because it could give the casual reader the impression of a far less complex relationship between DNA and human action than a single adjectival name can express. However, most of you, the readers of this book, are not scientists and would have a hard time remembering what behaviors different genes influence if I called them all solely by their scientific names: MAOA, DRD2, AVPR1A, COMT, and so on. To remind you that the monikers I give the genes don't mean that the named gene is the only one that affects the outcome being discussed, I put the descriptive name in quotes and provide the scientific name in parentheses.)

Fourth, I'm not saying that the genetic factors that influence the likelihood of engaging in certain work-related behaviors, such as the tendency to start businesses, *only* affect those things and nothing else. In fact, most genes almost certainly impact more than work in organizations, given the number of generations necessary for our genes to evolve and the length of time that the concept of business has existed. Over the period that people have engaged in organized work, very little of our genetic makeup has changed.[17]

For instance, the human genome hasn't changed enough over the relatively short period since human beings first began starting their own companies for us to have developed genes that govern *only* our tendency to engage in entrepreneurship. Because we had pretty much the same genes in prehistoric times that we have now, it seems much more likely that the genes that influence the odds of going into business for oneself also encode for something else that was present in prehistoric times, such as intelligence or temperament.

Fifth, I am definitely *not* saying that genetics accounts for racial or ethnic differences in work-related behavior. These types of arguments have given genetics a bad name and have very little scientific basis. The differences among groups of people (e.g., races) in the characteristics that genes influence, such as general intelligence, are very small relative to the differences among individuals within those groups.[18] Therefore, the genetic effects on work-related behavior discussed in this book are effects on differences among *individuals*, not groups of people.

Finally, I am starting with the assumption that genetic differences across people exist and focusing my attention on how that variance influences work-related behavior. A whole literature on evolution exists to describe *why* human beings have different versions of their genes, including those that affect behavior. This book doesn't discuss these evolutionary accounts because the subject is so vast that it would take another entire book to do it justice. Moreover, the evolutionary explanations for human behavior aren't yet well developed, and the theories remain controversial. From an academic perspective, the absence of an evolutionary context for the material presented in this book might be a limitation, but, for most of you, it shouldn't be a problem. I suspect that most readers of this book are interested in *how* genetic differences affect workplace behavior, not *why* that variance has emerged.

Why Should You Care?

Two genetics researchers made a very straightforward statement in a scientific journal recently. They wrote, "It has become increasingly accepted that traits, attitudes, and behaviors relevant to the workplace have a genetic component."[19] This statement shows that the scientific community doesn't view the effect of DNA on workplace behavior as controversial. Scientists recognize that what you do at work is influenced by your genes. In fact, studies show that over *one-third* of the difference between people on virtually every employment-related dimension investigated, including work interests, work values, job satisfaction, job choice, leadership turnover, job performance, and income, is genetic.

Don't you think you should know about things that affect more than one-third of the difference between you and the person in the next cubicle over? I'll bet that if something nongenetic accounted for a third of the variance between you and your coworkers in things like job satisfaction and income, you'd want to know what that was.

Second, the effect of your genes on work-related behavior is becoming more important over time. Genetics accounts for more of the difference among people when variation in environmental conditions narrows. And the environment in developed countries has been affecting people more equally over time. Think about how people were treated 250 or even 50 years ago as compared to how they are treated today. Two hundred and fifty years ago, if your father was a merchant, then you'd probably have been a merchant too; if he was a farmer that is what you'd have become. If your dad was a member of the aristocracy, then, well, your life would have been quite good.

If you were a man, that is. If you were a woman, your role in the world of commerce would have been very limited, regardless of whether you had the genetic makeup to be a true business leader. Even 50 years ago, if you were black, your odds of attaining a leadership position in business or politics were very small, regardless of your genetics. Now, we have a black president of the United States. As the environment places fewer restrictions on what we can become, genetics has emerged as a more powerful influence. Over time, genetics is accounting for more and more of the difference among us in our work-related behaviors and attitudes.

Third, seeing how your genes affect you on the job will help you understand why you do what you do. Research shows that most people are very poor at self-assessment. Because most of us generally don't have a good sense of how we think and why we act, we don't do as well at most activities as we could. Anything—genetic or environmental—that helps us to better understand ourselves helps to improve our work performance. So seeing how genes affect employment-related behavior will help you in the same way that recognizing other influences on how you act at work, from the temperature of your office to the tone of your boss's voice, impacts the way you do your job.

Fourth, your success in the work world depends on your ability to make the most of "what you've got"—your skills, personality, attitude, and so on. Knowing where your strengths and weaknesses lie helps you to accentuate the former and compensate for the latter, making you more effective at leading, managing, making decisions, or just being happy in your job.[20] This is true whether your advantages and disadvantages are the result of how your parents raised you or the genes they gave you.[21] As Tom Harrison, author of *Instinct*, a book about how people's genes influence their entrepreneurial abilities, asks, "If you are born with a predisposition to being analytical or outgoing or emotional, doesn't it make sense to take advantage of these natural strengths instead of trying to fit yourself into a mold that forces you to work against who you are?"[22]

On the other hand, knowledge of how genetics influences your behavior is also useful for acting in ways contrary to your "nature." How you behave at work is not genetically predetermined; your genes just make you more likely to conduct yourself in certain ways and not others. You can always overcome your genetic predispositions, and information about your natural tendencies helps you to identify where to put your efforts to do so.

For example, suppose you have a genetic proclivity to be risk averse. You can become just as much of a gambler as someone who is genetically predisposed to take chances. But training yourself to become a risk taker will be more difficult for you than for your genetically inclined counterpart. That's where information about your innate tendencies is valuable. Knowing that you have to work twice as hard as other people to become a risk taker tells you how to spend your time and effort. You might need to practice the 10 steps to becoming a better risk taker outlined in the book recommended by the human resource consultant to your company, even though the guy in the office next to yours seems to manage fine without cracking it open.

Sixth, understanding the influence of genetics on work-related behaviors highlights the importance of fit between people and organizations. People have different attitudes, skills, and abilities, and organizations are looking for employees with certain of these and not others. That's not controversial. In fact, it's standard human resource management practice. But attitudes, skills, and abilities aren't easy to change because they depend, in part, on genetic factors. Even though people can alter their beliefs and abilities, innate tendencies create resistance to change, pushing attitudes and skills to be consistent with genetic predispositions. Because your attitudes, skills, and abilities are relatively difficult to shift, having the right fit for your job is important to your performance and your happiness.

Take, for example, the case of an applicant for a customer service job. Certain people are genetically predisposed to display negative emotions; they tend to see life from the perspective of a half-empty glass, rather than a half-full one. These pessimistic people can train themselves to be rosy and optimistic, but that's difficult for them. So, typically, they don't change their brooding nature.

This genetic predisposition shows why it is so important for people to find jobs that fit. People with a pessimistic outlook don't do very well in customer service because their negativity undermines the customer experience. And if a glass-is-half-empty worldview is largely a function of genetic factors, those genetically predisposed to pessimism will find training to be optimistic difficult. As a result, people with a genetic proclivity to display negative emotions may be better off finding something to do other than customer service work.

This doesn't mean that people who are genetically predisposed to have a less-than-rosy outlook on life won't be able to find good jobs. Pessimism is useful for some activities, which makes these individuals a better fit for some jobs than optimists. For example, people with an innate tendency to be pessimistic probably make better hedge fund managers, or at least superior investors in financial markets. Researchers have found that people with a more negative worldview invest more successfully in the stock market than those with a more positive outlook on life because they are more cautious investors and are more willing to abandon losing positions.[23]

Seventh, knowledge of genetic effects on work-related behaviors helps to make sense of the concept of fairness in the work world. We often assume that everyone has equal odds of achieving a variety of organizational outcomes: earnings, promotion, job satisfaction, and so on. But, in reality, their chances are not the same. People have different personalities, attitudes, skills, and abilities, and these individual attributes influence our odds of making a lot of money, or becoming a company CEO. Of course, this point really shouldn't surprise you. If you watch *American Idol*, you almost certainly realize not everyone has the voice to become a professional singer.

Whether you have the right personality to be a good salesman, the leadership ability to be a CEO, or the voice to become a rock star, depends on how you were raised, your life experience, and your genetic endowment. While the first two factors are beyond the theme of this book, the third one has implications for understanding our sense of workplace fairness. Genetic effects on personality and leadership, as well as on other attitudes and abilities, highlight the fallacy of assuming that everyone has an equal chance of playing in the NBA, being a rock star, achieving high earnings, getting a promotion, or even being satisfied with a job. Because of their DNA, some people have better odds of achieving certain outcomes than other people.

The unlevel playing field raises the fairness question. If some people, but not others, have genetic predispositions to achieve certain outcomes, rewarding employees for reaching those goals, treats individuals with different genetic endowments unequally. For instance, as chapter 7 explains in greater detail, some people have an innate tendency to be good leaders. Is it fair to reward employees financially for successfully completing leadership training programs, as Frito-Lay does? After all, that is tantamount to paying some employees, at least partially, for being born with the right genes.

This isn't very fair, especially when you realize that we don't give people bonuses for other victories in the genetic lottery. For instance, we don't pay employees extra for being good-looking, even though their attractiveness affects their performance as leaders, in sales, and at a host of other things. So why should we reward people for being born with a genetic predisposition to develop charisma but not an innate tendency to be attractive, when both of these attributes increase the odds that someone will be a good leader? If we are rewarding employees for having "good genes," why not compensate for all of them?

Eighth, knowing about the influence of genetics helps us to be more realistic about our ability to alter people's work-related behavior through organizational design initiatives, incentive programs, changes to work climate, or any of the myriad of other things that business books and human resource consultants tell us to do. Perhaps because offering advice sells consulting work, and explaining the difficulty of changing workplace conduct does not, there's a cottage industry advising managers how to shift employee behavior by altering external factors, such as the incentives people are given or the structure of the organizations in which they work.

Take job satisfaction, for instance. The prevailing wisdom is that we can make people happier with their jobs by increasing their pay or improving their working conditions. But when companies make these changes, they often find that the average job satisfaction of their employees doesn't improve very much. Genetics helps to explain why. Genetic effects on workplace behaviors mean that some portion of how people act at work is *not* the result of external factors, such as pay or working conditions, but is caused by something innate.

Understanding genetic effects on behavior tells us *how much* changes in external factors should influence work-related behaviors. If genetic factors were to account for all of the difference in people's on-the-job behavior, then environmental factors, such as pay or working conditions, would have no effect *at all*. So the genetic portion of the variance in work-related outcomes tells us whether changing external factors is likely to have a small or a large impact.

Consider job satisfaction again. Research shows that genetic factors account for 30 percent of the difference among people in whether they are happy with their jobs.[24] This means that external forces, such as pay or working conditions, influence no more than 70 percent of the variance in job satisfaction. Because environmental factors can only work on 70 percent (rather than 100 percent) of the difference among people in their workplace contentment, it's harder to use tools, such as higher pay or better working conditions, to improve employee job satisfaction than many people think.

Ninth, understanding genetics will help you to identify the right external forces to alter workplace outcomes. Genetic factors often interact with environmental influences to affect behavior. So, if you want to alter how people act, you need to know what external factor will trigger a behavioral change. Once again, consider the example of job satisfaction. Anyone interested in improving employee happiness among those with a genetic tendency to be content at work needs to know whether incentive pay or better working conditions is the right trigger for job satisfaction. If your DNA predisposes you to become happier at work if you get a raise, but makes your job satisfaction immune to the nastiness of your boss, then your employer's ability to enhance your contentment on the job depends on increasing your pay, not changing your supervisor.

Onward to the Details

Having made the case for why you should care about genetic effects on work-related behavior, I now turn to the details of how genetics influences different aspects of work life. What follows might frighten some people and intrigue others. But if I do my job right, it certainly won't bore you.

2

DNA at Work: Your Genes and Organizational Behavior

An Australian company called Genetic Technologies offers a test to identify the version of the ACTN3 gene people have. With a simple swab of the mouth, a person can gather some DNA and ship it to the company's lab. Within four weeks, the company will send back a report that identifies which sports the person is best suited for.

The company's product is based on research that shows that people with a certain version of the ACTN3 gene, which I will call the "sports" gene, don't make alpha-actinin-3, a protein that allows muscles to contract powerfully and quickly. People who received copies of one version of this gene from both of their parents are predisposed to be good at endurance sports, such as running or swimming long distances. Those who didn't receive this version of the gene from either parent are more likely to be skilled at power sports, such as weightlifting and football.

Although scientists point out that as many as 200 genes influence athletic ability, and environmental factors also matter a great deal, people are beginning to send away for this genetic test. They want to know if their kids are predisposed to become professional athletes (or at least good at certain sports), and if they are, how to coach them to develop their natural talents. While the test might only indicate the presence of one of many genes that help a child to be a better athlete, parents are interested in learning that information.[1]

This example raises some important questions. How do your genes influence your odds of becoming a professional athlete, or leader or entrepreneur? How do they shape your interest in different domains, such as business, the arts and sports? How do your genes affect whether you are happy with your job and prone to stay in it, or perennially dissatisfied with work and always looking to leave? The "how" question is a fundamental one for most people interested in understanding how heredity influences work-related outcomes, and a good place to start a discussion of a genetic basis for organizational behavior.

Unfortunately for those of us without a background in molecular genetics, the relationship between your genes and your behavior at work isn't straightforward. There's no gene for leadership, "liking baseball," "favoring detail-oriented jobs," or becoming an Olympic athlete. Unlike Huntington's disease (for which a single gene controls whether or not you get the disorder), there is no one gene that *determines* anything about your work life. So we can't just look at the map of the human genome and identify genes that govern the tendency to engage in different on-the-job activities. And even if we could, those genes probably wouldn't directly affect your work-related behavior. Rather, they would probably interact with each other and a variety of external factors to influence how you act at work.[2]

In short, while your genes influence your work life, *how* they do it is a lot more complicated than most people think. This chapter explains how differences in DNA lead us to take divergent approaches to many aspects of our jobs.

What Genes Do

Before we get into a detailed discussion of how your genes influence your workplace behavior, you need to understand what genes do. While you don't need a scientist's knowledge of genetics to grasp how your DNA affects how you act at your job, you do need to know the basics.

Your genes are spiral-shaped particles made up of a chemical called deoxyribonucleic acid (DNA) that contains the instructions for producing proteins, which, in turn, determine how the cells of your body are structured and what they do.[3] As Figure 2.1 shows, DNA comes in four different varieties, called bases, which are labeled with the letters A, G, C, and T.[4] The bases are put together in long strands, with two strands coming together to form a DNA molecule by matching the A with the T and the G with the C.[5] The order in which the bases are put together provides the instructions that tell your body how to create different proteins from amino acids (small organic molecules that are the components from which proteins are made).[6] Speaking simplistically, all genes do is serve

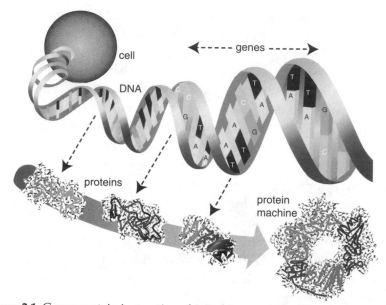

Figure 2.1 Genes contain instructions for making proteins. *Source*: http://www. ornl.gov/info/ornlreview/v37_1_04/article_12.shtml

as templates for proteins (which, in turn, work as enzymes to change one chemical into another) or as structural building blocks for the cells in your body.[7]

It takes a lot of DNA to provide the instructions necessary to produce the proteins to make you. In fact, in humans, there are about 3 billion base pairs of DNA.[8] Much of this DNA doesn't provide instructions that result in any differences between people. Roughly 99.9 percent of human DNA is identical across all of us. But the one out of every thousand pieces of DNA that differs across people accounts for the entire range of genetically influenced variety among human beings.[9] For instance, one person might have a C at position 3,426 on a chromosome where another person has a T, and that difference results in different protein-construction instructions.[10]

If you've been following this short digression into high school biology, you probably realize that your DNA can't affect your behavior directly because genes only determine the creation of proteins, and behavior is not a protein.[11] But, there's another step that takes us from your genes to how you act. The proteins, which are made according to genetic instructions, create the different parts of your body, from your muscles to your skin to your central nervous system.[12]

While genes that code for proteins to create skin cells or blood cells probably don't have much effect on your behavior, the ones that provide instructions for proteins that affect brain structure, neurotransmitters, and glandular systems do.[13] Because the way that your central nervous and glandular systems work affects your cognitive functioning, personality, interests, values, and physical capacities, your genes for these things influence how you act, whether you are starting a business, quitting a job, or going to church.[14] Thus, your DNA indirectly affects your tendency to favor certain types of jobs, or to become a leader, or have high job satisfaction, and a host of other aspects of organizational behavior.

Neurotransmitters are the chemicals that nerve cells use to communicate with each other. They are probably the most important genetically influenced parts of your body in terms of impacting the way we work in organizations. Scientists have found that the versions of the genes we receive influence the amounts of different neurotransmitters in our brains, which, in turn, affect the way we think and feel. And, of course, how we think and feel influences our behavior.

DNA affects neurotransmitters in several different ways. Take, for example, the case of dopamine, a brain chemical that influences how you feel and act. Your genes provide instructions for the creation of dopamine receptors, or the part of the nerve that the chemical stimulates, as is the case for the gene DRD2. They also code for the creation of dopamine transporters, or the structures that carry the chemical to the nerves. Finally, your genes provide instructions for other neurotransmitters, like monoamine oxidase (MAO), which metabolize, or break down, dopamine and other brain chemicals. The genetic codes for these receptors, transporters, and metabolizers all play a role in how much dopamine you have in your brain, which, in turn, affects how you feel and act.

Small Differences, Big Effects

You might wonder how one or two genes that code for a couple of enzymes that ramp up a few chemical reactions in the body can have much of an effect on your behavior. That's a fair question. The answer is twofold. First, the size of a gene's influence isn't necessarily of the same magnitude as the difference between the two variants of a gene. A tiny divergence of only one or two nucleotides between alternative alleles (versions) of a gene can cause a large disparity in phenotypes, or what people look like, and how they behave. For instance, the small distinction between two versions of the ACTN3 gene described in the introductory section of this chapter could result in major differences in whether a person is good at power sports.

Second, the influences of genes on behavior operate through a chain of steps in which the effects get magnified across each successive stage.[15] Take, for example, dopamine, which is released by certain cells in the brain in response to some type of stimulus, like a tasty meal or good sex. This release sets off a series of chemical reactions in the brain that influence how you feel and, consequently, behave.[16]

Within your cells, you have genes that code for the production, transportation, and breakdown of dopamine. This means your DNA influences virtually every aspect of the dopamine in your body. Because some people have the variants of dopamine genes that instruct brain cells to produce, transport, or break down a lot of dopamine, while others have the versions that tell brain cells to produce, transport, or break down less of this chemical, some individuals are more impulsive and excitable than others.[17]

Now suppose you are one of those people with a genetic predisposition toward impulsiveness and excitability that comes from your endowment of DNA. (The genes for dopamine are just a few of many genes thought to relate to impulsivity, but I'll focus on the dopamine genes here to avoid making things too confusing.) You hear about a new investment opportunity that promises a very high potential return. Given your genetic tendency, you impulsively take half of your 401K (a type of retirement plan used in the United States) and put it into this deal without doing much to investigate it. The investment turns out to be a bust, and you are out a big chunk of your savings. In the end, a tiny difference in your genetic code—perhaps as small as the divergence between one version of a dopamine gene and another—results in a major financial loss.

How This Works: The Example of the CREB1 Gene

So how could genes affect you at work? Let's take a look at one example: how you respond to anger. Everyone who has ever had a job knows that sometimes you have to deal with animosity in the workplace. Bosses get angry at subordinates, subordinates get angry at bosses, customers get angry at suppliers, suppliers get angry at customers, and team members get angry at each other.

As you have no doubt noticed, some people are better than others at dealing with this distemper. Instead of storming around, punching walls, or fighting back, these individuals calmly accept the anger of others and deal with it productively. The version of the CREB1 gene (which I will call the "emotional response" gene) that these people have might explain at least part of the reason why. This gene codes for the formation of enzymes that influence the reward and aversion functioning of the brain—that is, how brain chemicals make you *feel* in response to external factors. One study has shown that people with one version of the "emotional response" (CREB1) gene had greater activation of the insula (the part of the brain responsible for visceral and emotional responses) at the sight of angry faces.[18] Some individuals, it seems, have a version of a gene that causes the emotional part of the brain to be more heavily stimulated by the sight of an angry person. Put simply, displays of distemper upset some of us more than others, in part because of our genetic makeup.

Because I am summarizing the effect of a study of a single gene here, it is important to highlight the limitations of the relationship that scientists have found between the variants of the "emotional response" (CREB1) gene and human behavior. While the versions of this gene are associated with different reactions, versions of other genes, perhaps dozens of them, might be linked to these responses as well. Moreover, all genetic factors together might account for only a small portion of the difference in how people react, resulting in the "emotional response" (CREB1) gene accounting for only a tiny part of the variance in this behavior. Furthermore, the finding of a relationship between the versions of the "emotional response" (CREB1) gene and how people respond to angry faces itself has not been replicated. Additional research might simply show that it was an accidental correlation (a measure of how similar two things are to each other; a correlation of 1.0 means that the patterns are exactly the same) that occurred in just one experiment. So we are still far off from the day when we could predict to any great degree people's emotional reaction from the identification of the variants of specific genes that they have.

And even if the "emotional response" (CREB1) gene were found to affect a large portion of people's reaction to anger in a number of studies, that is *not* to say that you would have to respond that way. The brain is capable of enormous plasticity, or flexibility to change. So even if you had the version of the gene that made you likely to be upset by a display of anger, you could learn to be stoic in its face. But people with this version of the gene, and the variants of other genes that have similar effects, will have to work much harder to make those behavioral changes. This is very much like sports, where some athletes can easily achieve what others find much more difficult to accomplish.

The Difficulty of Identifying the Relevant Genes

Having completed your biology refresher course, you might be wondering about other genes that influence workplace behavior. While I'd like to give you a straightforward description of these genes and their effects, doing so is surprisingly difficult. One problem is that behaviors and attitudes are abstract concepts and difficult to measure in quantitative terms. For instance, we might know that a variant of a gene increases your level of extraversion by 3 percent and that this genetic effect is of the same magnitude as working in a particular organizational culture. But what does that mean? Extraversion is something abstract that is measured by psychologists with paper-and-pencil tests. So a 3 percent increase in your level of extraversion isn't tangible like a 3 percent raise in your salary. You know what you could buy with an additional 3 percent of your income, but you don't know what you would get from 3 percent greater extraversion, or even how, precisely, you would act if you were 3 percent more extraverted.

Second, to figure out how specific genes influence how we act on the job, researchers first need to identify what our 20 to 25,000 different genes do.[19] That's not so easy, because genes interact with one another, making the task extremely complicated. Moreover, a number of genes that researchers didn't think would influence behavior turn out to matter. For example, scientists recently suggested that a gene that acts on heart function also influences the development of borderline personality disorder.[20] As a result, researchers have only identified the purpose of a small portion of our genes and haven't yet come up with a list of all the ones that impact behavior. And scientists don't yet have a firm understanding of how many genetic effects operate, for even those genes that they have found to influence how we act.

Some Likely Mechanisms

While we aren't sure of all of the ways that genes affect work-related behavior, we have evidence of several routes. Before getting into a discussion of these different pathways, I want to point out that your genes could easily affect how you act through all of them or just some of them, and there are, undoubtedly, still other mechanisms through which your DNA exerts its influence that aren't discussed here. In fact, given the size of the genetic effects on some behaviors, multiple pathways are probably nearly always at work. And it's very likely that there are some mechanisms that have yet to be discovered.

Direct Effects

The most straightforward way that your genes influence your behavior is through direct physiological effects. For instance, you might be more likely than other people to be very good at interior design because you have the variants of genes that control the production of the brain cells responsible for spatial recognition. As a result, you are simply better than others at visualizing the orientation of objects in a room. Or you might be predisposed to be talented at jobs that demand a lot of concentration because you have certain versions of the COMT gene, which inactivates dopamine and adrenaline. Of course, being endowed with the variant of this gene might make you worse at work that demands calmness because the same genetic variant is also associated with agitation and worry (which is why I will call COMT the "worrier" gene.)[21]

The genes that are most likely to influence some aspect of organizational behavior through direct physiological effects are the ones that code for some dimension of brain function, such as those responsible for neurotransmitter activity.[22] Because genes provide the instructions for enzymes that help make these brain chemicals, different genetic variants influence how your body produces and shuttles around neurotransmitters, including our old friend dopamine and another one called serotonin (which helps regulate mood and thought).[23] Neurotransmitter activity, in turn, can affect decision making.[24] For instance, serotonin levels influence how people feel physically in response to taking chances. As a result, some people might make riskier decisions than others, such as quitting a job without having another one lined up or buying speculative stocks, because they have a particular version of one of the genes that influences the amount of serotonin that their brains produce.

But genes that relate to neurotransmitters aren't the only ones that influence behavior. The DNA that controls the making of hormones, such as testosterone, matters as well. Testosterone levels affect how much we want to dominate others. Some of us might be more likely to adopt a take-no-prisoners attitude toward rising to the top of an organization or be less willing to work cooperatively as part of a project team because we have versions of genes that cause our bodies to produce higher levels of testosterone than people without those genetic variants. Those with more testosterone in their systems literally feel differently from other people when engaged in social interactions. Higher levels of testosterone lead these people to receive less of a physical boost from talking to, and cooperating with, others. As a result, they are more likely to try to dominate others in the workplace.

Through Individual Attributes

Another likely path through which your genes influence your work-related behavior is through their effect on individual attributes, such as personality and temperament. These personal characteristics have a biochemical component to them; all are related to the performance of your neurobiological and hormonal systems.[25] For example, researchers have found the way your body produces and shuttles around neurotransmitters like dopamine and serotonin influences the type of personality that you develop, with variations in genetically affected serotonin levels making some people more likely to be anxious and neurotic, and others to be emotionally stable.[26]

In fact, numerous studies show that roughly 50 to 60 percent of the difference in personality is genetic.[27] This is true for all personality traits: for men and women, for people of all ages and nationalities, and across different measurement instruments and time periods.[28]

Your personality influences a great deal about you—how much you eat, whether you are shy, whether you easily get stressed out by life's experiences, and how you act. Therefore, it should come as no surprise that your personality influences your behavior at work. In fact, a long line of research shows that personality influences whether people are leaders or followers, whether they like sedentary or active jobs, and even whether they are satisfied or unhappy with their jobs.

Leadership is a good example of the way your genetic endowment influences your behavior through its impact on your personality. Researchers have shown that self-confidence affects your odds of becoming a leader because leaders need to stick to their positions even if others are skeptical or indifferent.[29]

But where does this self-confidence come from? While some of it comes from your life experiences and how your parents raised you, part of it comes from having a certain genetic composition. For instance, research indicates that much of the difference between people in domain-specific self-esteem is genetic.[30] In short, your genes affect aspects of your work behavior by influencing the type of personality you develop.[31]

Through Interaction with External Forces

Many researchers believe that genetic factors don't influence behavior equally across all environmental conditions. (The environment is every-thing other than one's genes, and includes such varied factors as life experiences, health, education, and exposure to toxins and illnesses.) Rather, having a particular version of a gene may make a person more sensitive to an external factor that increases the odds of displaying a behavior. Take, for example, the interaction between the "antisocial" (MAOA) gene and being mistreated as a child. When coupled with being abused as a youth, people with one variant of this gene are less likely than people with another version to develop an antisocial personality.[32] Becom-ing antisocial depends on the combination of the version of the gene and emotional or physical maltreatment. People who experience abuse but don't have the version of the gene, or who have the genetic variant but aren't treated badly aren't as likely to develop this type of personality.

One could easily think of parallels to this type of interaction between genetic variants and external factors in the work world. And we prob-ably should, because some researchers believe that the most important way our genes affect our work life is in interaction with environmental forces. For instance, some people might have a version of a gene that increases their odds of making large financial bets (as chapter 4 dis-cusses in greater detail), but the influence of this gene on risk taking might only be manifest in high-pressure, short-time-to-make-a-decision situations, such as currency trading operations. Thus, the gene might not influence managers' decisions to gamble billions of dollars on new technologies after months of careful evaluation, but it might affect traders' choices to bet billions of dollars on currencies in a few seconds on foreign exchange markets.

Influencing organizational behavior depends a lot on identifying the right triggers to get different people to take desired actions. Thinking in terms of these types of interactions will help organizations to choose the right stimuli for the outcomes they are looking for. For instance, suppose that your company is interested in enhancing worker creativity. People who are hardwired to be conscientious cannot be taught to be innovative the same way as those without this genetic predisposition because the potential for failure is often too much of a threat to con-scientious people for their creativity to emerge from training efforts. The highly conscientious are simply too concerned about their performance to "let themselves go" and innovate. To effectively teach people with a genetic tendency to conscientiousness to be creative might require decoupling the efforts to encourage innovation from the measurement of performance so that the experience of failure does not undermine the training process. Therefore, efforts to apply research on gene-environment interactions to creativity training might prove very beneficial to a large number of companies.

Through Selection (Gene-Environment Correlations)

The relationship between our genes and our behavior is made more complicated by the fact that our genes and the environments we face are not really independent of each other. Rather, our DNA affects the odds that we experience certain situations, things like having a particular job or going to a certain school. As a result, some part of what first appears to be an environmental effect is actually genetic, and teasing that apart is extremely difficult.[33] For instance, studies show that a portion of the differences between people in financial events, such as declaring bankruptcy (which we tend to think of as brought upon by external forces like the loss of a job), are actually accounted for by our genes.[34]

This somewhat counterintuitive idea means that the differences between people's behavior that we think are explained by divergence in their education, jobs, and life experiences are actually accounted for by variance in their genes. For instance, researchers have recently found that children with a particular version of the dopamine receptor gene DRD2, (which I will call the "impulsiveness" gene) are less likely to go to college than other kids. One explanation for this genetic effect lies in the tendency of children with this variant of the "impulsiveness" (DRD2) gene to behave worse than other children. This more negative behavior leads their parents to become less involved in their education. This lesser parental involvement, in turn, reduces the school performance of the children, lowering their odds of going to college.[35]

It is easy to see how these patterns might be manifest in work-related outcomes. Take, for example, the great performance appraisals you've received since your transfer to Birmingham. You might think that your better job performance is the result of the company's decision to send you to a place you like much more than where you used to live. But a geneticist might explain that your transfer (an environmental factor) might not have *caused* you to do better. Your DNA might account for both your ability to negotiate for a favorable move and your happiness living in the new city.[36]

Choosing Your Environment

Your genes influence the situations that you are in and the experiences that you have because they affect your tendency to choose those experiences and situations.[37] Take, for instance, the duties that you have as the chief financial officer (CFO) of a Fortune 500 company. Only CFOs of public corporations have the responsibility for making certain types of financial disclosures to regulators. You might not think that your genes could have a hand in foisting such duties on you, but they can.

Suppose you were born with versions of certain genes that made you better than other kids at math. Your genetic gift led you to gravitate toward mathematics in school because you liked all of the positive feedback that your parents and teachers provided when you did a good job. Your quantitative skills made you a good student, which increased the odds that you would choose to go to college. At college you majored in finance, which you found very easy, given your innate mathematical aptitude. Of course, going to college and majoring in math was key to being able to get a job in the finance department of a Fortune 500 company. There, you rose through the ranks to become the company's CFO 20 years later. Your genes influence your CFO responsibilities because your innate ability at mathematics led you down the road to the job as CFO, as opposed to becoming a Broadway actor like your best friend from high school.

The Immigration Story

The kinds of selection processes that your genes trigger can be quite profound. For instance, having a particular version of one of the dopamine receptor genes (DRD4, which I will call the "novelty-seeking" gene), increases your odds of moving to another country. Studies have shown that this genetic variant is more common among immigrant groups than it is among the native-born population.[38] Researchers believe that this version of the "novelty-seeking" (DRD4) gene is associated with the development of a personality trait called novelty seeking, which makes people more likely to seek new life experiences. While the effects of having this gene variant can manifest themselves in a number of different ways, from having a large number of sex partners to a fondness for extreme sports, it is also associated with leaving one's home country and moving to another.

Three Types of Gene-Environment Correlations

Geneticist Robert Plomin has identified three different types of gene-environment correlations (that is, three different ways that your genes lead you to certain situations more often than would be expected if the settings you found yourself in occurred randomly), which he calls *passive, evocative*, and *active*.[39] To illustrate how these three types of gene-environment correlations might affect work-related behavior, I give the example of a professional musician.

A *passive* gene-environment correlation might look something like this: suppose you are the child of two musicians. Because musicians need to have good hearing, your parents probably are good at differentiating sounds, which would make you more likely than the average person to get the versions of the genes that give a person an ear for music. You might think that the good-hearing genes are the only way that your DNA affects your chances of becoming a musician, but your genes also affect the way that the environment contributes to those odds. Being born into a family of musicians makes you more likely than the average person to receive piano and singing lessons at an early age, have an unlimited opportunity to purchase music CDs, and get the chance to meet Miles Davis at Thanksgiving dinner. The music lessons, CD purchases, and the chance to pass the gravy to Miles Davis also increase your odds of becoming a professional musician. But these "environmental" effects are really partially the result of your parents' DNA, leading to a correlation between the genetic and environmental effects on becoming a musician.

The second type of gene-environmental correlation—the one that Plomin calls *evocative*—looks something like this: suppose you are born with a genetic gift that makes you an exceptionally good child musician. When you display that ability, it is likely to evoke a response in other people. Your ability to play Beethoven's Fifth Symphony on the piano at age three and a half might lead your parents to spring for piano lessons instead of ice-skating classes. And taking lessons might make you a better pianist than you otherwise would have been. As a result, you become so good that when you grow up, you turn professional and play for the New York Philharmonic. In this case, your genetic endowment both made you good at playing the piano and gave you a supportive environment for becoming a professional pianist because other people responded to your genetic gift by favorably shaping the situations you experienced.

The third type of gene-environment correlation, which Plomin calls *active*, looks like the following: suppose you are born with the version of the good-pitch genes (the ones that my wife reminds me I definitely do not have). Because people experience greater pleasure from doing things well than doing things poorly, you are more likely than other children to practice singing. You thus have greater odds of joining the church choir, taking part in the school musicals, and pressuring your parents for singing lessons. Kids who take singing lessons after school, join the choir, and participate in school musicals have a higher probability of going to the Berkelee College of Music than those who take tae kwon do lessons, participate in martial arts competitions, and practice breaking pieces of wood with their foreheads. And graduating from music school dramatically increases your chances of becoming a professional musician. As a result, the "good" versions of the music-pitch genes you have make you more likely to become a professional musician than people with the "bad" versions, because they make you more likely to choose situations that reinforce your innate strengths.[40]

Gene-Environment Correlations for Preferences

The influence of your genes on your environment holds whether your genes affect your skills, as was the case in the pitch example above, or merely your interests. For instance, you might be born with the versions of the genes that lead the social and communication centers of your brain to develop more than average, which will likely increase the appeal of verbal communication. That interest could translate into a greater investment of time in talking-related activities, making you better than average at them.[41] So it could be that you are born with more than typical odds of becoming a broadcast journalist because you received the versions of genes that lead to bigger communications centers in the brain, which, in turn, might lead you to develop a disproportionate interest in talking. As a result, you might spend much more time on drama, debate, and the school radio station than most kids, and end up with a greater chance of a career in radio or television.

Missing Mechanisms

As you read through this book, you are bound to notice that some chapters discuss the effects on job-related behavior of interactions between genes and environmental factors and gene-environment correlations, but others do not. The absence of discussion does not mean that these interactions and correlations are unimportant in explaining the aspects of work outcomes described in the chapter. On the contrary, these two mechanisms will probably prove to be the *most important* ways that genes affect behavior. Unfortunately, to date, researchers have conducted little research on them. Where no studies have been conducted, there are none to summarize, leading some chapters to be devoid of sections devoted to gene-environment correlations or gene-environment interactions. Someday, hopefully soon, researchers will turn more attention to these mechanisms and these sections can be filled in. But for now they remain empty.

Magnifying the Effects

One or two genes can have profound effects on activities as complicated as learning to read or starting a company because our genes influence our tendency to choose situations that reinforce our genetic predispositions. A small genetic difference might create only a tiny initial innate advantage at reading or risk taking or leadership. But because we prefer to do those things that we are good at, this small advantage leads us to choose to be in certain situations and not others. (The better reader spends more time reading; the risk taker puts him or herself in more risky situations; and the leader looks for opportunities to be in charge.) The cumulative effect of these choices, and the subsequent reinforcement of the effect that comes from the situations themselves, can result in very large downstream effects, much the way that a decision to read a single book might open a person up to a new subject and send him or her down a particular career path.[42]

The effect of our genes on our tendency to choose situations that reinforce our genetic predispositions may also explain the somewhat counterintuitive observation that genetic effects appear *stronger* in older people than in younger ones. Take the ability to reason and solve problems (otherwise known as intelligence).[43] Studies show that our genes are the most important factor in predicting our intelligence, and that their effect *increases* with age, whether measured as g (a measure of general intelligence called general cognitive ability), IQ test scores, or a variety of other aspects of mental ability.[44] The explanation that researchers give for genetic effects becoming larger with age is that people choose to be in situations that support their genetic propensities. Thus, over the course of their lives, their innate predisposition leads more intelligent people to read more, have more intellectually challenging jobs, choose more intelligent friends, and so on, expanding the magnitude of the genetic contribution to intelligence as they get older.[45]

More Than One Gene

Unfortunately for those of us interested in genetic effects on human behavior, no single gene has a large effect on any one work-related behavior. For example, researchers have found that the portion of the difference in personality explained by any individual gene—whether the examined trait is extraversion, neuroticism, open-mindedness, or something else—is almost always less than 5 percent, and averages about 2.5 percent.[46]

For the most part, our DNA influences our workplace behavior in complex ways that combine the effects of a number of genes.[47] Take, for example, the personality trait of novelty seeking. A noticeable portion of the difference across people in this personality trait is accounted for by a combination of genes that govern neurotransmitters. One study found that four genes: the "impulsiveness" gene (DRD2), the "novelty-seeking" gene (DRD4), another dopamine receptor gene (DRD1), and a gene (SLC6A3, previously known as DAT1) that provides instructions for the creation of a dopamine transporter—the structure that carries the chemical to the nerves—together account for 5.25 percent of the differences between people in novelty seeking.[48] (I will call SLC6A3 the "activity" gene.) A later study showed that approximately 10 percent of the variance between people in this same personality trait could be attributed to the combination of the effects of the "impulsiveness" gene (DRD2) and the "novelty-seeking" gene (DRD4).[49]

Moreover, the combined effects of genes are not limited to those that code for the production of a single brain chemical, like dopamine. Other studies show that differences between people's levels of novelty seeking are better explained by a combination of their dopamine *and* serotonin system genes than the effects of their dopamine system genes alone.[50]

Although any single gene only accounts for a small portion of the variance in our personalities and behaviors, we can identify a lot of the difference between people by looking at the combined effect of many genes. For instance, one study found that, when taken together, a group of 59 genes explained 38 percent of the difference between people in novelty seeking, 32 percent of the difference in harm avoidance, 41 percent of the difference in reward dependence, and 32 percent of the difference in persistence.[51]

If we just focus on the last measure for a minute, we can see the potential impact of genetics on understanding work-related behavior. The results of this study show that if we tested you and your coworkers to identify which versions of these 59 genes all of you had, we could account for almost one-third of the difference among you in how persistent you are.

Now think about the number of tasks at your job for which persistence is important. Maybe you're in sales, where persistence is the key to closing sales. Maybe you're in product development, where this personality trait is important to bringing new products to market. Maybe you're running your own business, where this characteristic is crucial to raising money from investors. Whatever your specific job entails, persistence is probably important for some part of it. And now we can account for about one-third of the difference between the quitters and those who persist in the face of obstacles if we measure their versions of 59 different genes.

Additive or Something Else?

The effect of our genes on our behavior is sometimes additive, with the impact of one gene being added to the effect of another to provide the total genetic influence.[52] Other times, our genes' effects combine in ways that are not additive, with one gene influencing the impact of another, complicating efforts to explain DNA's impact on work-related outcomes.[53]

Sometimes genes have multiplicative effects on behavior, which means that the impact of one gene multiplies the influence of another.[54] For instance, the "novelty-seeking" gene (DRD4) gene interacts with the "worrier" gene (COMT) to affect novelty seeking.[55] People who have certain versions of each gene are much more likely than other people to seek out new situations and experiences, even if doing so involves taking some risks. This is similar to the situation in which a version of the "worrier" gene (COMT) combines with a variant of the "impulsiveness" gene (DRD2) to enhance drive and fun seeking.[56]

The "novelty-seeking" gene (DRD4) also interacts with one of the genes (HTR2C, also known as 5HT2C) that code for receptors for the brain chemical serotonin to affect reward dependence, a personality trait in which people have a strong tendency to respond to social approval.[57] (I will call HTR2C the "concern" gene.) People with certain versions of both the "novelty-seeking" (DRD4) and "concern" (HT2RC) genes tend to be very sensitive to what other people think of their behavior.

Perhaps Henry Ford had the opposite versions of both of these genes. That would be consistent with his reputation as someone who didn't give a damn about what anyone else thought of him.

The "novelty-seeking" gene (DRD4) also interacts with the "concern" gene (HTR2C) to affect persistence.[58] People who have certain versions of both of these genes tend to work hard to overcome all obstacles at work and other settings. Maybe Thomas Edison, the man who said invention is 1 percent inspiration and 99 percent perspiration, had the persistence-promoting versions of these two genes.

Finally, people who have certain versions of one of the genes (GABRA6) that provides instructions to receptors for the gamma-aminobutyric acid gene—gamma-aminobutyric acid is a chemical released by neurons to calm their response to stimuli—and one of the serotonin genes might be more likely than other people to be anxious and hostile.[59] (I will call GABRA6 the "cooperativeness" gene.)

Some of these interactions between pairs of genes have been found to have substantive effects on behavior. For example, a version of one of the dopamine receptor genes interacts with a version of a serotonin gene to account for 30 percent of the difference between people in persistence and 13 percent of the variance in reward dependence.[60]

These are only the interactions between two genes. Three or more genes can also combine to influence personality and behavior. For instance, one study showed the joint effect of a difference in the DNA sequence involving genes for serotonin, dopamine, and catechol-O-methyl transferase on the personality trait of novelty seeking.[61] People with certain versions of these three genes were found to have a higher likelihood than other people of seeking new and varied experiences.

A Single Gene to Many Behaviors

A single gene can also influence many different aspects of behavior.[62] For instance, the very same genes that make some people more likely to be dyslexic also increase the odds that they will be hyperactive. Additionally, two of the dopamine receptor genes (DRD4 and DRD5) affect the odds that people will be both aggressive and novelty seeking. And the "activity" gene (SLC6A3) and the "novelty-seeking" gene (DRD4) increase susceptibility to attention deficit hyperactivity disorder (ADHD), several types of addictive behavior, and a number of personality traits.[63]

What does the single-gene-to-multiple-behaviors pattern mean for understanding how people act in the workplace? Because many genes affect more than one outcome, having a version of a gene that predisposes you to a particular behavior doesn't mean that you are going to display it. Take the effect of the "novelty-seeking" gene (DRD4) described above. A version of this gene increases the odds that people will be both novelty seeking and aggressive. While one individual with this gene variant might be more likely than the average person to seek out new experiences, another might find the genetic difference manifest in higher-than-average aggressiveness. Add in the fact that people choose situations that reinforce their innate tendencies, and interactions between multiple genes and between genes and external factors, and you can see that it is not easy to predict the odds that a person with a certain version of a gene will display a particular behavior.

How Do Researchers Figure This Stuff Out?

At this point you might be wondering how anyone knows any of this. You also might be thinking that it would be easier to understand how genes affect work-related outcomes if you had some insight into the approaches that researchers take to figuring this out. For these reasons, it is worthwhile to summarize the different ways that scientists explore how genes affect behavior.

In general, researchers use two different approaches to study genetic effects on behavior: an older approach of behavioral genetics and a newer one of molecular genetics.

Behavioral Genetics

Behavioral genetics is the study of hereditary differences in how people act and think.[64] Typically, it involves studies of twins and adopted children.

Behavioral geneticists like to study twins because twins provide a natural experiment (a situation in which the effect that the researcher wants to examine is found randomly across a group of people) that allows them to examine the portion of behavior that comes from genetic and environmental factors. To understand how twins provide this type of natural experiment, you need to know a little bit of biology. Identical twins are identical because they share 100 percent of their DNA. This makes their genetic similarity different from fraternal twins, who, like all siblings, share half of their genes.[65] (On average, your biological mom and dad each provide 50 percent of your genes.)

This difference in the proportion of shared genes—100 percent versus 50 percent—allows researchers to get a handle on how much of our behavior comes from our DNA. Researchers know that all of our behavior must be accounted for by either our genes or the environment (everything else that we experience in life). They also know that the similarity of the effects of external factors are generally no different for pairs of identical twins than they are for pairs of fraternal twins, meaning the source of divergence between identical and fraternal twins is the degree to which they share the same genes.[66]

The fact that the environment affects the pairs of twins similarly, combined with the 100 percent genetic commonality of identical twins and the 50 percent genetic commonality of fraternal twins, is what allows researchers to figure out the proportion of the genetic effect on behavior. They do this by looking at the correlation between how pairs of identical and fraternal twins think and act. If something is 100 percent genetically determined—like eye color—then the correlation between pairs of identical twins would be 100 percent; every pair of identical twins would both have the same color eyes, whether blue, brown, green, or what have you. If something has no genetic effect—like the tendency to live in brick houses, for instance—then there would be no difference between the correlation of the identical and fraternal twins. Whether both twins reside in brick homes, both live in wooden houses, or one lives in a brick house and the other does not is no different for identical and fraternal twins.[67]

Any time the correlation between pairs of identical twins is higher than that between pairs of their fraternal counterparts, genes must influence what is being measured. And if certain genes are associated with particular work-related results, then the genes must be the cause of the outcomes, and not the other way around, because behavior cannot cause genes to change within a single generation. For example, we know that our DNA affects our ability to direct groups of people because pairs of identical twins are more likely to show the same level of leadership talent than pairs of fraternal twins.

Behavioral geneticists also study adopted children because adoption creates what researchers call an experiment of nurture. Adopted children carry the genes of their biological parents, but not the DNA of their adoptive parents. The difference in the correlations between the behavior of the children and their two sets of parents identifies the size of the innate effects. If genetic influences exist, then how a child acts will be more highly correlated with (be more similar to) the behavior of his or her biological parents than his or her adoptive parents.[68] But if no genetic effects exist, there will be no difference, on average, in this correlation.

For example, we could compare the similarity between children's selection of professions and those of their biological and adoptive parents to see whether job choice has a genetic component. Researchers who have done this have found that the correlation is much higher between the selections of children and their biological parents than between the picks of kids and their adoptive parents. This means that there is a genetic component to job choice.[69]

Molecular Genetics

Molecular geneticists approach the process of figuring out how DNA affects work-related outcomes differently. They focus on identifying specific genes that are associated with behaviors, such as leadership or risk taking, through linkage studies, association studies, genome-wide association studies, and "knockout" studies.

Because human beings have so many genes, it is very difficult to identify the specific genes associated with a particular behavior. Often, the first step in this process is a linkage analysis. These studies are efforts by scientists to identify the tendency for two or more genes to be passed on together because they are located in similar parts of the same chromosome.[70]

The idea behind linkage analysis is straightforward. All chromosomes are inherited in twos—one from each of our parents. Mom and Dad's versions of the gene tend to get mixed up during the making of the child, but the odds of mixing is greater for genes that are further apart on a chromosome than ones that are close together. Those that are near each other, as it turns out, tend to be passed on to children together. The difference in the rate of mixing of proximate and distant genes helps researchers to get their initial clues about the relationship between a gene and a behavior. Because nearby genes tend to be passed on to children together, if parents and children tend to both show a behavior and an identifier gene, then researchers have a clue that the gene responsible for the behavior is located on the chromosome somewhere near the identifier.[71]

In association studies, researchers take a different approach. They collect data on a group of people, some of whom display the behavior that they want to explain and some of whom do not. Then the researchers figure out which versions of a gene the different people have. The final step is to see if there is a correlation between the version of the gene and the action being investigated. If so, that implies an association between the gene and the behavior.[72]

In genome-wide association studies, researchers look across the genome for small variations that are more common among people with certain characteristics. Unlike in traditional association studies, the researchers don't assume that the variants of the gene they are investigating are found in a particular part of the genome. They simply look across the entire genome and examine hundreds of thousands of genetic variations at one time.[73]

A final type of molecular genetics study is the "knockout study." While this approach is used frequently by geneticists who study animals, it isn't used very often to identify the genetic factors that influence workplace behavior among humans, for reasons that will become obvious in a moment. Knockout studies involve removing or changing a version of a subject's (usually a mouse's) gene. By comparing the genetically altered subject to a normal one, researchers can identify the effect of the modified gene.[74]

The reason that these studies aren't used to identify most employment-related outcomes is probably obvious to most readers. Most animals don't engage in workplace behavior, and knockout studies of human beings are unethical. So the only evidence of work-related behavior from knockout studies is that inferred from research on animals.

A good example of the kind of inference to humans that researchers make from knockout studies are investigations of the effects of vasopressin genes on mountain and prairie voles' social behavior. Prairie voles are monogamous animals, but mountain voles are not. One research team inserted the prairie voles' vasopressin receptor gene into mice, which aren't very social or monogamous animals. They found that the mice who received the prairie voles' gene became highly social. From these animal studies, researchers surmised that vasopressin genes influence how social we are.[75]

Some Important Cautions

Scientists have discovered a great deal about the effects of genes on human behavior, and much research is currently being conducted to learn even more. In the process of coming up with these insights, researchers have identified several important cautions that you should keep in mind when you read the evidence presented in this book. First, we need to be careful not to conclude that genetic effects exist from accidental correlations between genes and behaviors. Scientists can never know for sure that a correlation is real and isn't just a chance occurrence. They conclude that a correlation (in this case, between a gene and a behavior) is true if there is no more than a certain percentage chance that the association was there by accident. However, the more correlations that scientists examine, the more "false positive" relationships they will find. (False positives are correlations that aren't real, but are just the result of random chance.) To ensure that they don't find a lot of false positives, scientists can set the threshold for certainty very high—perhaps as high as a one-in-a-million chance that the correlation occurred by accident.

However, elevating the standard for confidence that the result is real comes with its own set of problems. Scientists need to examine very large samples or they won't have enough cases to find anything at all. Moreover, with a very high threshold for certainty, some true correlations won't be identified, a problem that scientists call "false negatives."

The end result of all this is a balancing act between too many false negatives and too many false positives. Because scientists must weigh these two alternatives, different researchers often set different standards to conclude that a correlation is real. Some scientists err on the side of being too conservative, while others err in favor of being too liberal. All of this means that future research will likely show that some of the relationships between genes and behaviors reported in this book were not really there after all. So you should think of the findings cited in this book as tentative, not definitive.

Second, we need to be careful not to attribute coincidental relationships between genes and behaviors to genetic effects. This point is probably best explained by the exemplar that genetics researchers have termed the "chopsticks example." It goes like this: Asians are, on average, better at using chopsticks than Caucasians because chopsticks are the main utensil used to eat food in Asian cultures. On average, Asians and Caucasians also tend to have certain genetic variants to greater or lesser extent because of their evolutionary histories. As a result, the ability to use chopsticks turns out to be correlated with the presence of certain gene variants for reasons having nothing to do with innate differences in manual dexterity, physiological traits, or anything else that might account for superior ability to use chopsticks. Rather, the correlation results from the random similarity between two things—the tendency of Asians to have different gene variants from Europeans and the lesser inclination of Europeans to eat with chopsticks—rather than from one thing causing the other.[76]

Third, the estimates of genetic effects on work-related behavior that come from the twin and adoption studies described in this book are just that, estimates, and are subject to countervailing influences that make them imprecise. These offsetting factors could make the estimates reported here either too low or too high. So the genetic effects described in this book should not be thought of as exact numbers, but rather as approximations.

There are too many countervailing influences on genetic effects to list them all here, but to illustrate my point about the potential inaccuracies in the estimates, I'll highlight a few of the most important ones. One effect that could make the estimates *too low* is "assortative mating." This is just a fancy term geneticists use to explain that people tend to have kids with people similar to them. If genetically alike people tend to have children together, then any fraternal twins that they have will be more similar than a standard twin-study design would assume. As a result, the size of genetic effects reported in twin studies will be lower than they actually are.

On the other hand, the estimates of genetic effects might be *overstated* if identical twins are treated more similarly than fraternal twins. For instance, if identical twins are more likely than fraternal twins to be dressed the same way, enrolled in the same after-school activities, or otherwise treated identically, then some of what researchers estimate to be a genetic effect is actually a misattributed environmental influence. The end result of more similar treatment of identical twins would be estimates of genetic effects that are too high. While most studies show that identical twins are *not* treated more alike than fraternal twins, and most researchers correct their estimates for this possible error, we need to be cautious that this effect may still be present in the results they report.[77]

Conclusions

This chapter explained *how* our genes influence our job-related behavior. While a large body of evidence shows that genes affect a variety of work outcomes, they don't do so directly. Because (simplistically speaking) genes are merely chemicals that provide instructions to our cells to produce more or less of certain proteins, genes must impact behavior indirectly. Alternative versions of genes lead people to produce different amounts of proteins that affect how our bodies function. Because body function, particularly brain activity, affects our cognitive abilities, personalities, interests, values, and attitudes, our genes influence our behavior.

The most straightforward way that your genes affect your behavior is through their effect on your body's production of brain chemicals and hormones. By coding for the speed of biochemical reactions, the functioning of receptors and transporters for neurotransmitters, and the creation of hormones, the versions of the genes that you were born with affect work-related outcomes.

Genes also impact behavior by influencing the development of individual attributes, such as personality, temperament, and intelligence. Your genetic variants affect your body's biochemical processes to make you more or less likely to take on certain attributes, such as personality traits. Because these characteristics, in turn, affect your behavior, your genes end up influencing your work-related actions.

Of course, not all of the effects of your genes on your behavior are independent of the contexts you find yourself in. Often, your genes interact with those situations to influence how you act. In these cases, your genes may make you more responsive to certain external factors (by increasing your physiological reaction to those stimuli). This heightened sensitivity increases your odds of engaging in certain kinds of behaviors and not others.

The relationship between your genes and your behavior is complicated by the fact that your genes influence the odds that you will find yourself in situations that make certain types of behavior more likely to occur. Through passive, evocative, and active gene-environment correlations, your genes lead you to select your experiences, making life events partially a function of your genes.

Figuring out how your DNA influences your actions is complicated by the fact that genes don't have a one-to-one relationship with behaviors. Most work-related outcomes are not explained by a single gene, but instead are found only when the influences of multiple genes are combined.

To figure out how our genes influence our beliefs and actions, researchers conduct behavioral genetics (twin and adoption) and molecular genetics (linkage, association, genome-wide association, and knockout) studies. While these efforts have provided much evidence of how our genes impact work-related behavior, not all of the reported relationships will hold up in future investigations. Accidental correlations, coincidental relationships, and under- or overstated effects mean that some of the correlations between genes and job-related outcomes that researchers believe they have found may not really be there.

It's also important to remember that genetics is about risk, not certainty. Your DNA influences the *probability* that you will behave in a particular way; it does not *assure* it. You can always overcome your genetic endowment; and many people do. But, as we will see in subsequent chapters, overcoming a "bad" genetic draw is like swimming against the current; it's harder than going with the flow. So if you want to act against your genetic tendencies, knowing those propensities is crucial to figuring out what to do.

Having established how your genes influence your work-related behavior, I turn now to a discussion of genetic effects on work interests, the subject of the next chapter.

3

Why That Job? The Genetic
Foundations of Your
Work Interests

Are some people born with a genetic composition that makes them more interested in buying and running companies, while others are born genetically predisposed to fighting fires or doing police work? Researchers who have studied identical twins reared apart often recount stories of the remarkable similarity in the work interests of the twins, stories that suggest a genetic effect. In her book *Indivisible by Two*, Nancy Segal recounts the story of twins named Mark and Gerry, who, despite being raised in separate households, had very similar jobs and work interests. She writes,

> Mark actually got into firefighting as a lark; his high school friends thought it would be fun to run red lights and see buildings burn. So Mark tried it. But when he rescued a girl from an accident and saw the gratitude on her face, he knew this was not a game. And he knew it was something he wanted to do. Gerry said that he always wanted to be a fireman; he had chased fire trucks as a kid and had visited fire stations with his father. He applied for membership in his local firehouse twenty-five years ago.... They both liked forestry, but Gerry studied it at school whereas Mark learned it in the field. When they met, Gerry installed chemical fire-suppression systems and Mark installed burglar alarms. Both twins have driven trucks in addition to fighting fires.[1]

Examples like this one have an attention-getting value that lead us to think that our work interests might, to some extent, be inborn, but they are hardly scientific evidence that our genes influence our vocational interests. After all, Mark and Gerry could be one of a small handful of cases of identical twins raised apart who happen to have similar jobs, and the rarity of these examples might be too great for there to be any evidence of a genetic effect on work interests. To figure out whether this example illustrates the influence of DNA or is an exception to the rule, researchers have conducted a number of studies.

As this chapter will show, scientists have amassed a body of evidence that your genes influence your work interests.[2] In fact, not only is your preference for certain types of work influenced by your genes, but even how focused you are on work relative to other things in your life is affected by your DNA.[3] For instance, one study shows that 52 percent of the difference between people in how important work is to them ("work orientation") is explained by genetics.[4]

In the sections that follow, you will see which aspects of your work interests your genes affect and how your DNA influences the type of work you choose to do.

The Effect of Genes on Work Interests

Are you a sports nut, an arts maven, a music fanatic, or a collector of ancient Roman coins? Whatever your interests, some part of your preference can be traced to your DNA. Take your intellectual pastimes, for example. Do you prefer to read books or listen to music? One study found that about 21 percent of the difference between people in the kinds of intellectual activities they prefer can be accounted for by their genes.[5]

But genetic effects on interests are not limited to preferences for types of intellectual endeavors. They extend to a wide range of activities, from public speaking to physical fitness to writing. Even an inclination toward academic achievement—the desire to be a professorial type, like me—has an innate component, with studies showing as much as half of the difference in this preference to be genetic.[6]

Although researchers have gathered evidence of genetic effects on interests from a wide variety of studies, their best evidence comes from studies of twins raised in different households, because identical twins raised in separate households have the same DNA but are subject to very different family and life experiences. So what do these gold-standard investigations show? One found that an average of 40 percent of the variance across people in interests is genetic, and that this effect is observed across numerous domains, from daily activities to hobbies.[7] Another showed that a genetic effect was present across 23 different topics, from public speaking to physical fitness to writing.[8]

What about work interests? Do our genes affect these as well? The answer is yes. In fact, as early as 1932, researchers had found statistical evidence of the greater commonality of the work-related preferences of identical than fraternal twins.[9] Whether people want to become doctors, commodities traders, ranchers, firemen, automobile salesmen, or any number of other occupations, identical twins are attracted to more similar jobs than fraternal twins, even same-sex fraternal twins.

The evidence of genetic influences on our employment interests is quite strong and is present across a number of different ways that researchers measure work preferences, from the actual jobs themselves, such as police officer or teacher; to skills-based occupational groupings, such as math-focused or writing-centered; to the type of work that people describe liking, such as working outdoors or making calculations.[10] Moreover, the effects have been found in studies that use all of the major vocational instruments, including the Minnesota Vocational Interest Inventory, the Jackson Vocational Interest Survey, and the Strong Vocational Interest Blank.[11]

For instance, Table 3.1 shows the share of the differences between people in responses to the Jackson Vocational Interest Survey accounted for by our genes, while Table 3.2 shows the genetic portion of the variance in the basic interest scales.

Even the studies of twins *raised separately* show that identical twins display astonishing similarity in their jobs, whether they are employed as university presidents, fire department captains, fashion designers, entrepreneurs, or astronauts in the NASA shuttle program, and that these twins have like jobs at a much higher rate than fraternal twins (see Table 3.3).[12]

Adoption studies also provide evidence of the effect of genes on work interests. Biologically related members of the same family tend to have similar job preferences, while adopted family members do not.[13] For instance, one study of Danish boys who were adopted before they reached age one shows that the children's jobs correlated significantly with the vocations of their birth parents but not their adoptive parents.[14] That is, the kids who became police officers tended to have biological parents who were in law enforcement, but not adoptive moms and dads who had that occupation; the children who became teachers tended to

Table 3.1 The percentage of the difference between people in the Jackson Vocational Interest Survey accounted for by genetic factors

Vocational interest dimension	Percentage of difference that is genetic
Creative arts	74
Physical science	68
Engineering	61
Nature/agriculture	61
Business	59
Technical writing	59
Personal service	58
Teaching	58
Authorship/journalism	56
Social service	54
Law	51
Skilled trades	50
Professional advising	49
Adventure	47
Human resource management	47
Performing arts	41
Mathematics	41
Social science	40
Life science	39
Medical service	39
Supervision	38
Finance	36
Elementary education	33
Office work	32
Sales	25

Source: Adapted from data contained in Roberts, C., and Johansson, C. 1974. The inheritance of cognitive interest styles among twins. *Journal of Vocational Behavior*, 4(2): 237–243; Betsworth, D., Bouchard, T., Cooper, C., Grotevant, H., Hansen, J., Scarr, S., and Weinberg, R. 1994. Genetic and environmental influences on vocational interests assessed using adoptive and biological families and twins reared apart and together. *Journal of Vocational Behavior*, 44 (3): 263–278; and Moloney, D., Bouchard, T., and Segal, N. 1991. A genetic and environmental analysis of the vocational interests of monozygotic and dizygotic twins reared apart. *Journal of Vocational Behavior*, 39(1): 76–109.

have biological parents who were teachers, but not adoptive parents who had that job, and so on. (Remember, if there is a genetic effect here, adopted children should choose employment more similar to that of their biological mothers and fathers, who gave them their DNA, but had no influence on their upbringing, than to that of their adoptive parents, who raised them but did not contribute to their genetic makeup.)

Table 3.2 The percentage of the difference between people on the basic interest scales accounted for by genetic factors

Dimension	Percent of difference that is genetic
Mathematics	50–52
Nature	41–44
Athletics	39–43
Law/politics	39–41
Medical service	39–40
Writing	38
Public speaking	38
Art	37–40
Music/dramatics	37–38
Science	35–54
Adventure	35
Social service	34–39
Teaching	31–51
Medical science	31
Merchandising	29–44
Mechanical activities	29–43
Military activities	28
Business management	25–45
Sales	19–22

Source: Adapted from data contained in Roberts, C., and Johansson, C. 1974. The inheritance of cognitive interest styles among twins. *Journal of Vocational Behavior,* 4(2): 237–243; Betsworth, D., Bouchard, T., Cooper, C., Grotevant, H., Hansen, J., Scarr, S., and Weinberg, R. 1994. Genetic and environmental influences on vocational interests assessed using adoptive and biological families and twins reared apart and together. *Journal of Vocational Behavior,* 44(3): 263–278; and Moloney, D., Bouchard, T., and Segal, N. 1991. A genetic and environmental analysis of the vocational interests of monozygotic and dizygotic twins reared apart. *Journal of Vocational Behavior,* 39(1): 76–109.

Even when work preferences of adopted children are similar to those of both their biological *and* adoptive parents, the correlation with the interests of the biological parents is higher. For example, one study found that people's occupation-related inclinations—such as a favoring of jobs that offer security, are highly competitive, or involve control over others—are more closely related to the job preferences of their biological parents than their adoptive ones.[15] Moreover, as adopted children get older, their vocational interests become more like those of their biological mothers and fathers (even when they have never met their birth parents) than those of the adoptive parents who raised them.[16]

The best evidence of the effect of genes on work preferences comes from combined studies of twins reared separately and adopted children. These studies show that about 36 percent of the difference between

Table 3.3 The correlations in occupational preferences between identical and fraternal twins raised together and apart

Dimension	Identical twins raised apart	Identical twins raised together	Fraternal twins raised apart	Fraternal twins raised together
Special interest scales				
Managerial potential	55	58	28	16
Religious occupational interests	55	43	9	23
Law enforcement orientation	28	22	−3	20
General occupational themes				
Social jobs	42	45	4	20
Enterprising jobs	41	41	4	25
Investigative jobs	39	46	0	24
Conventional jobs	24	49	10	22
Artistic jobs	23	51	17	29
Realistic jobs	20	49	15	20
Basic interest scales				
Athletics	45	49	−3	21
Science	43	47	11	14
Medical service	38	45	7	13
Writing	36	47	9	18
Public speaking	36	45	18	20
Merchandising	35	34	1	??
Business management	35	32	−8	20
Mechanical activities	33	49	25	18
Teaching	33	41	5	21

Source: Adapted from Betsworth, D., Bouchard, T., Cooper, C., Grotevant, H., Hansen, J., Scarr, S., Weinberg, R. 1994. Genetic and environmental influences on vocational interests assessed using adoptive and biological families and twins reared apart and together. *Journal of Vocational Behavior*, 44(3): 263–278; Bouchard, T., McGue, T., Hur, Y., and Horn, J. 1998. A genetic and environmental analysis of the California Psychological Inventory using adult twins reared apart and together. *European Journal of Personality*, 12(5): 307–3290; Bouchard, T., and McGue, M. 2003. Genetic and environmental influences on human psychological differences. *Journal of Neurobiology*, 54(1): 4–45.

people in vocational interests, as shown by both the basic-interest scales and general occupational themes, is accounted for by genetic factors.[17]

In short, the evidence is clear; your genes influence your work interests. But, remember, your DNA affects the *odds* that you will develop particular preferences; it doesn't *ensure* that you will have them.

The Specific and the General

While the discussion thus far has focused on general work interests, research shows genetic effects on fairly specific dimensions as well. Take, for example, the desire to become a member of law enforcement or a teacher. One study shows that 21 percent of the difference between people in what researchers call "law enforcement orientation," and what the rest of us might describe as wanting to be cops, corrections officers, and FBI agents, is genetic. Similarly, about 46 percent of the difference between people in what researchers call "academic comfort," and what most of us would call an interest in teaching, is explained by genes.[18]

Although genetic effects exist for specific job preferences, they tend to be stronger for broader categories that represent the major skills and activities involved in those positions. For instance, one study showed that 32 percent of the difference between people on single questions to measure occupational interests—for instance, do you like carpentry, or buying and selling, or public speaking—are genetic. A higher share, 48 percent, of the variance on scales that combine specific questions into measures of more general interests, such as a preference for writing, reading, or working with animals, is a function of our genes. And an even larger portion still, 53 percent, of the difference on factors that combine these different scales, such as interest in adventurous work, intellectual work, or agrarian work—is hereditary.[19]

The fact that DNA accounts for more of the variance in general categories of interests than in the specific positions themselves suggests that people have innate preferences for types of activity more than for particular jobs. This makes sense, since human beings have engaged in different categories of work, like physical labor or interpersonal communication, ever since we began to walk the earth, but many specific jobs, like selling life insurance and annuities, have existed for only a couple hundred years.

Vocational Assessment

Some studies of genetic effects on work interests have a very practical use. They examine innate preferences for the very job categories used in vocational assessments to tell people what type of employment they are best suited for.

To evaluate what jobs are right for people, human resource experts often use a typology of occupations developed by former Johns Hopkins University professor John Holland. This categorization places all jobs into six groupings: conventional, realistic, investigative, social, artistic, and enterprising.[20] Realistic jobs are those in which the work is very tangible, such as mechanic, assembly-line worker, or farmer. Investigative jobs are those that involve the search for information, as is the case for biologists, economists, and news reporters. Social jobs are ones that involve helping others, such as teacher, counselor, or social worker. Conventional jobs include such occupations as accountant, bank teller, or file clerk. Enterprising jobs are those that involve business activity and transactions, such as business owner, lawyer, or real estate agent. Finally, artistic jobs are those that involve one of the arts, such as musician, writer, or interior designer.[21]

While the human resource experts who conduct vocational assessments rarely consider *why* some people are better suited to certain jobs than to others when recommending occupations to those tested, research shows that one reason involves genetic differences. Studies of twins and adopted children show that between 21 and 44 percent of the variation between people in these six occupational categories are explained by their genes (see Table 3.4).[22] So the next time you take one of these tests, keep in mind that a good portion of the explanation of

Table 3.4 The percentage of the difference between job themes accounted for by genetics

Job theme	Percent of difference that is genetic
Investigative	34–42
Artistic	33–39
Realistic	28–43
Social	26–40
Conventional	23–39
Enterprising	21–44

Source: Adapted from data contained in Roberts, C., and Johansson, C. 1974. The inheritance of cognitive interest styles among twins. *Journal of Vocational Behavior*, 4(2): 237–243; Betsworth, D., Bouchard, T., Cooper, C., Grotevant, H., Hansen, J., Scarr, S., and Weinberg, R. 1994. Genetic and environmental influences on vocational interests assessed using adoptive and biological families and twins reared apart and together. *Journal of Vocational Behavior*, 44(3): 263–278; Moloney, D., Bouchard, T., and Segal, N. 1991. A genetic and environmental analysis of the vocational interests of monozygotic and dizygotic twins reared apart. *Journal of Vocational Behavior*, 39(1): 76–109; and Bouchard, T., McGue, M., Hur, Y., and Horn, J. 1998. A genetic and environmental analysis of the California Psychological Inventory using adult twins raised apart and together. *European Journal of Personality*, 12(5): 307–320.

why you are the right fit for certain kinds of jobs and not others comes from your DNA.

Altruistic, Socially Responsible, and Nurturing Jobs

What about Bobby's desire to be a social worker or Suzy's interest in joining the Peace Corps? Do our genes have anything to do with our preference for jobs that demand a high degree of altruism? Again the answer appears to be yes. Our genes influence how interested we are in work that involves helping others, perhaps because our genes affect how altruistic we are. Studies show that about 30 percent of the difference between people on this dimension is genetic.[23] Stated differently, a little under one-third of the variation in whether individuals put themselves or others first appears to be innate.

Moreover, researchers have even identified specific genes associated with altruism. One gene, AVPR1A, (which I will call the "altruism" gene) provides instructions for the production of a brain receptor for the hormone arginine vasopressin. (Don't forget, there are probably many genes that affect altruism; naming AVPR1A the "altruism" gene is just a mnemonic device to help you remember one of its many functions.) In one study, people with the long version of this gene were more altruistic than people with the short version when they played an online game that involved giving away money.[24] It's true that this result has not yet been extensively replicated, and the "altruism" gene (APVR1A) might just be one of many that influence this behavior. Nevertheless, this finding indicates that researchers can identify a path from specific genes to important workplace behaviors.

The "novelty-seeking" gene (DRD4) also appears to affect altruism. Some scientists believe that people with a particular version of this gene are more altruistic than others because they get a stronger physiological response from helping those around them. As Richard Ebstein, a researcher at Hebrew University in Israel, explains, "Dopamine probably plays a key role in pro-social behavior. People with the altruism gene may do good works because they get more of a thrill out of their good works."[25]

Because altruistic people are more likely than non-altruistic people to choose jobs—like joining the Peace Corps—that involve helping others at expense to themselves, genetic effects explain the choice of self-sacrificing jobs.[26] So, if you are wondering why your son wants to spend the next two years building wells for the poorest of the poor in Africa or your daughter wants to be a social worker and minister to your city's homeless, you might be responsible in ways that you might not have considered. Something in their DNA is influencing their choice.

Similar to altruism is the concept of social responsibility. Both involve acting in ways that might be counter to one's own self-interest, but social responsibility focuses on a person's sense of duty to others. People high in social responsibility feel that they have an obligation to more than just to themselves and their families; they have a duty to society. For instance, a socially responsible approach to managing a company would involve worrying about whether the business engaged in perfectly legal actions that harmed others. If someone were to tamper with an over-the-counter medication to make it unsafe after it was on store shelves, a socially responsible manufacturer might voluntarily recall the product even though it would not be legally responsible for any adverse effects of the drug on customers.

People differ in their levels of social responsibility, and some part of this variation is genetic. Studies have shown that as much as 73 percent of the variance between adolescents in their level of social responsibility is accounted for by their genes.[27] So your teenage son may criticize your company's failure to help clean up the environment, while your cow-orker's kid doesn't care at all, because of differences in their DNA.

Social responsibility often takes two forms: what experts call normative altruistic obligation and normative civic obligation. The former measures the duty people feel to engage in charitable activities, such as volunteering money or time for social causes. The latter measures the obligation people feel to fulfill civic responsibilities, such as testifying in court about an auto accident they witnessed. One study examined the genetic portion of the difference between people in the two types of social responsibility and found more than 30 percent of the variation in altruistic obligation and 37 percent of the difference in civic obligation are genetic.[28]

The genetically influenced variance in both types of social responsibility affect the jobs we choose, with people high in both being more likely to choose jobs, like public service, that benefit society. (Ironically, those high in Machiavellianism—who are willing to manipulate others to achieve their goals—are also drawn to this line of work. Public service provides the opportunity to influence the behavior of others to benefit oneself; something that is all too clear to anyone who follows the news of political corruption. As we will see in chapter 6, Machiavellianism has a strong genetic component. So, indirectly, our genes affect how willing we are to choose jobs heavy on social responsibility, whether we have a genetic tendency toward altruism or Machiavellianism.)

Some jobs require a lot of empathy and nurturance. For instance, nannies need to be more caring than lawyers, and nurses need to be more compassionate than investment bankers. Therefore, more empathetic and nurturing people tend to choose nannying and nursing much more than law and investment banking.

Who is caring and compassionate isn't random, nor does it depend solely on how we were raised. It's partially a function of the genes our parents gave us. Studies have shown that 40 percent of the variance in warmth is genetic.[29]

Moreover, our DNA also affects the likelihood that we develop other characteristics that would lead us to favor certain types of jobs and shy away from others. Many people think that short-sellers, who make their living betting on the price declines of stocks, tend to be callous and cynical, or at least more callous and cynical than people who run soup kitchens. And people rarely switch back and forth between the two occupations. That's not surprising because the traits associated with the two jobs are in part genetic.[30]

Business Interests

Consider famed investor Warren Buffett. According to his biographer, Alice Schroeder, Buffett was always interested in commerce, starting his first business to sell chewing gum at age six, reading and rereading a book called *One Thousand Ways to Make $1,000* at age ten, and making his first investment in the stock market at age eleven.[31] Is there a genetic effect for having a strong interest in business like he had? Given the earlier discussion of the effect of our genes on our preferences in general, it's natural to think that they would also influence how attracted we are to business.

The data clearly show evidence of this genetic effect. Take, for example, studies of identical and fraternal twins. Identical twins, whether raised together or apart, tend to display more similar levels of interest in business jobs than their fraternal counterparts.[32] In fact, the rate at which identical twins raised apart express a common preference is higher than that for fraternal twins who grow up together, with fraternal twins raised separately having almost no similarity of interest in working in the business world.[33]

Adoption studies show similar patterns. Adopted children are much more likely to want to work in the business world if their biological parents express similar interests than if the parents that raise them do. Specifically, at least one study shows that the correlation between the preference for business jobs between adopted children and their adoptive parents is much lower than that between the kids and their biological moms and dads. In short, both studies of twins and studies of adopted children show that some portion of our interest in the business world is genetic.[34]

But how much of this attraction comes from our DNA? A substantial amount, it appears. One study, done way back in the 1960s, showed that, among boys, 41 percent of the variance in interest in a business career is accounted for by genetic factors.[35] As was mentioned earlier, another study showed that approximately 44 percent of the difference in a vocational interest dimension called "enterprising" (which captures interest in business, finance, professional advising, law, supervision, merchandising, and business management) come from our DNA.[36]

Genetic effects on interest in business are smaller in the very best studies (those that jointly examine twins raised together and apart and adopted children), but they remain substantial even in these "gold standard" investigations. For instance, one study found that genetic factors accounted for 31 percent of the difference between people in their attraction to business-related jobs, while growing up in the same household only accounted for 11 percent of the variation.[37]

Aspects of Business

Business is a broad domain. Within it, there are many different kinds of jobs, from human resource management to sales to finance to accounting. So you might wonder whether our genes influence our preference for functional areas of business as well. "Yes" is the answer. Let's take a look at what some of the studies show.

One aspect of work in the business world is managing other people. Like the character Michael Scott on the hit TV show *The Office*, supervising others is what many businesspeople do on a day-to-day basis. You might be surprised to learn that your interest in this kind of work is more heavily influenced by your genetic endowment than by how your mom and dad raised you. About 25 percent of the variation in interest in managing people is attributable to genes, while only 8 percent is accounted for by family environment.[38] (Note to the producers of *The*

Office: you might consider an episode that explored the genetic origins of Michael Scott and Dwight Schrute's desire to manage others.)

Another kind of work in the business world involves managing the ongoing operations of companies, what researchers have called "the day-to-day functioning of business and commercial organizations."[39] After all, companies don't order their own raw materials, manage their own inventory, or run their own assembly lines. Someone has to do that for them. Like managing other people, this aspect of business attracts some people more than others. And, as with managing other people, in the appeal of this work is affected by your genes. Studies show that genetic factors account for approximately 59 percent of the variation in people's interest in "the day-to-day functioning of business and commercial organizations."[40]

A third type of work that takes place in the business world is merchandising, which the Merriam-Webster online dictionary defines as "sales promotion as a comprehensive function, including market research, development of new products, coordination of manufacture and marketing, and effective advertising and selling."[41] Again, this type of work is preferred by some and is disliked by others, in part because of genetics. Studies show that about 29 percent of the variation in people's interest in merchandising is attributable to our genes, while only 6 percent is explained by the families in which we were raised.[42]

A fourth kind of business work, and one related, in part, to merchandising, is sales, or the process of convincing people to buy a product or service. Sales, as I am sure you are aware, attracts some people more than others. Genetics explains part of the reason why. Studies show that approximately 19 percent of the difference between us in our preference for sales work is the result of our DNA.[43]

A final type of work is finance, or what might be defined as an interest "in meeting the financial needs of the public, in solving financial problems, and in investment and trade."[44] Again, the interest that some people have in this type of work appears to be partially innate. Research shows that approximately 36 percent of the difference in people's interest in finance jobs, such as being an accountant, controller, investment banker, stockbroker, or insurance underwriter, is genetic.[45]

How Do Our Genes Influence Our Work Interests?

While the information presented in the previous section painted an interesting picture of genetic influences on work interests, it didn't explain how we get from a set of chemical instructions to form proteins to wanting to be a Wall Street tycoon. The evidence that some of us are genetically more predisposed than others to have certain work interests and to choose particular occupations begs the question: *How* do our genes influence job preferences and occupational choice? A variety of different mechanisms could be at work. Among them: genetic effects on hormone levels, brain function, personality, temperament, and cognitive abilities. To date, we don't have enough research to definitively suggest which of the paths is most important, or even to identify all of the mechanisms at play. But the evidence gathered thus far suggests some fascinating alternatives, which are described below.

The Hormone Story

One mechanism could be hormonal. Hormones are chemicals produced by cells in one part of your body that influence the activity of cells in other parts. You are probably familiar with the names of some of the hormones you have in your body, including testosterone, estrogen, thyroid hormone, and adrenaline. Your genes affect your body's production of hormones, and some of those hormones influence the kind of jobs that you prefer. Thus, your genes impact your occupational preferences, in part, through their role in hormone creation. While this might sound far-fetched, there is considerable science behind it.

Your genes probably exert their influence through a number of hormones. However, the evidence is greatest for testosterone, so I'm going to focus on that example. All people, male or female, have this hormone in their bodies. The amount present changes over the course of the day and as a function of external stimuli, but this variation occurs around a base level that is very much affected by a person's genetic makeup. Studies show that genetics accounts for 80 percent of the difference between men in the base rate of testosterone production.[46]

So testosterone levels are influenced by our genes, but how do genetic differences in base testosterone levels affect our work interests? Perhaps as follows: a particular genetic variant leads some men to have higher base testosterone levels than others. The hormone level, in turn, influences behavior, with higher testosterone leading to more aggression and dominance. Because higher testosterone men tend to be more aggressive than lower testosterone men, they might prefer jobs that permit such behavior, leading them to disproportionately choose certain occupations over others.

Evidence from several studies supports this proposition. Research shows that managers, on average, have higher testosterone levels than computer programmers; and salesmen, on average, have more of this hormone than teachers. Even within specific professions, men with certain types of jobs tend to have higher testosterone levels than those with other jobs. Trial lawyers, for instance, are more testosterone laden, on average, than other kinds of attorneys.[47]

High-testosterone men might also prefer jobs that are less sedentary. Testosterone enhances the development of muscle mass and other body features that facilitate physical activity, leading high-testosterone men to prefer less desk-bound jobs.[48] Several studies have shown a relationship between men's base testosterone levels and their choice of occupations in ways consistent with this idea. For instance, high-testosterone men are more likely than low-testosterone men to have blue-collar jobs.[49]

Genetic differences in base testosterone levels might also influence work interests and occupational choice by affecting brain development. Some researchers believe that testosterone increases the development of the right hemisphere of the brain instead of the left, resulting in greater mathematical, mechanical, and computing ability at the expense of talent for communication.[50] The more-developed right brains and less-developed left brains of people with higher base testosterone levels might draw them disproportionately away from jobs that demand strong social skills. For instance, research shows that high-testosterone women are found in occupations that involve communicating with others at a much lower rate than low-testosterone women, a pattern consistent with the effects of base testosterone on brain development described above.[51]

Differences in job preferences might also result from testosterone's effects on skill at spatial problem solving (the ability to imagine objects from different perspectives or to re-create combinations of images). A variety of studies show that testosterone levels are related to talent at solving problems that involve the orientation of objects in three-dimensional space. For example, men with higher testosterone levels are better than those with low testosterone levels at envisioning the rotation of three-dimensional objects.[52] Moreover, a lack of this hormone is associated with worse spatial memory in men, and the taking of testosterone supplements increases spatial memory among women.[53] Furthermore, very "feminine" women, who tend to have low testosterone levels and high estrogen levels, tend to show the lowest spatial ability among groups of women. Finally, female-to-male transsexuals show better spatial performance after receiving testosterone treatment.[54]

Another piece of evidence for how genetic differences in testosterone levels affect work interests comes from studies of girls with congenital adrenal hyperplasia (CAH). CAH is a disorder that causes girls to produce excess testosterone prenatally.[55] Girls with this disorder tend to display more masculine behavior than their counterparts without the disorder. They are significantly more likely to play with "boys' toys" when growing up, and tend to have better spatial ability than other girls. They are also more interested in careers than in marriage, and are more likely than girls without the disorder to have typically "male" job preferences, like engineering or flying airplanes. In fact, the job interests of girls with CAH appear to be related to the amount of exposure the girls had to testosterone; the greater the exposure, the more "masculine" their later work preferences.[56]

Genes and Brain Function

Genetically influenced differences in levels of testosterone production are not the only mechanism through which our DNA might affect our work interests. Another possible path is through the impact of genes on brain formation and brain function. Take, for example, the preference for science and engineering jobs. Some researchers believe that these job interests might be affected by the same genes that influence Asperger's syndrome, a disorder that comes from an overdevelopment of the right hemisphere of the brain, resulting in normal intelligence but underdeveloped social skills. Those who are good at engineering and science tend to have many characteristics prevalent among those with Asperger's, including a better-than-average understanding of the mechanical properties of physical objects and worse-than-average comprehension of human behavior.[57] As noted author Oliver Sacks has written, those with a talent for science and engineering tend to have "a striking literalness and directness of mind, extreme single-mindedness, a passion for calculation and quantitative exactitude, unconventional, stubbornly held ideas, and a disposition to use rigorously exact language—even in his rare nonscientific communication—coupled with a virtual incomprehension of social behaviors and human relationships."[58]

Other evidence also supports the link between genetics, Asperger's syndrome, and a tendency toward science and engineering occupations. Not only has research on twins shown that Asperger's syndrome has a genetic component,[59] but also the fathers and grandfathers of children with the related condition of autism are more likely to be employed in engineering and related occupations than the fathers and grandfathers of children without the disorder.[60]

These patterns have led some observers to believe that the genes that influence the propensity to suffer from Asperger's syndrome might also affect how the human brain is wired more generally. One thought is that certain versions of these genes give people a greater tendency to understand the mechanical properties of physical objects, but a lesser likelihood of grasping the nuances of human behavior. This brain wiring, in turn, leads people toward occupations that demand different skills, such as a preference for engineering, rather than sales.

Through Personality

Our DNA also influences our work interests through its effect on our personalities. That is, the versions of the genes that we get from our parents predispose us to develop certain personality traits, and these characteristics, in turn, lead us to favor some jobs and occupations over others. This should not be surprising to most of you, as you probably have encountered few introverted car salesmen and only a handful of extraverted librarians.

The OCEAN Model of Personality

Let's take a look at how this process operates for one of the dimensions of the OCEAN model of personality: Neuroticism, which manifests itself in worry, insecurity, and emotional instability.[61] Genetic factors account for between 27 and 68 percent of the difference between people in this trait.[62] Moreover, certain variants of genes affiliated with serotonin and dopamine are found to a greater extent among neurotics than among emotionally stable people.[63]

The strong genetic component to neuroticism is important because a number of studies show that people who are neurotic are more sensitive to hygiene factors in their jobs, things like physical working conditions, salary, or benefits.[64] Thus, certain versions of dopamine and serotonin genes might affect the tendency to choose high paying jobs in comfortable working environments by influencing the odds that people will be neurotic.

But this is only one example. Much psychology and organizational-behavior research shows robust relationships between a number of other personality traits and work interests. For instance, a meta-analysis combining the results of 24 different studies showed the following consistent links:

- People who are imaginative, creative, and inventive—characteristics that psychologists combine in a trait called *openness to experience*—tend to prefer artistic, investigative occupations, such as acting and research.
- Extraverted people tend to prefer enterprising and social jobs, such as business and nursing.
- Agreeable people tend to prefer social jobs, such as child care and sales.[65]

All three of these personality dimensions have a strong genetic component. Studies show that between 45 percent and 61 percent of the variation across people in openness to experience comes from our DNA,[66] and that this trait is more common among people with certain variants of dopamine system genes.[67] Studies also show that genes account for as much as two-thirds of the difference between people in extraversion,[68] and that people with certain variants of neurotransmitter genes are more likely than others to be extraverted.[69] Furthermore, research shows that between 33 and 66 percent of the variance between people in agreeableness is genetic[70] and that versions of several neurotransmitter-related genes are more common in agreeable people.[71]

Harm Avoidance

Your genes also affect your occupational preferences through personality dimensions that are not part of the OCEAN model. Take, for example, the trait of harm avoidance, which manifests itself in frequent worry and pessimism. Noted geneticist Dean Hamer explains how this characteristic, which researchers have shown is very much influenced by your DNA,[72] affects job preferences. He says,

> A person's level of harm avoidance will have a definite impact on careers and relationships, especially at the high end. Just as a physically frail person would be wise to steer clear of physically demanding jobs, a person with a high level of harm avoidance most likely will shun occupations that require cutthroat competition or jobs that require unfailing cheeriness or constant contact with the public. Low scorers can take advantage of their self-confidence and interest in people, working in sales, public relations, contracting, hands-on health care, everything from cashier to corporate CEO.[73]

In short, people whose DNA predisposes them to be harm avoiding tend to also avoid highly competitive and public-facing jobs.

Self-Efficacy

Another genetically influenced personality trait that affects your occupational preferences is self-efficacy, a psychological measure of how much confidence you have in yourself. Self-efficacy has a significant genetic component; one study showed that 32 percent of the difference in people's interpersonal confidence is explained by their genes.[74]

The genetic predisposition to have high or low self-efficacy extends to self-confidence specific to the workplace. Many aspects of work, from selling to leading others to even just providing input in a meeting, demand self-confidence. A particularly important aspect of work-related self-confidence is the belief that you can do your job. One study showed that 44 percent of the difference in people's confidence in their workplace skills, and 51 percent of the variance in their belief in their trade skills, is genetic.[75]

Genes influence work preferences because people with high self-efficacy prefer different jobs than people with low self-efficacy. Those high in self-confidence tend to like work settings where self-assurance is important, whether that self-efficacy is needed to talk to strangers, to speak confidently about many topics, or to believe you have the ability to achieve your goals.[76]

Novelty Seeking

Your genes might influence your work preferences by affecting whether you have a novelty-seeking personality. As we saw in an earlier chapter, this trait has a strong genetic component. Moreover, researchers have identified a probable causal path through which genes make some people more novelty seeking than others. In his book *Living with Our Genes*, noted geneticist Dr. Dean Hamer explains that the genes that code for the brain's dopamine receptors affect the development of this personality trait.

Dopamine, like all brain chemicals, needs to bind with special receptors called, as one might expect, dopamine receptors. Like everything else in the body, the production of these receptors is controlled by instructions provided by your genes. These genetic codes are not all the same. Some people have versions of the dopamine receptor genes that lead them to react less than other people to stimuli that trigger the dopamine system. This lesser response means that, to get the good feeling that comes from dopamine, these people need to experience stronger stimuli than people with other versions of the genes. As a result, the individuals with the low-reaction versions of the genes pursue more novelty through their jobs and activities.[77]

High-novelty seekers are more likely than low-novelty seekers to choose risky jobs and to take chances at work. They are also more willing to undertake activities that could crater their careers.[78] High-novelty seekers even think about new opportunities differently than their low-novelty seeking counterparts, seeing activities they haven't done yet as less risky than the others view those same choices.[79] For instance, Dr. Hamer explains that

> a person who scores extremely high for thrill seeking could work as a pilot, firefighter, stock broker or bank robber.... Low scorers tend to be... accountants, librarians, editors, machine tool operators, dentists, and computer programmers.... They are cubicle dwellers.... They prefer jobs with long-term projects and goals rather than rapidly changing priorities. They will feel more comfortable at IBM than at a start-up company that might not exist next week. Lower thrill seekers make excellent middle managers because they are willing to perform the difficult, often thankless tasks required to turn a new idea into reality.... Low scorers tend to be orderly and precise, and a routine can be comforting, rather than confining.[80]

In sum, the path from genes to job preferences through the personality trait of novelty seeking looks something like this: being born with one type of dopamine system genes and not another makes a person more likely to be novelty seeking, and having this personality characteristic increases the odds that the individual will choose more thrilling jobs, like flying planes or trading stocks.

Calmness and Stress Reaction

Research shows that your genes also affect your vocational interests through relatively narrow aspects of personality, such as stress reaction. (This personality characteristic refers to the degree to which people experience anxiety in response to stressful situations.) Some people, we know, are calm in almost all settings. The media refers to the 44th president of the United States, Barack Obama, this way, calling him preternaturally calm.

Stress reaction is partially innate, with studies showing that DNA accounts for between 43 and 45 percent of the difference between people in this trait.[81] Being high or low in stress reaction affects the kind of employment that people are suited for and, consequently, their job preferences. Certain jobs, such as that of airplane pilot or air traffic controller, demand the ability to react to stress with calmness; an anxious response could prove deadly. On the other hand, extreme calmness may be less useful among teachers where it might be misinterpreted by many as a lack of enthusiasm or interest.[82]

Through Temperament

Closely related to the concept of personality is temperament. According to the Merriam-Webster online dictionary, temperament is a "characteristic or habitual inclination or mode of emotional response." People often think of temperament as being positive or negative. Those with a positive temperament see the world as a glass half full, while those with a negative temperament see the world as a glass half empty.

As most parents of newborn children realize, part of temperament is genetic.[83] Some babies greet the world positively, being mostly cheery, while others are cranky and irritable. These genetic differences aren't just something present in infants; they last our entire lives. Research shows that some of us are genetically predisposed to have consistently more positive moods than others, whether those differences in state-of-mind are measured every day, once a week, or once a month.[84] Moreover, studies of people of all ages, from infants to the elderly, show that between one-quarter and one-half of the difference between people in measures of temperament, including optimism and pessimism and positive and negative emotionality, are genetic.[85]

Psychologists have found that happiness tends to have two components: a stable part that persists over time, and a variable portion that goes up and down frequently. The stable part reflects how happy you are with your lot in life, while the variable component reflects your pleasure with recent events, such as winning a raffle. It's probably intuitive that the changing part of happiness would have a small genetic component—it's harder for your genes to affect your reaction to winning the lottery than to influence how you feel about your life in general. However, your basic cheerfulness is something you are, to a large extent, born with. While events, such as being promoted at work or being laid off, move your day-to-day happiness up and down, they do so around this base level.[86]

Recent research has provided clues about how genes influence your tendency to see the world as a glass half full or as a glass half empty.

Those mechanisms revolve around the workings of several brain chemicals. Although the research hasn't been completely replicated and the genes involved might only have a small effect on your worldview, the results are intriguing. For example, a version of the "novelty-seeking" gene (DRD4) is associated with having a more positive outlook on life.[87] In contrast, a version of the ADRA2A gene, which controls the pace at which neurotransmitters are released from your sympathetic nerves, is more prevalent among people who are irritable, hostile, and negative.[88]

Another important brain chemical affecting your temperament is MAO, which as an earlier chapter explained, is an enzyme that accelerates the process of breaking down other neurotransmitters, like serotonin, dopamine, and adrenaline.[89] The more MAO there is in your brain, the less of these other substances there will be.

So what explains how much MAO you have in your system? You guessed it: your genes. Studies show that genetic factors account for approximately 86 percent of the difference between people in the amount of MAO found in their bodies.[90]

MAO levels are important to the story because they affect your overall outlook on life. People whose bodies produce a lot of MAO tend to have a more negative worldview than people whose bodies make less MAO, because the low-MAO producers decompose other brain chemicals—like the feel-good neurotransmitter dopamine and anxiety-reducing neurotransmitter serotonin—more slowly.[91]

These genetic differences in our temperaments influence the jobs we have. Research shows that, on average, people who have more pessimistic dispositions work in lower-skill jobs than people with more optimistic worldviews. In addition, those with negative affect tend to avoid high-stress jobs. Finally, research shows that people with a cheerful outlook on life tend to advance higher in organizations than their less chipper counterparts.[92] Thus, the versions of the neurotransmitter genes that you got from your parents predispose you to have either a positive or a negative worldview. This outlook on life, in turn, affects the kind of job you select.

Through Cognitive Abilities

Your genes also influence your vocational interests through your cognitive abilities.[93] Cognitive ability is a term that the experts use to refer to both intelligence and the types of mental activity that you are good at, whether that is mathematics, writing, problem solving, or other things.

Through Intelligence and General and Specific Cognitive Ability

Researchers have spent a lot of time investigating genetic effects on intelligence and cognitive skills and have found that they are very large, much bigger than the influence of genes on personality or temperament. A wide variety of adoption and twin studies (including those of twins reared together and apart), conducted in many different countries and using a range of test designs (including nonverbal tests of intelligence), show that as much as 75 percent of the differences in IQ scores are explained by our genes.[94] In addition, numerous studies show that genes have a substantive effect on *g* (a measure of general intelligence). Furthermore, genetic effects are significant for all aspects of cognitive ability, from verbal comprehension to spatial visualization to mental processing speed to memory, with estimates that between 38 and 75 percent of the difference between people on these dimensions comes from genetic sources.[95] In fact, one meta-analysis showed that 48 percent of the variation between people in verbal ability, 60 percent of the difference in spatial ability, 64 percent of the variance in perceptual speed and accuracy, and 48 percent of the difference in memory is explained by genetics.[96]

Research also shows that genes account for about half of the difference between people in cognitive skills,[97] and impact word fluency, verbal reasoning, number skills, and inductive and deductive reasoning.[98] Genes also affect performance in a wide variety of academic subjects, including mathematics, reading, writing, natural and physical sciences, and social studies.[99]

But genetic effects on cognitive skills are not limited to those needed to succeed at school. They also influence many workplace skills, including being well organized, having talent at buying and selling, and being precise. They affect trade skills, such as the ability to put together mechanical or electrical devices; interpersonal competences, such as the ability to persuade others; and intellectual skills, such as writing and public speaking.[100] They even have been shown to affect physical abilities, such as fine motor skills.[101]

Clearly, your genes have profound effects on your overall intelligence and the specific mental activities that you are good at. But what does this have to do with your work preferences? A lot, actually. People's jobs depend a great deal on their intelligence and cognitive skills. It's an unfortunate fact of life that not everyone is smart enough to do every job. Brain surgery and nuclear engineering, for example, demand higher levels of intelligence than making ice cream and cleaning houses. While some people manage to get and hold jobs despite being less intelligent than others who have the same position, and other people are much smarter than the average person doing their job, research shows that the difficulty and complexity of people's jobs is related to their general cognitive ability.[102] That is, roughly speaking, brighter people work at more difficult jobs.[103] And because a majority of the difference between people in intelligence comes from their DNA, vocational interests are very likely to be affected by genetic differences in overall smarts.

Genetic differences in specific cognitive abilities, including spatial visualization, number skills, verbal comprehension, and so on, also affect work preferences because, on average, people tend to choose jobs that fit their abilities, or at least those they think they have the skills to do.[104] For instance, people who believe that they are poor verbal communicators tend not to take jobs like teaching, which demand a lot of speaking.[105] Similarly, we would expect that a person with a genetic predisposition to:

- numeracy might have higher odds of becoming an accountant, since accountants spend their days analyzing numbers.
- verbal understanding (the ability to comprehend written and spoken words) might be more likely to become a book editor, since editors need to read and understand authors' books.
- high perceptual speed (the ability to see similarities in between disparate things quickly) might have greater chances of becoming a pilot, since pilots need to react quickly to changing circumstances.
- deductive reasoning might have higher odds of becoming a market researcher, since market researchers use deductive analysis to identify attributes to put into products.
- spatial visualization might be more likely to become an interior designer, since interior designers need to envision the design of rooms.[106]

Learning Disabilities

Your genes can even influence your vocational interests by predisposing you to develop certain learning disabilities. Take, for example, the case of dyslexia, which makes processing written words more difficult. Researchers have found that genetic factors affect the odds of having this disability.[107] Twin and adoption studies, for instance, show that between 25 and 50 percent of the difference between people in the development of language disorders is genetic.[108]

Moreover, molecular geneticists have mapped the location of the genes contributing to dyslexia, finding that this disability is related to a particular part of chromosome 6.[109] They also have discovered that certain connections between parts of the brain are absent in dyslexics,[110] and have shown that the genetic factors accounting for dyslexia also influence mathematical skills.[111]

Dyslexia also affects job preferences. Dyslexics are less likely to select occupations, such as those in science, information technology, management, or finance, which require a lot of reading of words and numbers, and are more likely to pick human-interaction-oriented jobs, such as nursing and sales, than people without the disorder.[112] Therefore, we can trace a path from genetic endowments to language disabilities to vocational preferences, which demonstrates another way in which genes affect work interests.

Education: A Gene-Environment Correlation Story

As you probably remember from the previous chapter, your genes affect several aspects of your work-related behavior by increasing your tendency to choose certain situations over others. This effect, called gene-environment correlation by geneticists, is another way that your DNA influences your job preferences.

The relationship between job choice and education is one example of a gene-environment correlation.[113] Studies show that genetic factors account for between 30 and 57 percent of the difference between people in their level of education.[114] In fact, the *same* genetic factors influence educational attainment as affect general cognitive ability, specific cognitive abilities (including verbal, spatial, speed and memory skills), intelligence, school performance, and academic achievement (in reading, math, and language).[115]

In addition, genetics are a strong predictor of how well children do in school.[116] Studies conducted in the United States show that about 40 percent of the difference between kids in their performance on the National Merit Scholarship Test is accounted for by their genes.[117] Similarly, studies done in Australia indicate that about 44 percent of the variance in the results of college entrance exams is genetic.[118]

But how, exactly, do gene-environment correlations in education explain the jobs that people have? Here is one possible path: A child might do marginally better at school if he or she has a genetic predisposition to be slightly more intelligent.[119] Because skill at different activities influences the amount of pleasure that we get from them, children with a genetic predisposition to be smarter, will, on average, enjoy school more than other children. The greater enjoyment that the children genetically predisposed to be brainier experience from doing schoolwork will lead those kids to try harder and learn more.[120] The result is better grades and a higher chance of going to college. Because some jobs, such as medicine or engineering, require a college education, kids who go to college are more likely than other children to get these jobs.[121] In short, kids who are born with the variants of genes that make them a little more intelligent tend to end up in different jobs than those born with other versions of these genes because the small genetic differences put in place a series of choices that lead the two sets of children down disparate educational paths.[122]

Conclusions

Our genes influence our work interests. This is true for broad categories of preferences, such as liking business or the arts, as well as narrower ones, such as a fondness for writing or a love of public speaking. Genetics has even been linked to preferences for specific jobs, such as interest in law enforcement. And within the corporate world, genetics has been shown to influence the job functions that people favor, whether that is finance, sales, operations, or other aspects of business.

Of course, none of this means that being an investment banker or astronaut is in your genes. Your genes only affect your *odds* of preferring one job over another; they don't determine your job choice. How your parents raised you and your early experiences in school also influence your work preferences. So you should think of your genetic makeup as just one among many factors that affect your occupational interests.

We don't yet know for sure how our genes influence our work interests, but research suggests some possible mechanisms, including through instructions provided for the creation of hormones and the development of different parts of the brain, and by predisposing people to form certain personality traits, temperaments, and cognitive abilities.

Having described how your genes influence your work interests, I now turn to a discussion of their effect on job satisfaction, the subject of the next chapter.

4

Happy at Work? How Your Genes Affect Your Job Satisfaction

Tom and Robert couldn't have had more different feelings about their jobs. Although both of them worked as insurance claims adjusters for the same Midwestern insurance company, their views of the company and their job were completely different. Tom really enjoyed his work, and experienced immense satisfaction from helping his company's clients when they needed to file claims on their homeowner's insurance policies. He felt that home-owner's insurance was an important product; it protected people against financial ruin when something happened to their dwellings. And he felt good about the fact that he could get people a check quickly, so they could begin to repair the damage to their homes.

He saw what he did as important. He was the one who figured out the cause of home damage and what it would really cost to fix. Although he sometimes had to root out fraudulent claimants among the homeowners he dealt with, it didn't bother him. Having to expose people who tried to pull something over on the company was just something he had to do to preserve the money for the legitimate claim holders.

Tom had worked as a claims adjuster for the same company for much of his career and intended to stay in that job until retirement. When asked if he would ever want to change jobs, Tom would often reply, "Why? I have a great job, working for a great company."

In contrast, Robert hated the job of being a claims adjuster, despite working at the same job and in the same company as Tom. He didn't like having to survey damage to people's homes and then decide how much money they should get to repair them. Although most of the time he gave the customers the money that they needed, the few occasions when people fought with him about the size of their claims left him upset for days. He particularly disliked having to root out fraudulent claims. He said it felt like being the assistant principal in a high school, always checking on everyone, just looking for the one person smoking in the bathroom. Even when he found people who abused the system, he got no satisfaction from saving his company the expense of illegitimate payouts.

Because he was so unsatisfied with his job, Robert was looking for a new one. Unlike Tom, he wasn't going to stay at one company his whole life, and had already changed jobs several times. In fact, each time he took a job, he found he didn't like it very much and began to search for another one.

Why does Tom like his job so much more than Robert? It couldn't be the position itself because both of the men have the same job. It has to be something about them. Something about Tom gives him higher satisfaction from doing the same job as Robert.

Their coworker Mary says it must have something to do with how they were raised, but neither man believes that. Could it be something else? Could it be that Tom's genes have predisposed him to have higher job satisfaction than Robert? The answer, research shows, is yes.[1]

The Importance of Job Satisfaction

Before we discuss the role of genetics in job satisfaction, it's useful to explain why this topic deserves an entire chapter. After all, I covered many different work interests in a single chapter. So, devoting an entire chapter to job satisfaction signals its importance for people interested in understanding the effect of genetics on work-related behavior.

Job turnover is a major concern for most companies, perhaps the most important human resource issue that companies face. Employee turnover is a drag on profits; it adds the costs of recruiting, selecting, and training people who leave the company. Job turnover also reduces the amount of revenue generated per dollar of human resource costs because new employees are often less productive than more experienced ones.

The magnitude of turnover expense is not trivial. Studies show that it costs approximately $34,000 to replace an information technology systems analyst who earns only double that amount, and $10,000 to replace a sales clerk in a retail store, who earns only about $18,000 per year.[2] And the reduced productivity that comes from employee departures makes the numbers even worse. Clearly, companies benefit from reduced employee turnover.

So companies need to know what makes people quit their jobs. While many factors are at play, one of the biggest is job satisfaction. Happy workers don't leave their jobs at the same rate as unhappy ones, so having contented employees lowers turnover costs substantially. That gives a lot of companies a financial interest in figuring out what would make their employees more satisfied with their jobs.

Companies would also like to enhance employee contentment on the job for other reasons. Job satisfaction increases productivity because happy employees work harder, allowing them to produce more at a lower cost. Moreover, in many service organizations, client satisfaction often depends directly on the attitudes of employees, who are the company's face with customers. Because people's purchasing patterns are affected by how they feel during the buying experience, happy employees matter. When workers are dissatisfied, their unhappiness makes the customer's experience worse. As a result, consumers buy less, and company performance suffers.[3] Clearly, it is important for companies to know what makes their employees satisfied with their jobs.

The Causes of Job Satisfaction and Turnover

So why do Robert, and many other people like him, dislike their jobs? There's no shortage of answers to this question. Many human resource experts say that it has a lot to do with company efforts to make jobs desirable or undesirable. Companies can improve employee job satisfaction and reduce costly turnover, the experts explain, by paying people more, improving working conditions, and creating a favorable work culture.

While these recommendations certainly affect how people feel about their jobs, something is missing in the consultants' focus on changing the work environment. I'm sure you see it when you look around your own workplace. Some people seem very resistant to efforts to improve their job satisfaction, while others seem happy no matter how bad their jobs are. Clearly, some portion of the difference between people in job satisfaction doesn't come from the characteristics of their work environment, such as their pay, hours, and working conditions. It comes from something inside the employees themselves. Moreover, the experts increasingly believe that a good part of that something is hardwired, and is very difficult to change.

The Genetics of Job Satisfaction

Research has confirmed that genetics account for almost a third (30 percent) of the difference between people in overall job satisfaction.[4]

Moreover, our DNA affects both intrinsic and extrinsic job satisfaction.[5] (Intrinsic job satisfaction is the kind of satisfaction that comes from the nature of the work itself, while extrinsic job satisfaction is the kind that comes from the context in which the work is done, such as the conditions of the workplace, the pay that a person receives, or the kind of boss that they have.) Some people just have an innate tendency to be content with the type of work they do, the pay that they receive for it, and the conditions under which they do it.

Genetic effects on our workplace satisfaction are present across a wide variety of jobs. They affect us whether we do office work or physical labor, conduct financial analysis or write prose, drive a vehicle or sit at a desk.

Our genes also affect how happy we are with different aspects of our jobs. They influence what we think are the key criteria for employees to be satisfied with their jobs.[6] For instance, one study found that genetics accounts for an average of 35 percent of the difference between people in the importance of different job criteria, such as level of pay, how interesting the work is, or the amount of job security.[7] In short, our genes affect a number of different aspects of job satisfaction.

Our Views of Our Employers

An important part of our job satisfaction is our view of the companies where we work. People who have a positive view of their employers tend to be happier with their jobs than people who have a negative view of those organizations. But why do some people have a rosy perspective on the companies they work for, while others have a more negative outlook? Much of what is written on this topic tells only one side of the story. Because most authors of business books are striving to be as practical as possible, they focus their attention on things that managers can do to make their employees view their employers more positively. While managers can, no doubt, take a variety of actions to make their employees adopt more favorable views toward the company, no matter what they try, they can't get everyone to develop a positive outlook. That's because some part of why employees have positive or negative views of their employers is beyond the company's control; it lies in the workers' genetic makeup.

For instance, studies show a genetic effect on whether we perceive a variety of dimensions of our jobs positively, including the support we receive from our supervisors, our level of autonomy, the pressure we feel, and the clarity of our jobs.[8] In fact, one study even showed that 22 percent of the difference between people in the perception that the company offers a "supportive climate" for employees, and 27 percent of variance in the view that the organization's culture is "annoying," are accounted for by genetic factors.[9]

Some part of employees' positive or negative views of their employers comes from their genetic predisposition to have a favorable or unfavorable outlook toward everything in their lives. But that is not the only way that genetics affects people's perceptions of the companies they work for. Another important factor is the fit between an employee and the organization. Human resource experts tell us that people have a more favorable view of their employers if those organizations have cultures—the set of characteristics about how people work and interact—that are consistent with their own beliefs.[10]

Organizations develop very different cultures. Some companies encourage autonomy, letting employees set their hours and choice of projects. Others closely monitor employees, carefully prescribing what the people who work for them can do, closely scripting their activity, and sometimes even specifying the words they are to use when they speak to customers.

Some businesses focus on safety and security; letting their employees know that nothing harmful will happen to them at work. Some even nurture the belief amongst their staff that no matter what happens to the company, their jobs will be secure. Other organizations develop a culture of risk taking. These organizations encourage people to take big bets, often rewarding those who take chances and succeed. Whether the company emphasizes autonomy or close monitoring, security or risk taking, or any of a number of other dimensions of organization culture, people have more positive views of those organizations whose cultures fit their personal beliefs.

Because fit between corporate culture and employee beliefs is beneficial, many organizations provide incentives, such as bonuses, raises, and promotions, to encourage their staff to align their thinking with that of the company. However, no business ever gets all its workers to conform their values to the corporate culture. Like Robert from the chapter's opening vignette, some people just plain disagree with the philosophy of the organization that they work for and can't seem to realign their beliefs.

Many researchers think that people like Robert can't easily change their work values because these beliefs are partially innate. Although we are accustomed to assuming that our values are shaped largely by how our parents raised us, the data show that, for many beliefs, genes account for more of the difference between people than the family context in which we grew up.[11] Take, for example, attitudes toward religion and politics. The majority of the variance between people comes from genetic factors.[12] Even the most rigorous studies of twins reared in different homes show that more than half of the difference in levels of "social conservatism" is genetic, regardless of the specific dimensions of "social conservatism" examined.[13] In fact, research shows that a wide array of different attitudes are at least partially innate, including beliefs about the death penalty, abortion, open-door immigration, and organized religion, with genetics typically accounting for more than one-third of the difference between people.[14]

Work Values

Our genes don't just influence our religious and political attitudes; they also affect our beliefs about business. For instance, studies show that a significant portion of the variance among people on whether capitalism is good, socialism is evil, unions are helpful, and the nationalization of industry is wise, are accounted for by differences in our genetic makeup.[15]

But what about beliefs in the different dimensions of organizational culture discussed earlier in the chapter? Do our genes affect those values, too? The answer is yes. As Table 4.1 shows, genetic factors account for between 37 and 68 percent of the difference in preferences for the following dimensions of organizational culture: achievement, comfort, status, safety, autonomy, and altruism.[16]

People look for all sorts of different things when deciding whether or not to take a job. For some people, security is of paramount concern. These people want "a job with a definite and predictable future," where they can "avoid taking social or economic risks on the job."[17] And they favor companies whose cultures emphasize job permanence.

Research shows that our genes affect our preference for this dimension of organizational culture. A study of identical and fraternal twins who were raised in different families shows that a significant portion of the variance in the importance that people place on job security is genetic.[18]

For other people, a key aspect of organizational culture is status. These people favor companies that have a brand name or cachet among their friends and neighbors. The desire to work for high-status employers

Table 4.1 Genetic effects on preferences for dimensions of organizational culture

Dimension	Definition	Share of the difference accounted for by genetics
Achievement	A work environment in which the chance to use one's abilities is encouraged	68 percent
Status	A work environment in which authority and social position are widely recognized	63 percent
Safety	A work environment in which policies and procedures are carefully followed	49 percent
Comfort	A work environment in which a job has pleasant working conditions	42 percent
Autonomy	A work environment in which freedom and independence are encouraged	38 percent
Altruism	A work environment in which moral values, social service, and concern for coworkers are stressed	37 percent

Source: Adapted from Keller, L., Arvey, R., Bouchard, T., Segal, N., and Davis, R. 1992. Work values: Genetic and environmental influences. *Journal of Applied Psychology,* 77(1): 79–88.

is partially genetic. One study showed that 37 percent of the difference in the preference for a job that lets a person "be 'somebody' in the community" comes from genetic factors.[19]

What about freedom to make your own decisions on the job? Some people are attracted to jobs where they can exercise their own judgment, while such opportunities are of less importance to others. The preference for employers whose cultures emphasize personal freedom is also partially innate. One study demonstrated that 30 percent of the difference in the desire for a job that provides the "freedom to use my own judgment" is genetic.[20]

From Misfit to Action

As the discussion at the beginning of the chapter pointed out, one of the effects of job dissatisfaction is turnover. People who don't like their work are more likely to quit than those who are happy with it.[21] This self-evident point raises an important question: since your genetic composition affects the odds that you will be satisfied in your job, doesn't it also influence your chances of shifting jobs? The answer is yes. More than one-third of the difference in the frequency of actual job changes—36 percent—is accounted for by our genetic makeup.[22]

What about the tendency to be a "job hopper," quitting a position every couple of years to find a new one? Is that in some people's DNA? As you probably suspect from the genetic effects on job satisfaction and turnover, the answer is "yes." There is a genetic component to the type of employment record that folks have. Over half (56 percent) of the difference in people's descriptions of their job histories as "stable" or "changing" comes from their genes.[23]

In fact, it's not just changing companies within an industry that your genes influence, it's also changing occupations. It turns out that 26 percent of the difference between people in occupational change (e.g., shifting from being a doctor to being a lawyer, or from being a manager to being a teacher) is genetic.[24] So one reason why certain people shift careers while others do not is found somewhere in their DNA.

Our genes might even explain whether or not we quit our jobs to go into business for ourselves. Studies show that the desire to have more autonomy at work is a key factor motivating many people to start their own companies. In fact, one study showed that agreement with the statement "being my own boss is vital in choosing a job" increases the odds that a person will be self-employed 10 years later, while accord with the phrase "job security is most vital in choosing a job" reduces the chances that a person will be self-employed a decade hence.[25] Because our genes have a strong effect on our preferences, some individuals may be more inclined than others to quit their jobs and start their own companies because of genetic variation that predisposes them toward work autonomy and away from job security. After all, research shows that genetic differences affect the odds that people will go into business for themselves.[26] (For more about genetic effects on entrepreneurship, see chapter 9.)

How Our Genes Affect Our Work Values, Job Satisfaction, and Job Turnover

How do genes affect work values and work outcomes, such as job satisfaction and turnover? After all, there is no "job-satisfaction gene," and no one exits the womb with a set of work-related values. So, clearly, genetic effects must operate through some indirect mechanism. But what is that pathway? How do genes, which code for the development of different proteins, end up influencing our work values and job satisfaction?

Researchers have found evidence for three different paths: through temperament, personality, and cognitive abilities. Let's take a look at how genetic effects operate.

Temperament

Tom, from the introductory vignette, is a happy guy, always seeing the best in everything, while Robert is a glass-is-half-empty type who has a more pessimistic worldview. This difference in temperament accounts for much of the reason that Tom has higher job satisfaction than Robert. Because he is a more positive guy in general, Tom is happier with his work than Robert.

Meta-analyses of many studies of job satisfaction conducted by psychologists in a variety of settings over a number of years show that between 10 to 25 percent of the difference between people in job satisfaction—particularly contentment with the work itself, happiness with coworkers, and perceptions of job stress—is the result of variation in temperament. People with a negative outlook on life tend to experience more stress on the job and are less satisfied with their work and relationships with coworkers than those with a more positive perspective.[27]

They are also more likely to quit their jobs. Research shows that happy people express more organizational commitment and have lower odds of leaving their employers than unhappy people.[28] The effect of temperament on job satisfaction is so powerful that it predicts job and career contentment as much as 50 years after it is measured. Moreover, temperament influences all aspects of job satisfaction, including happiness with income, opportunity for advancement, freedom to develop ideas, and job security.[29]

Okay, so your temperament affects your level of job satisfaction, but is the source of those effects genetic? We have some compelling evidence that the answer is yes. As chapter 2 explained, twin and adoption studies show that more than half of the difference in some aspects of people's dispositions is explained by genetic factors.[30] In fact, as Table 4.2 shows, identical twins have much more similar temperaments than fraternal twins, even if they were raised in separate households with no contact with one another.

Table 4.2 Correlations between identical and fraternal twins raised together and apart on different measures of temperament

Dimension	Identical twins raised apart	Identical twins raised together	Fraternal twins raised apart	Fraternal twins raised together
Negative emotionality	61	54	29	41
Stress reaction	61	52	27	24
Well-being	52	44	−2	8
Emotionality—fear	37	49	4	8
Positive emotionality	34	63	−7	18
Emotionality—anger	33	37	9	17
Emotionality—distress	30	52	26	16

Source: Lykken, D., and Tellegen, A. 1996. Happiness is a stochastic phenomenon. *Psychological Science*, 7(3): 186–189. Plomin, R., Pedersen, N., McClearn, G., Nesselroade, J., and Bergeman, C. EAS temperaments during the last half of the life span: Twins reared apart and twins reared together. *Psychology and Aging*, 3(1): 43–50; Tellegen, A., Lykken, D., Bouchard, T., Wilcox, K., Segal, N., and Rich, S. 1988. Personality similarity in twins reared apart and together. *Journal of Personality and Social Psychology*, 34(6): 1031–1039.

Moreover, molecular genetics studies show that differences in serotonin, dopamine, and MAO genes influence temperament.[31] Because people with a positive outlook on life tend to have different versions of neurotransmitter genes than people with a negative worldview, genes for brain chemicals might affect job satisfaction through their effect on temperament.

Some researchers have examined the evidence for this causal path. They looked at whether there was a genetic component to job satisfaction, and if there was, how genes exerted their influence. The researchers found that almost half (45 percent) of the genetic difference in job satisfaction comes from the effect of genes on temperament.[32]

Personality

Another way that our genes impact our job satisfaction is through their effects on our personalities. Psychologists and human resource experts have found that people with high core self-evaluation (those with high self-esteem, self-efficacy, and emotional stability, and an internal locus of control) tend to be satisfied with whatever job they have.[33] Moreover, genetics affects all four of the components of core self-evaluation. As much as 55 percent of the difference in locus of control,[34] 49 percent of the variance in self-esteem,[35] and 68 percent of the difference in emotional stability[36] comes from genetic factors.[37]

Research shows that people with other personality traits are also more satisfied with their jobs. For instance, neurotics have lesser job satisfaction and experience more work stress than emotionally stable people, perhaps because the former feel greater anxiety from adverse job events. Conscientious people have greater job satisfaction than other people, possibly because they tend to be more involved in their work, which makes them more likely to receive rewards, such as pay increases and bonuses. Extraverts experience less job stress and more job satisfaction than introverts, perhaps because the former are more social, which leads them to form more friendships at work.[38]

Genetics influences the development of all of these personality traits. Numerous studies show that more than half the difference between people in the OCEAN model of personality is genetic.[39] Moreover, certain variants of genes responsible for the brain chemicals monoamine oxidase, serotonin, and dopamine are found to a greater extent among people with particular personality traits.[40] So it is quite plausible that a person's neurotransmitter genes affect his or her personality, which, in turn, influences his or her level of job satisfaction.

In fact, some researchers have examined this causal path, looking at whether there is a genetic component to job satisfaction, and if there is, how the genetic effects work. The scientists found that 24 percent of the *genetic share* of job satisfaction operates through the OCEAN personality traits.[41] That is, your genes affect your job satisfaction by influencing the kind of personality you have.

There is also evidence that genetic differences in personality lead to job satisfaction and turnover by influencing the fit between people's beliefs and the cultures of the organizations they work for. Research shows that your work values are related to your personality.[42] For instance, novelty seekers favor work environments that offer autonomy and independence,[43] neurotics seek settings that emphasize job status and employment security,[44] and the self-confident prefer places that offer the chance to make one's own decisions.[45] Whatever the specific work values that people with different personality traits seek, those who find themselves in organizations whose cultures do not support those values tend to be dissatisfied and prone to quitting their jobs.

Cognitive Abilities

Genetics also influences job satisfaction through its effect on cognitive abilities. As we saw in chapter 2, genes have a profound effect on these individual attributes, accounting for the majority of the variance between people in intelligence and cognitive skills.[46] This genetically influenced variation in mental ability could lead to differences in job satisfaction, given the negative relationship between intelligence and contentment with work.[47] Smarter people, research shows, tend to be less satisfied with their jobs. Therefore, having versions of the genes that enhance intelligence could account for some of the difference among people in job satisfaction.

Moreover, your genes might affect your job satisfaction by influencing the fit between your cognitive abilities and the requirements of your job. People have low job satisfaction when their skills and abilities don't fit position requirements, as occurs when, say, an innumerate person is assigned to a company's accounting department.[48] Because genetics affects people's skills and abilities, making some of us better at math, others at writing, and so on, a portion of job dissatisfaction might stem from having the wrong genetic makeup for your job.[49]

Furthermore, your cognitive abilities affect the kind of employment you can get. As we know from surveys, if not from common sense, some jobs are more satisfying than others. For instance, college professors tend to have higher job satisfaction than septic tank cleaners. Because people need different skills to get their positions—you need to know calculus to become a college math professor, but not a septic tank cleaner—your genes might influence your job satisfaction by affecting the abilities that you develop, which, in turn, constrain the kind of work you can find.[50]

Conclusions

Your job satisfaction is in part genetic. Regardless of who your employer is, what you are paid, or what your working conditions are like, your genes affect the odds that you will be happy with your job. This is true for how satisfied you are with the nature of the work itself as well as with your pay and chances for advancement. Moreover, because people who are less satisfied with their jobs are more likely to quit them, your genes also affect how likely you are to change employment.

Does this mean some people are predestined to hate their work, never to enjoy employment anywhere? Of course not. No one's DNA *guarantees* that they will have low (or high) job satisfaction. Some people's genes just make them *more likely* to be content with their jobs than others. Sure, good pay, a pleasant work environment, and a nice boss make a difference in your job satisfaction, but those of us born with the "right" versions of key genes will be more likely than others to be happy in a job with lousy compensation, a poor work setting, and a terrible supervisor. And people with the "wrong" versions of those genes will have greater odds of hating a high-paying position, working for a sainted boss in a great company.

Because there is no such thing as the "job-satisfaction" gene, your genes don't affect your work happiness or your odds of changing employers directly. Rather, they do it by affecting your temperament, personality, and cognitive abilities. Genetic differences in temperament influence job satisfaction because people with more positive worldviews look favorably upon just about everything, including their jobs. Genetic differences in personality also matter; conscientious, extroverted and emotionally stable people have higher job satisfaction than others. Genetically influenced personality traits also impact people's work values and their fit with the cultures of their employers, as well as their attitudes toward their jobs. Genetic differences in intelligence and cognitive abilities affect job fulfillment because smarter people tend to be less satisfied with their work than the less intelligent, because our intellect affects the types of employment we can get (and some jobs are better than others), and because job satisfaction is higher for people whose cognitive abilities are more appropriate for their positions.

Having described how genetic factors influence your job satisfaction and the odds that you will change employment, I now turn to the effect of your genes on how you make decisions, the subject of the next chapter.

5

Instinctive Choices: Genetic Influences on Decision Making

Alice was a senior manager at a consumer products company. Her job required her to make a large number of decisions every day. She had to make choices about the strategy of her division, hiring managers, setting budgets, selecting new projects, and a host of other things.

Alice had received an MBA from a prestigious university and had been taught decision making by some of the greatest experts on the topic. So she understood exactly how to make choices using the types of complex decision tools taught in business school. In part, that's why her company hired her. They wanted someone to use state-of-the-art tools to make decisions about new projects.

There was only one problem. Alice never used the tools. She always went with her gut. She believed intuition was the way to go with most business decisions. This, of course, caused some conflict with her boss, who was a big believer in rational decision making. So far, Alice was okay. Her choices had mostly been right, and that has protected her from criticism in her company environment.

But one of these days, she would pick poorly, and would be criticized for not using the decision models taught to her in business school. Despite this risk, Alice couldn't bring herself to use the tools. She just didn't think they were as good as her intuition.

Like Alice, all of us make decisions every day as part of our jobs. These choices might be about the strategic direction of the company where we work, or they might be about how to design the firm's operations. They might concern which new products to make or what production schedule to adopt. They might be about whom to hire, or how to treat customers, or even just whether to come to work on a given day. But no matter who you are or where you work, you need to make decisions as part of your job.[1]

More important, these choices matter. The performance of organizations depends on the sum of the decisions made by the people in them. If everyone—frontline employees, middle managers, and senior executives—selects poorly, then the organization will falter. But if everyone makes great decisions, then the business will do well. No doubt about it, decision-making skills are central to company performance.[2]

So why do we make choices the way we do? Why do some of us make gut decisions, while others use complex decision tools? Why do some of us make choices without doing much due diligence, while others analyze reams of data before selecting between alternatives?

Of course, there are a lot of reasons behind the way we make choices. So many factors, in fact, that people have written whole books about them. We might have learned how to make decisions in certain ways from our parents, or at school, or on the job—at least, these are the explanations that experts tend to provide.

But there's another force at work: genetics. We are born with a predilection to make choices in certain ways. In fact, our DNA influences several aspects of decision making, from how rational our choices are, to the degree to which we discount the future, to how much information we need to select between alternatives, to how intuitive our decisions are.

For instance, do you think quickly, but make decisions calmly? That might be because of the combination of serotonin and the human-brain-derived neurotropic genes (BDNF) that you have. (I will call BDNF the "memory" gene.) What about being a risk taker? That might come from your versions of the "worrier" (COMT) and "impulsiveness" (DRD2) genes.[3] (Keep in mind that there are many genes that affect memory, worry, and risk taking; the names I have given these genes are just a way to help you remember some of their many functions.)

While researchers have only begun to scratch the surface of how your genes affect the way you make choices, already they have found interesting patterns. Are you curious about what aspects of decision making your genes affect, how your DNA influences the way you select between alternatives, and what genes are involved? That's probably at least partially genetic—so go ahead, read on.

The Effect of Genes on Decision Making

Decision making is a complex process, one worthy of far more discussion than I have space to give it. Numerous components go into the process of selecting between alternatives, from the gathering of information, to its analysis, to an assessment of its probability of occurring. Moreover, the topic can be approached on a number of levels, from the mental process that a single individual engages in to the efforts of a group of people to reach an outcome. Decision making is simply too vast a subject for me to attempt to cover all the ways in which genetics affects it. Therefore, I will focus instead on highlighting how your genes influence a few selected aspects of choice taking. Readers should note that I have chosen five dimensions I think are interesting and easily understood by most people: intuition, insight, information gathering, risk taking, and group decision making. These aspects represent neither the totality of choice taking, nor the sum of genetic effects.

Are You an Intuitive Decision Maker?

Academics like to teach people how to make choices rationally. Whether in decision theory courses in MBA programs or undergraduate economics and management classes, people are shown how to select between alternatives according to a rational model of balancing costs and benefits. Often, the decision is arrived at by mathematically calculating the best choice from a set of alternatives, because math relies on logic, not intuition.

However, many people don't use these decision tools. They don't calculate out the best alternative from a set of choices. They don't balance the costs and benefits. They don't make rational decisions. They make intuitive choices, without gathering and evaluating evidence to justify their selections.[4] That is, they go with their gut.

One can easily see the value of intuitive decision making in the business world. Going with your gut may be particularly useful when the future is uncertain and you don't know ahead of time if your selection will be correct. Having intuition might help you to pick stocks or to decide whether a new product makes sense to launch. It might help to choose whether a prospective employee is likely to be good or stands a high chance of doing five to ten in the state pen.

Take a look at how successful entrepreneur Sam Wyly describes making business decisions. He says it involves "paying attention to the ideas and trends floating around out there, studying them, coming to some intellectual conclusions, and then, ultimately, listening to your own gut about how to apply your conclusions to the business ventures you elect to pursue."[5]

As you might imagine, intuition is a tricky thing to measure. It's hard to figure out whether a person has a gut feel for something that isn't readily seen by others. But researchers do the best that they can.

One way they do this is to ask people how they make choices. Surveys reveal that some people make rational decisions, while others take a more intuitive approach. So why are there differences between us in our methods? There are many reasons, but one of the most interesting is genetics.

Studies show that genes account for close to half of the variance between people in the tendency to rely on intuition to make choices. In fact, genetics affects the tendency to use inductive versus deductive reasoning, to collect data through the senses, to focus on a small amount of information versus taking a more global view, and a number of other dimensions of rational and intuitive decision making.[6] Researchers have even found evidence of a genetic basis to the concept of "women's intuition."[7] In short, the use of more intuitive approaches to making choices is something that some of us are born more predisposed to do.

Information Gathering

Suppose you need to make a decision. It could be about which candidate to hire for a job, or which stock to buy, or how to make a case to your boss that your department needs an increase in its budget. Whatever that decision is, you need to collect some information to make it.

Take the example of choosing a new employee. You need to decide how much to investigate the backgrounds of the job applicants. Do you interview prospective employees and stop there? Do you also check their references? What about references that they didn't supply? Do you hire a company to conduct a background check on them? Do you look at their college transcripts and SAT scores?

You might need more information than your coworkers require to hire someone new. That's because people generally gather different amounts of data to make decisions. Some need to gather very little before they make their choice, while others need to collect volumes before they feel comfortable deciding.

Why do people require such different amounts of information to make decisions? Like many things, some of the difference is learned. It's just how they were taught to make choices in school or by their parents. But another part of this variation is innate.

Human beings are hardwired to seek out information. When people find rich sources of data, their brains release opioids, which are brain chemicals that enhance pleasure.[8] Some scientists believe that not everyone's body releases the same amount of opioids in response to a given amount of information. The size of the reaction depends on which versions of the opioid genes a person got at birth. Certain people have the versions that cause their brains to release a lot of opioids, while other people have the variants that cause a smaller release of these pleasure chemicals. Perhaps people whose DNA hardwires them to get a bigger opioid release from the discovery of information will be more likely than other people to gather a lot of data before making any decisions.

Risk Taking

"He's a born risk taker." I'm sure you've heard that phrase, whether it was used to describe your boss, one of your subordinates, or the motor-cycle-driving, helmet-eschewing, hang-gliding-champion who is dating your 18-year-old daughter. That phrase developed for a reason. Some people, it seems, are much more willing than others to take chances—all kinds of chances—starting when they are first born and continuing throughout their entire lives.

Why? Again, genetics appears to be at work.

Studies that compare identical and fraternal twins have shown that as much as 55 percent of the difference between people in their willingness to take risks is genetic.[9] That's a pretty hefty portion of the variance between people, one larger, in fact, than that accounted for by environmental factors, such as how people are raised or the experiences that they have had over the course of their lives.

DNA affects the type of risks that businesspeople take every day. Consider for example, the choice between more and less certain financial outcomes. One set of researchers examined the effect of genetics on preferences for different payoffs, using a portion of a questionnaire employed by an investment management company to assess the risk tolerance of its clients. This questionnaire asked people to select between alternatives in the following three investment settings:

- You won a lottery and have to choose between a certain payment of $2,000, a 50–50 chance of getting either a $5,000 payment or nothing, and a 20 percent chance of a $15,000 payment and an 80 percent chance of receiving nothing. Which do you select?
- You have to allocate between three investment opportunities: (a) "a money-market fund or guaranteed investment contract, giving up the possibility of major gains, but virtually assuring the safety of your principal," (b) a "50–50 mix of stock and bond funds, in the hopes of getting some growth, but also giving yourself some protection in the form of steady income," and (c) "aggressive growth mutual funds whose value will probably fluctuate significantly during the years but have potential for impressive gains in the long term." Which do you pick?
- You have to choose how much to invest in stock at a private employer that has plans of going public in three years, but which offers no possible return if the company fails to do so. How much of your salary do you invest: (a) "none," (b) "two months' salary," or (c) "4 months' salary?"

The study showed that 63 percent of the difference between people in these choices was genetic.[10]

The effect of your DNA on financial risk taking isn't just seen in experimental settings. One set of researchers looked at *actual* portfolio allocations and found that 25 percent of the difference between people in their tendency to select different types of investments is genetic.[11]

Researchers have identified several genes (among many that will likely be discovered in coming years) that each have a small effect on risk taking. A version of the "worrier" (COMT) gene is associated with the tendency to be a risk seeker.[12] So is a version of the "impulsiveness" (DRD2) gene.[13] People with certain versions of the latter gene also tend to respond strongly to the opportunity to gamble. One variant of the FAAH gene (which I will call the "Warren Buffett" gene) reduces the brain's fear mechanism and increases its reaction to money making.[14] One study showed that people with a variant of the "novelty-seeking" (DRD4) gene took 25 percent more risk than individuals with another version.[15] Another study showed that men with a variant of this gene were more tolerant of risk in a game that involved financial decision making than those with another version. In fact, the difference in the gene accounted for 5 percent of the difference in risk preference, roughly one-fifth of the share of financial risk taking that comes from genetic sources.[16]

The association between specific genes and risk taking is intriguing and suggests the influence that our genes have on how we act at the office. However, we must treat these findings with caution. As I have mentioned when discussing other genes, we don't yet have extensive replication of the results (which could subsequently be proven wrong), and any one gene might account for only a small portion of the difference between people in this behavior.

So far I have implied that risk taking is always good. But that's not really true. We know that some people take too many chances, and may even destroy their own lives through their bets. One example of self-destructive risk taking is pathological gambling, what the clinicians define as wagering so much money so frequently that it interferes with a person's job or family. (Studies confirm that pathological gambling is related to general chance taking because pathological gamblers tend to score high on general tests of risk taking.[17])

This type of destructive betting occurs for many reasons, including genetic predisposition. Researchers have found that 55 percent of the difference between people on one aspect of pathological gambling—"gambling with larger amounts for longer periods than intended"—and 51 percent of the variance on another aspect of this disorder—"increasing bets to maintain interest"—are genetic.[18]

Genes might also affect risk taking in more complex ways. They might, for instance, influence how people perceive opportunities. To see how, consider two people—one who is genetically predisposed to take chances and another whose genes incline her to shun risks. The first person might be perfectly comfortable placing a bet, while the second might feel sick to her stomach bearing the same risk. As a result, when making a risky decision, such as whether to develop an unproven technology, the first person sees the opportunities opened up by the invention, while the second sees only the downside loss from choosing wrongly.

Now suppose that the person with the predisposition to shun risks has the version of the stathmin protein gene that leads her to recall all of her bad experiences with previous downside losses. Combined with the non-risk-taking version of the first gene, the variant of the second gene would lead to a further negative reaction to the risky situation. As a result, the person with the "negative" versions of these two genes might be unable to see business opportunities in uncertain situations that are plain as day to other people.[19]

Group Decision Making

Have you ever been in a meeting where you anticipated that the group around the table was going to have a long discussion of the different options to solve a problem before reaching an agreement? But two minutes after the first person spoke, everyone else was agreeing with her, and no one was willing to bring up anything different. For the next five minutes, each person in the room made some brief statement that essentially restated the position of the first speaker. Then the meeting adjourned, having reached consensus on the approach brought up by the first speaker without considering any other alternatives. Well, that's groupthink.

Unfortunately, groupthink can play a big role in how people make decisions in business. And it can be a real problem. While consensus is good, if people come to agreement too quickly, they often fail to consider better alternatives. So it's important for companies to make sure their employees don't engage in too much groupthink. Doing that involves understanding *why* groupthink occurs in the first place.

Researchers have found that organizational structures, pressures and stressors present at the time that the choices are being made, and a host of other factors external to the decision makers, play a large part in explaining groupthink. But environmental conditions aren't the only forces that account for why we engage in groupthink. Our genes also play a role.

Two important aspects of groupthink are social conformity—being consistent with the norms and beliefs of the groups we are part of—and compliance—obeying the rules imposed by the groups we are in. Compliance and social conformity contribute to groupthink. When people believe that they must adhere to a group's norms and ideas and obey its rules, they are unlikely to disagree with the positions expressed by others. As a consequence, the group will often converge quickly on a position, resulting in groupthink.

People differ in their tendency to conform socially for genetic reasons. For instance, research shows that 48 percent of the difference between people in how compliant they are is innate.[20] This means that some people are more genetically predisposed to engage in groupthink than others.

Groupthink isn't the only aspect of group decision making that genetics effects. While researchers are only beginning to explore this topic, they have made some fascinating discoveries that are worth mentioning. One of these is the way people make decisions that affect others.

When people make choices, they often need to select between alternatives that help others at their own expense or benefit themselves at a cost to the others. For instance, a team leader responsible for assigning overtime might allot it in a way that helps himself to the detriment of his subordinates or in a manner that aids the subordinates at a cost to himself.

Scientists have found some people tend to act selfishly when making decisions, while others tend to act selflessly. While there are a number of reasons why these differences exist, researchers have recently discovered a genetic explanation—one that was discussed in chapter 3 in the context of preferences for altruistic jobs. Approximately 20 percent of the difference between people in selfless behavior is innate.[21] And 42 percent of the variance in the willingness to give up financial gains to punish unfair behavior is genetic.[22] Moreover, the tendency to make benevolent decisions depends, in part, on which version of the "altruism" gene (AVPR1A) you have.[23] Individuals who produce a lot of the hormone that this gene codes for feel good toward others even when they are not treated well, and act in more trusting ways than people who produce less of it. Thus, some people may be born predisposed to make decisions more selflessly than others, at least in part because they have a version of a gene that stimulates greater production of a hormone that generates feelings of emotional attachment.

How Our Genes Influence Decision Making

Let's assume that you accept the evidence that your genes influence how you make decisions. The next question is how they do it. Research suggests several different paths, including through their influence on neurotransmitters, hormones, temperament, personality traits, and cognitive skills.

From Genes to Neurotransmitters to Decision Making

To understand how your genes affect the way you make choices through the instructions they provide for the production of neurotransmitters, let's take a look at the example of risky decision making. As you no doubt know, some people are more prone to taking chances than others. Whether they have a penchant for buying penny stocks, going hang gliding, or having unprotected sex, some people are less concerned about risk than others. Many researchers believe that this difference comes, at least in part, from how different versions of certain genes code for the release and decomposition of neurotransmitters in the brain.

Scientists have found that differences in a DNA sequence for one of the serotonin genes are related to the willingness to take chances. People with a particular version of this gene score higher on psychological tests of risk taking and are more likely to choose uncertain options than people with an alternative variant of the gene.[24]

Some researchers think this genetic effect occurs by influencing people's attention. When asked to choose between alternatives in a gambling game, people with the version of the gene associated with less risk taking focused more on the odds of winning the game, and paid less attention to the overall expected value of the different choices, than people with the other version of the gene.[25]

In contrast to the effect of serotonin, which appears to moderate risk taking, the neurotransmitter dopamine seems to accelerate it.[26] Researchers believe that the level of this brain chemical affects how people feel about taking risks.[27] Studies indicate that people with certain versions of the "impulsiveness" (DRD2) and "novelty-seeking" (DRD4) genes take more chances than those with other variants.[28] In addition, people with those versions of the two genes are more likely to be diagnosed with a gambling disorder.[29] And people with Parkinson's disease, which is a disorder of the dopamine system, have a tendency to become compulsive gamblers when they take dopamine drugs to treat their symptoms.[30]

Related to the effect of the serotonin and dopamine genes is the impact of the MAO genes. Genetically influenced MAO levels are associated with the tendency to take chances; low levels of MAO in the bloodstream are correlated with high levels of risk taking and impulsivity;[31] and people with low levels of MAO are more likely than those with high levels to be pathological gamblers.[32] In short, genetic factors account for part of the difference between people in the amount of three chemicals in their brains—dopamine, serotonin, and monoamine oxidase—and these levels, in turn, influence the tendency to make risky decisions.

Thinking with Your Gonads: The Path Through Hormones

Have you ever heard the expression that "he is thinking with his gonads"? Well, it turns out that there is some truth to it. Our sex hormones (as well as our other hormones) influence the way in which we make a variety of decisions in the workplace. Because the evidence is strongest for the effect of testosterone, I'll focus here on that hormone.

Some evidence suggests that the genes that provide instructions for the production of testosterone affect how willing you are to take chances. As was mentioned earlier, a person's DNA influences how much testosterone his or her body produces. Evidence that high-testosterone men take more risks than low-testosterone men suggests that differences in genetic instructions for the production of this hormone might impact your risk tolerance.[33]

Your testosterone genes might also affect how rational a decision maker you are. Studies show that higher testosterone levels are associated with a less analytical process. For instance, women tend to perform worse on tests of rational decision making after receiving testosterone supplements than before.[34]

Moreover, experiments designed to force men to choose between alternatives show that high-testosterone men act less rationally than their low-testosterone counterparts. For example, high-testosterone men tend to reject low offers when playing the ultimatum game. In this game, two people have the opportunity to split $10. The first person makes an offer of how the money is to be divided, and the second person gets to accept or reject the proposal, with the payout to them being zero if the offer is rejected and the amount proposed if it is accepted. The rejection of low offers in this game indicates a desire for dominance rather than economic rationality.[35] So it's quite plausible that men born with the "high-production" versions of their testosterone genes are less rational decision makers than those born with the "low-production" variants.

Although I mentioned that I would focus on the effect of testosterone genes, I want to provide one example of the effects of genes that provide instructions for the production of another hormone, cortisol, because this body chemical affects something that is absolutely central to decision making in business: assessing the time value of money. As I am sure you know, money paid today is worth more than money paid in the future. That's why people generally need to receive more to be willing to choose future payments in place of payments today. (Just think about how much more of your salary would need to get for you to agree to be paid once a decade, rather than weekly or monthly, as you are now.) But people differ on how much more money they need to receive in the future to make up for not being paid today (something that economists call time discounting). More important for our purposes, your time discounting depends, in part, on what instructions your genes provide for your body's base level of cortisol. People with a higher base cortisol level tend to want to be paid sooner than people with a lower base cortisol level, even if the amount of the future payment is much larger than the compensation today. Thus, some people are genetically predisposed to have lower time discounting than others, which affects how they make decisions that involve calculations of the time value of money.

Genes, Personality, and Decision Making

Your genes also influence your decision making through their effects on your personality. Take, for example, the impact of genes associated with extraversion. Extraverts are more willing than introverts to make decisions based on vague and incomplete data, perhaps deciding to launch a new product on the expressions of interest of just a few customers.[36] They also tend to gather information informally—chatting with people rather than surveying them—and prefer to gather non-confirming rather than corroborating data.[37] And they are better than introverts at making group decisions,[38] participating more in both electronic and face-to-face group meetings, further embellishing their comments in electronic meetings, and acting more reflectively in face-to-face gatherings.[39]

As we saw in other chapters, as much as 67 percent of the difference between people in extraversion is genetic;[40] and people with certain versions of neurotransmitter genes are more likely than other people to develop this personality trait.[41] Therefore, it is quite plausible that the amount and completeness of data that you need to make decisions, your willingness to gather that knowledge informally, your interest in hearing disconfirming information, and the amount that you contribute in group meetings are all affected by the versions of genes that you were born with, particularly the neurotransmitter genes associated with extraversion.

Your genes affect your decision making through other personality traits as well. Consider neuroticism. While people who are emotionally stable feel comfortable taking a variety of risks, including financial, career and strategic ones, anxious people don't like to take chances.[42] Moreover, neurotics aren't very good at gathering information. Because they are uncomfortable hearing negative news, they tend to seek confirming data and feel a lot of time pressure when gathering facts and figures.[43] Of course, neuroticism isn't something that people get randomly; your genes affect your odds of developing this personality trait.[44] So your allotment of DNA might affect your decision making by influencing the likelihood that you are neurotic rather than emotionally stable.

But the relationship between these genes and making choices is more complicated than a "bad" version of a gene leading to "poor" decision making by increasing the odds that a person will be neurotic. Some of the genes have versions that make neuroticism more likely, but also increase the odds of developing characteristics that enhance aspects of decision making. For instance, one version of the "worrier" gene (COMT) reduces risk taking. However, the same version of the gene also lowers aggressiveness, which can facilitate decision making, particularly in groups.[45]

Your genes might influence how you make choices by making you more likely to be open to experience. People with this personality trait tend to gather a wide range of information. They often consult a variety of sources, from people to archival records. They also tend to exercise a lot of critical judgment when evaluating facts and figures, and are very willing to consider disconfirming information.[46]

Some people are born with a genetic predisposition to be open to experience.[47] Therefore, your mom and dad might affect how you make choices—just not for reasons that most people think. Rather than affecting your decision making by how they raised you, your parents might do it through the DNA they gave you.

Your genes might also influence how you select between alternatives by increasing the chances that you develop an agreeable personality. More agreeable people make decisions differently than less agreeable ones. Agreeable people tend to believe that time is not a constraint to making choices; if they need more data to come to a conclusion they have time to get it.[48] Because much of the difference between people in agreeableness is genetic,[49] and versions of several genes are more common among agreeable people than among disagreeable ones,[50] your DNA might affect your decision making by influencing your predisposition to develop an agreeable personality.

Your genes also might influence how you make decisions through their effect on another of the OCEAN personality traits: conscientiousness. This psychological attribute impacts many aspects of decision making. People high in conscientiousness tend to gather disconfirming information to make sure that their decisions are truly valid. They tend not to feel a lot of time pressure when gathering data, believing that they can find additional time if they need it.[51] However, they have a tendency to look backward when making choices, suffering more from hindsight bias than other people (because of their need to justify their decisions).[52] This makes conscientious people more likely than others to interpret the past as more predictable than it actually was, as occurs when an investor explains, after the fact, that the direction of the stock market was always clear to him.

Genetics accounts for as much as 61 percent of the difference between people in conscientiousness;[53] and a variety of genes are associated with this personality trait.[54] In short, you might make decisions differently than others because you were born with the versions of genes that increase the odds of developing a conscientious personality.

The OCEAN traits are not the only aspects of personality through which genes impact your choice making. For instance, the versions of the neurotransmitter genes that you receive influence your odds of being novelty seeking,[55] and that personality trait, in turn, is associated with the following aspects of decision making:

- **Speed**: High-novelty seekers have shorter attention spans and make faster decisions than low-novelty seekers. They often make choices before all the data have been collected, in contrast to low-novelty seekers, who tend to gather large amounts of information before selecting between alternatives.[56]
- **Taking chances**: High-novelty seekers are more willing to place bets than low-novelty seekers, and prefer high-risk/high-reward outcomes, particularly in the pursuit of things that are new.[57] As Dr. Dean Hamer, a geneticist at the National Institutes of Health, writes in his book *Living with our Genes*, "A high novelty seeker may be more likely to . . . make a killing on the stock market, but he is just as likely to lose it all on a bad bet. A low novelty seeker may never hit the jackpot and might keep his money in low-yield CDs, but neither is he likely to . . . lose everything on a risky venture."[58]

Your genes might also influence how you make decisions by affecting your self-confidence. People who are unsure of themselves often have a hard time making choices, and avoid risky actions because they don't believe their own judgment. In addition, they are more likely to engage in groupthink because they are unwilling to challenge the wisdom of others.[59] People high in self-confidence, on the other hand, tend to be self-serving, taking credit for good outcomes and passing blame for bad ones. Because genes account for more than one-third of the variation between people in self-confidence,[60] they might account for some of the reasons why people make different choices, particularly those that are influenced by surety in one's own beliefs.

Genes for Temperament and Making Choices

In previous chapters, we've seen the role that genetically influenced differences in temperament play in many aspects of work-related behavior. This variation also affects decision making. As you have already seen, many studies show that genetics accounts for much of the variance between people in their general worldview,[61] with the genes that code for the production of neurotransmitters being plausible candidates for the source of these differences.[62] Temperament, in turn, affects decision making in a variety of ways. For instance, pessimists tend to have a harder time solving problems[63] and make worse choices than optimists because they tend to get bogged down in evaluating all possible alternatives, unable to see the forest for the trees.[64] Moreover, people with positive temperaments tend to make faster selections than people with negative temperaments because they are more willing to use heuristics to make decisions.[65] Optimists' willingness to extrapolate from a few data points, what researchers call representativeness, helps them make choices more quickly about everything from hiring employees to selecting new products to purchasing office supplies. But people with negative temperaments are better critical thinkers than people with positive temperaments because they are more accurate at judging risk and identifying causal effects.[66] In short, the instructions our genes provide for neurotransmitters (among other things) appear to influence how optimistic or pessimistic we are, which, in turn, affects how we make decisions.

Genes for Intelligence and Decision Making

Legendary investor Warren Buffett is known to have high intelligence, laser-like focus, a photographic memory, and tremendous skill at seeing patterns in numbers and data.[67] Buffett has made so many shrewd investment decisions over such a long period of time that many people believe his success isn't just the result of luck; something about him helps him choose wisely. How important intelligence, memory, focus, and quantitative skills are to Buffett's success at investing is unknown. But if I had to hazard a guess, I'd say that these attributes probably didn't hurt.

If our intelligence is useful for anything in this world, it is that it helps us to make better choices. The idea that, on average, smarter people make superior decisions is reflected in the tendency of modern societies not to hold individuals with severe cognitive impairments legally responsible for their actions. In general, we don't believe that these people are able to reason through their alternatives and the consequences that those choices have. But, even among people within the normal intelligence range, studies show that smarter people tend to make better decisions, particularly in complex and dynamic situations.[68]

The relationship between intelligence and decision making suggests that the genes that affect our mental abilities also influence how we make choices.[69] After all, genetics has a powerful effect on the development of cognitive skills,[70] and these skills are the building blocks of higher-order aspects of decision making, such as reasoning and planning. For instance, the genes that affect memory and perception are also thought to influence how fast people make decisions.[71]

Not only do studies show that genes affect all aspects of cognitive ability, including verbal comprehension, verbal fluency, mathematical skills, reasoning, spatial visualization, perceptual speed, mental processing speed, reaction time, attention, and memory, but these studies also show that the *same* genetic factors influence a variety of cognitive abilities. For instance, the genes that make people smarter also speed perception, and give people better working memory. The genes that speed reaction time also accelerate inspection time and increase IQ. The genes that improve spatial ability also enhance verbal ability and memory. The genes that increase cognitive skills also accelerate processing speed.[72] And the same genes increase processing speed, working memory, general cognitive ability, and IQ.[73]

Many researchers believe that the genes most likely to account for differences in intelligence and mental capacity are those that affect the density and connectivity of neurons in the brain, as well as the ones that impact brain size and structure.[74] Over 80 percent of the difference in brain volume and the amount of gray and white matter is accounted for by genetic factors,[75] and the amount of white and gray matter and brain volume are both related to general cognitive ability.[76] Moreover, the same genes that affect the growth of neurons also influence memory, which is important because the routine experiences that we have over the course of their lives do little to change the density of the neurons packed into our brains.[77]

Other researchers think that dopamine genes are at least partially responsible for differences in our intelligence and cognitive skills. Dopamine tends to be concentrated in the parts of the brain that are involved in memory, mental effort, mathematics, and complex planning. This neurotransmitter also speeds reaction time, which is positively associated with IQ,[78] and affects reasoning, analysis, planning, and prediction.[79]

Researchers have traced a path from several of the genes that affect the production of dopamine to intelligence. While far from definitive, research has shown that the "worrier" gene (COMT) affects intelligence by coding for catechol-O-methyltransferase, a substance that gets rid of dopamine. Thus, people with the version of the "worrier" gene (COMT) have less dopamine in their systems. One study has shown that the presence of this version of the "worrier" gene (COMT) accounts for 4 percent of the difference in scores on the Wisconsin Card Sorting Test,[80] "a widely used test of abstract thinking, planning, and ability."[81]

But the "worrier" gene (COMT) is far from the only gene associated with intelligence and cognitive skills. For instance, studies have shown that:

- a sample of young Chinese women with a particular version of the "impulsiveness" gene (DRD2) had lower average IQ scores than those with another version of the gene.[82]
- a version of the insulin-like growth factor-2 receptor gene (IGF2R), which influences some of the body's growth receptors, accounts for about 2 percent of the difference between people in intelligence.[83] (I will call IGF2R the "growth" gene.)
- a version of the gene for cholinergic muscarinic 2 receptor (CHRM2), which slows the heart after it has been stimulated, also affects learning and memory, particularly the ability to organize information logically, and accounts for some of the difference between people in IQ test scores.[84] (I will call CHRM2 the "logic" gene.)
- A version of a gene (CTSD), that codes for the production of an enzyme called cathepsin D, which breaks down certain complex cell chemicals, accounts for some of the difference between people in their IQ.[85] (I will call CTSD the "cognitive change" gene.)
- A variant of the cystathionine B-synthase gene (CBS), which provides instructions for the creation of an enzyme that helps to metabolize certain substances, is "underrepresented among children with high IQs."[86] (I will call CBS the "high IQ" gene.)

- The GABA-A-y3 subunit gene (GABRG3), which codes for the formation of receptors for a neurotransmitter, also affects working memory. (I will call GABRG3 the "working memory" gene.)
- The nerve growth factor beta polypeptide gene (NGF, previously known as NGFB), which provides instructions for the formation of a protein that affects the survival of brain cells, also influences visual ability, spatial ability, and memory. (I will call NGF the "nerve growth" gene.)
- The alcohol dehydrogenase 5 gene (ADH5), which codes for the creation of an enzyme that speeds certain aspects of cell metabolism, also affects memory and spatial ability. (I will call ADH5 the "spatial ability" gene.)
- A version of the prion protein gene (PRNP), which provides instruction for the production of a brain protein, is also associated with decreased memory, and global cognitive scores and skills.[87] (I will call PRNP the "information recall" gene.)

Conclusions

Whether you are a CEO or an entry-level employee, making choices is a large part of what you do at work. Therefore, understanding why and how people select between alternatives should be important to you. While a wide variety of factors impact your decision making, one that is rarely discussed is your DNA. Your genes influence many aspects of this process, including whether you tend to make intuitive decisions, how insightful you are, your tolerance for risk, and the amount and type of information that you seek.

Influence is an important word here. Your genes matter, but so do where you work, how you were raised, your education, and a variety of other factors. So I'm not saying that you should focus solely on DNA if you want to understand how people make decisions. Rather, I'm suggesting that to understand decision making, you need examine all of the forces that shape it, genetics included.

Scientists are in the early stages of learning how genes affect decision making, but they have found some intriguing patterns. DNA affects the way neurotransmitters function, which, in turn, affects the biochemistry of choice. In addition, your genes influence your hormones, personality, temperament, and cognitive processes, and through these attributes impact how you make decisions. Researchers have even identified specific genes associated with different aspects of the process, indicating that they have begun to outline the path from the versions of the genes that your parents gave you to the choices that you make.

Having described how your genes affect the way in which you make decisions, I now turn to their effect on your management style, the subject of the next chapter.

6

DNA at the Office:
How Your Genes Affect Your
Management Style

Joyce worked as a senior accountant at a large accounting firm. She supervised a team of junior staffers who did tax and audit work for businesses. Joyce was a control-oriented manager. She felt that it was very important to stay on top of all the details of her subordinates' work. To facilitate control over her team, she delegated very little and remained deeply involved in everything they did.

Joyce was also fond of planning. She asked all of her junior accountants to write a memo describing how they would conduct each audit before they started, setting milestones and laying out the process. This approach to planning also was something that Joyce did herself in her efforts to manage her department. She frequently updated her strategic plan, and always brought it with her when discussing the future of her department with senior managers.

Joyce thought rules were very important and always needed to be followed. Perhaps this is why she became an accountant in the first place. In college, accounting courses appealed to Joyce much more than marketing ones because accounting had hard-and-fast rules, while marketing seemed squishy, without any real tenets to follow.

Joyce's preference for rules extended to her management style. She was fond of saying that accountants who bent rules were the ones who got in trouble and that her subordinates should never, ever, contravene regulations. Any time a junior accountant asked her about skirting a rule in an audit, she pointed out that no auditor ever had a bad audit if the audit was done by the books.

All of us know someone with a management style like Joyce's. Control-based, planning-oriented, rule-adhering managers are pretty common. But we also know managers with the opposite style: a delegation-oriented, rule-breaking, improvisational approach. In fact, there's a great deal of variation in how people manage. Moreover, views toward control, planning, and rules aren't the only dimensions on which supervisors vary. They also have different approaches to negotiation, competition, frugality, and a host of other aspects of administration.

While most people recognize that managers have different styles, they don't always think about *why* those approaches vary. Conventional wisdom offers two explanations. One has to do with where people work. People manage a certain way, the experts say, because of the rules or norms of the industries, companies, or departments they are in. For instance, fire chiefs are much more regulation-oriented than movie directors because rule breaking isn't something that is encouraged among firefighters the way it is in Hollywood. This school of thought says management style isn't about the supervisor, it's about the organization or industry where that person works.

Other experts explain that management style depends a lot on the person. People with a certain psychological makeup, attitudes, or skills, administer one way, while those with other characteristics manage differently. More risk-tolerant individuals, for instance, tend to allow more rules to be broken under their watch than more risk-averse managers.

What causes people to develop their management styles and the psychological traits and attitudes associated with them? Experts tend to focus on learning. They explain that people develop their personalities, attitudes, and skills from their experiences—with their parents, at school, and on the job—and these personalities, attitudes, and skills lead them to favor one supervisory style over another.

What's missing in this discussion is the notion that anything innate affects how people manage others. But genetic factors do matter. Although rarely discussed, differences in DNA influence whether people are aggressive or laid-back negotiators, planning-focused or laissez-faire organizers, frugal or expansive spenders, among a host of other dimensions that make up a person's supervisory style. In fact, the data show that our genes even affect our management potential, with about half of the difference between people on tests of management capability being accounted for by genetic factors.[1]

This chapter examines which aspects of management our genes impact and how those genes exert their influence. While you might expect some of these effects, others will probably be new to you. Let's take a look.

The Effect of Genes on Management Style

As with decision making, a person's approach to management involves a variety of different dimensions, far too many, in fact, to cover in a comprehensive manner in a book like this. (After all, people write whole books on each of these topics.) Therefore, I will highlight how genes affect a few selected aspects of administration rather than trying to take a comprehensive approach. The dimensions on which I'll focus include: control, planning, rule breaking, social approval, power and politics, persistence, self-directedness, communication, competitiveness, change management, and negotiations. I'll start with the topic of control.

Born Control Freaks

Have you ever had a manager like Joe, the boss in the following example? He is so control-oriented that he even insists on going through his subordinates' travel expense forms and calculating whether the mileage they reported is consistent with what MapQuest shows is the shortest route between the two locations. If you've had a supervisor like Joe, you probably thought that he was a real pain. You might have even referred to him as being quite anal. And even if you have not had a manager like Joe, you probably know what these kinds of bosses are like.

Why do managers like Joe need to exercise so much control over their subordinates that they feel compelled to go through expense reports with a fine tooth comb? One common explanation has do with the setting in which the person works. Joe's employer might give managers bonuses for cutting expenses or for tightly monitoring what's going on in their units, which provides an incentive to be control-oriented.

Another common explanation focuses on the way in which people are raised. In fact, your reference to this type of manager being quite anal is an implicit statement that his control-oriented behavior was learned in early childhood, as a result of toilet training.

Few people invoke genetics to explain a supervisory style that involves checking expense reports for the shortest route between two locations. But they probably have an effect, even on this type of compulsion to micromanage. After all, studies show that some of the difference between people in the need for control is explained by our genes.[2] So, while your company's culture and rules, and the toilet-training style of your boss's parents, might contribute to his control orientation, his DNA probably also plays a role.

Innate Planners

Joyce, from the introductory vignette, is a planner. Psychologists explain that such people are high in constraint, and are apt to be cautious, careful, reflective, rational, and sensible. In contrast, non-planners tend to be more impulsive, acting suddenly without thinking through the potential impact of statements or actions.

Being high in constraint, Joyce frequently formulates and updates plans—hiring plans, budget plans, work-flow plans, strategic plans, contingency plans, and even plans for the company office party. Of course, not everyone at Joyce's company schedules and forecasts as much as she does. Some don't even plan at all. For instance, another manager, Tim, is far more impulsive than Joyce. Where Joyce makes hiring, budget, work-flow, and strategic plans, Tim makes decisions without those plans.

Part of Joyce's preference for scheduling and forecasting comes from the corporate environment in which she works, and a portion was learned over the course of her life. But some of Joyce's preference for planning comes from her DNA.

Some people are born with a genetic predisposition to design, schedule, forecast, and provision. One study, for instance, showed that 45 percent of the difference between people in what psychologists call "planfulness," is explained by our genes.[3] If we look at the specific questions that psychologists use to measure this orientation, it's clear that genetics affects work-related dimensions of this behavior. Evidence of a genetic effect on the inclination to plan comes from agreement or disagreement with the following statements (and ones similar to them):

- "I tend to begin a new job without much advance planning on how I will do it."
- "I very seldom spend much time on the details of planning ahead."
- "Before I begin a complicated job, I make careful plans."[4]

Other studies show a genetic predisposition for the converse of planfulness, what researchers call impulsiveness. A good example of an impulsive manager is Joseph Galli, the former Newell Rubbermaid CEO. Here's how a *Wall Street Journal* reporter described Galli: "While making one investor presentation, he grabbed a pen from an analyst's hand, threw it on a table and handed over a Newell pen."[5] This action showed Galli's lack of control over his feelings, even though they reflected his devotion to the company and his displeasure at seeing an investor using a competitor's product.

Much of the difference between people in impulsiveness is genetic, with the specific amount depending on the gender of the subjects, their age, the scale used to measure the trait, the nationality of the sample, and the design of the study.[6]

Other studies show the effect of our genes on dimensions related to being impulsive or having an orientation to plan. For instance, genetic effects account for:

- Differences in people's level of organization[7]
- Variation in the amount of time they spend in deliberation
- Differences in their self-control
- Disparity in their tendency to be careful[8]

So, if your manager is an organized, non-impulsive, deliberative, and careful planner who is always in control of him- or herself, genetics might be responsible.

Rule Breaking Is in Their Blood

What about Joyce's emphasis on adhering to rules? Is the DNA she inherited from her parents responsible for this, too? Again, the answer is yes, at least in part.

While psychologists interested in genetic effects on behavior haven't focused on rule breaking per se, we can measure the willingness of people to do so by looking at specific questions on the Eysenck personality questionnaire, a paper-and-pencil test used by psychologists to understand how people think about a number of different topics. Among the items that make up one of the scales are questions that get at the concept of rule breaking. For instance, one asks, "Do you prefer to go your own way rather than act by the rules?" Another inquires, "Is it better to follow society's rules than go your own way?"[9] Research shows that genetics accounts for part of the difference between people in the scale that these questions are part of.[10] So maybe Joyce was born with a genetic predisposition to be intolerant of rule breaking, a tendency that other managers in her company, like Tim, don't have.

DNA and the Need for Social Approval

Did you ever notice that some people at your workplace are willing to take an independent point of view even when everyone else disagrees with them, while other people tend to adhere to the majority's outlook and are very sensitive to the approval of others? Laurie, for instance, is an example of a manager who needs the approbation of her coworkers. She usually sits in meetings and waits to hear what other people say. Once the direction of the majority is clear, she chimes in with something consistent. Derrick, on the other hand, is a manager who doesn't really worry about the opinions of others. He figures out what he thinks is correct and states his view, not caring if everyone, or no one, agrees with him.

These different management styles reflect differences in reward dependence, a tendency to want the social approval of others. People who are highly reward-dependent tend to be very responsive to social cues and not very independent or objective.[11]

No doubt, many factors account for why some people are more reward-dependent than others, but that does not negate the fact that our genes play an important role. Studies show that they account for over a third of the variance between us in this dimension.[12] In fact, a few researchers even think they have identified some of the genes responsible for these differences. While many of these results have not been replicated, and we don't know how many other genes impact reward dependence or the size of each effect, we now have evidence for the influence of the following genes:

- APOE,[13] a gene that provides instructions for the production of Apolipoprotein E, which breaks down the protein part of certain enzymes. (I will call APOE the "Alzheimer's" gene because a variant of this gene has been found to be associated with the development of Alzheimer's disease).
- CYP19A1,[14] a gene that provides instructions for the development of sex hormones (which I will call the "sex hormone" gene).
- PNMT,[15] a gene that provides instructions for the production of the brain chemical adrenaline (which I will call the "adrenaline" gene).

- The "concern" gene (HTR2C).
- The "impulsiveness" gene (DRD2).
- The "novelty-seeking" gene (DRD4).[16]

(Don't forget, there are many genes involved in each of these behaviors and each gene likely affects several outcomes. The names I have given them are only to help you remember one of each gene's many functions.)

Laurie and Derrick's genetic inheritances influence their sensitivity to the social approval of others, and hence, how they manage people. Not only are the differences between these two individuals in reward dependence impacted by a combination of genes for neurotransmitters and hormones, but research also shows that we can trace the effects of these genes through to variation in management style.

Evil Genes and Their Effect on Power and Politics

As long as people have banded together to achieve their goals collectively, power and politics have been a part of the work world. As a result, experts on organizational behavior have long recognized that a good part of management involves exercising authority and political influence.

As with many other aspects of work-related behavior, people differ in their ability to manage power relationships up and down the hierarchy, and to navigate the minefield that is organization politics. Some people are very good at it, while others—yours truly included—are not. Because of the importance of power and politics to organizational life, much has been written about why people differ in their performance at these activities. In fact, one might say that dealing with power and politics is a central theme in many books on business, from textbooks to books for practicing managers.

While these books offer much useful information and needed advice about the topic, they often fail to discuss the source of differences between people in these aspects of organizational life. However, it isn't just a random accident that some people are bad at managing power and politics (and therefore in need of advice books), while others excel at this.

Among the myriad of factors that influence skill at the two P's is DNA. Some people have a genetic predisposition to be better at these aspects of organizational life than others. Take, for example, the tendency to exploit others to gain power. While people can gain authority in a variety of ways, including through the use of charisma and appeals to technical expertise, one time-honored approach is through manipulation of others. Experts call this approach Machiavellianism, after the Renaissance political scholar Niccolo Machiavelli, who was the author of the treatise *The Prince*.

Much evidence shows that people differ greatly in Machiavellianism, with some of us being much more willing than others to employ deception and manipulation for our own benefit.[17] Take, for example, this description of Jeffrey Skilling, former CEO of Enron, and current occupant of the Federal Correctional Institute in Lakewood, Colorado:

> Skilling thrived on confrontation and had a perfect command of the minutiae of deals. In interviews he could stun financial writers with his grasp of details, but that same superiority made corporate meetings enervating for his colleagues.... From the beginning, colleagues say, Skilling's pattern was to scapegoat others without leaving a trail that could lead back to him. In meetings that Ken Lay chaired, Skilling was often silent, letting Lay believe he was completely in control. But at other times Skilling could be very volatile.[18]

Although Niccolo Machiavelli did not recognize this when writing his treatise for the Medici family, part of the difference between people in the tendency to manipulate others for personal gain is inborn. Not only do studies show that DNA influences how greedy and selfish people are, but also that genetics accounts for 31 percent of the difference between people in the trait of Machiavellianism.[19] Stated differently, differences in how people tend to get and retain power—whether they manipulate others, appeal to technical expertise, or take advantage of their charisma—come, in part, from our genes.[20]

Genes for Persistence?

Steven is a car salesman. He's good at his job and earns high commissions. A lot of people envy his success, but he knows few of them would be able to sell as well as he does. Hawking cars isn't easy work. It takes a lot of convincing to get people to spend $20,000 or more on a vehicle. Most customers raise a lot of objections that have to be overcome to close a sale. And many people who become customers aren't ready to buy when they first walk onto the lot. When asked what makes him a successful salesman, Steven explains that the trick lies in persistence. "You can only close a sale," he explains, "if you keep trying until the sale is made or the customer tells you to stop."

Salespeople aren't the only people for whom persistence is crucial. It's also important to middle managers who want to influence more senior managers to change their company's business strategy. Rarely do top executives alter the direction of a company as the result of a single half-hour conversation with a mid-level employee.

Entrepreneurs also need persistence to accomplish their goals. Take the example of Harland Sanders, the founder of Kentucky Fried Chicken. At age 65, Colonel Sanders, set out to sell his chicken to restaurants. Traveling from town to town, often sleeping in his car, Sanders was turned down by 1,009 restaurants before number 1,010 bought his product, or so the story goes.

So what makes some people more dogged than others? Research shows that tenacity is partly inborn, with genetics accounting for a substantial portion of the difference between people in this characteristic.[21] In fact, we even have some tantalizing evidence of specific genes that influence this trait. While these results still need to be replicated, studies have shown that versions of the following genes are associated with persistence:

- The "impulsiveness" gene (DRD2)
- The "concern" gene (HTR2C)
- The "worrier" gene (COMT)
- The "activity" (SLC6A3)[22] gene.[23]

Scientists have even genetically engineered super persistent monkeys by turning off the "impulsiveness" gene (DRD2) in the modified primates. As Tom Harrison reports,

Researchers at the National Institute of Mental Health turned ordinary monkeys from procrastinators to workaholics simply by switching off a gene that helped them to know when they would be rewarded for completing their work.... The researchers shut off the function of a gene called D2 which affects a chemical involved in how our brain processes rewards for learning. The monkeys could no longer tell how close they were to getting their [reward]. They began working more efficiently and making fewer errors, as if the reward were constantly just around the corner.[24]

Of course, no one is proposing genetic engineering on humans to make people more tenacious.[25] The monkey studies just provide scientific evidence for what nature already does. Researchers believe that some people are more dogged than others, in part, because they have a version of a gene, or set of genes, that reduce signals of reward. As a result, the individuals with these gene variants experience a more pleasurable physiological response than other people to continuing with tasks, leading them to be more persistent. In short, being indefatigable appears to have a biochemical basis that is influenced by our genes.

Innately Self-Directed

At one time or another, almost all of us have had to do work that is self-directed. Perhaps you had to draft a legal brief, or conduct an audit, or manage a store. You might have been tasked with the assignment, but not supervised in carrying it out. You were simply asked to do the job and to report back with a finished product.

Are you good at this type of work? Some of us are and some of us aren't. Did you ever wonder why?

Genetics is once again a key contributor. Some people, it turns out, are born with an innate predisposition to perform well unsupervised, while others are not. Moreover, our genes affect multiple aspects of our self-directness. For instance, genetic factors account for some of the difference between people in their sense of responsibility, and 24 percent of the variance in their sense of accountability.[26]

While we don't yet know the source of this genetic predisposition, researchers have unmasked several intriguing clues. People who are more self-directed are also more likely to have a particular version of the ADORA2A[27] gene, which provides instructions for a neurotransmitter that inhibits arousal and promotes sleep (which I will call the "sleep" gene), and a difference in the DNA sequence for a gene involved with the production of the brain chemical serotonin.[28] While these two genes certainly aren't the only things that influence how self-directed people are, it does appear that they play a role in explaining who works well without direction from others and who does not.

Interacting and Communicating with Others

As you no doubt already realize, social relationships are the cornerstone of management. Because people are communal creatures, the organizations we create are built on interpersonal ties. In fact, in many ways, an organization is nothing more than a web of relationships between its members.[29] So being a manager involves forming and maintaining bonds between people.

But not all managers are great at social relationships. For example, Joseph Galli, the former CEO of Newell Rubbermaid, was ousted from that position in part because he took action too fast, without building personal ties first. In reflecting on his tenure at Newell Rubbermaid, Galli explained that he made "every mistake you can make in restructuring" because he "often lacked diplomacy."[30]

While you might think that building personal ties is something that you learned to do, perhaps on the playground as a child, it turns out that genes account for a lot of the difference in people's ability to create social relationships. Studies show that genetics is responsible for more than 40 percent of the variance between people in sociability. Moreover, these patterns are found whether researchers are studying children, teens, or older adults, men or women, or Americans or people of other nationalities.[31]

Research shows that the converse of sociability—not-so-creatively called the lack of sociability—is also influenced by genetics. Here, studies indicate that more than half of the difference between people in social avoidance—the tendency to be asocial—is explained by our genes.[32]

While a lot of the evidence for the effects of genes on sociability comes from tests that measure scales put together by psychologists, a few studies show DNA's influence on the actual quantity and quality of our social ties. For instance, researchers have found a genetic effect on the number of confidants and friends that people report having, how often they get together or talk with their friends and family, and the intensity of their personal relationships.[33] They have even found that about 26 percent of the difference between people in the amount of social support their friends provide them is genetic.[34] Put differently, genes affect a wide range of measures of how much people interact with others.

Okay, so maybe our genes affect our sociability, but how do we get from genes that provide instructions for the production of particular enzymes to building social relationships with other people? One plausible path that has received some research attention involves the genes that provide instructions for the production of a MAO, which, as was explained earlier, is a neurotransmitter that breaks down dopamine and serotonin.

Dopamine and serotonin influence how sociable you are and, conversely, whether you suffer from social anxiety. Studies show that more sociable people have lower levels of MAO than other people, suggesting that the friendliest among us are not breaking down dopamine and serotonin as quickly as everyone else.[35]

Of course, MAO levels aren't randomly set. They are affected by our genetic endowment.[36] Some people have versions of genes that lead them to develop more MAO than others. Those people whose bodies are genetically predisposed to produce more of this neurotransmitter tend to have less dopamine and serotonin in their brains, which inclines them to be less social.

Trusting Others

One important part of effective social relationships is your ability to trust other people. It's hard to work effectively in an organization, and even harder to manage others, if you don't have confidence in anyone else. After all, you can't do everything yourself. So you have to believe that other people are going to work with you, not against you, if you are going to get anything done.

The need to trust makes interesting the recent discovery that oxytocin, a hormone produced in the hypothalamus that also acts as a neurotransmitter in the brain, plays a role in helping you to believe in others' honesty.[37] In recent experiments, scientists have found that people become more social and more trusting when they are given oxytocin. For instance, one group of researchers asked people to play a game that measured how much they were willing to entrust others with their money. The researchers gave the experimental subjects oxytocin and gave the control group a placebo. They found that the group that received the oxytocin was much more willing to have faith in the fairness of their counterparts than those who didn't get the treatment.[38]

In another study, different researchers examined the effects of oxytocin on the ability to decipher others' emotional reactions. The researchers found that receiving this hormone increased the ability to read emotions and intentions in other people's faces.[39]

What makes all of this relevant to a book on genetics and work-related behavior is the identification by scientists of a genetic effect on oxytocin levels. Researchers have found that certain genes influence the production of oxytocin receptors, which, in turn, impact the amount of this hormone present in your brain.[40] If some people have genetic variants that lead to more receptors, and others have the versions that result in fewer receptors, then some of us will be predisposed to be more trusting than others because of the amount of oxytocin in our heads.

Dealing with Violators of Social Norms

Another important dimension of managing social relationships at the office is what to do about free riders, disruptive employees, and other people who violate the norms of the work group. As anyone who has ever worked in an organization knows, some people just won't go along with what the rest of the team is doing, and someone needs to ensure that they don't undermine everyone else's efforts.

Some people are much more effective at this task than others. Why? There are a lot of reasons, but here's one I bet that you never thought of: they have certain versions of the genes involved in the production of arginine vasopressin, which we first talked about in chapter 2. In one experiment, researchers gave some subjects arginine vasopressin and other subjects a placebo. The scientists found that those who received the hormone were more likely to punish people who behaved inappropriately when working together in small groups.[41] That is, arginine vasopressin affects how people respond to those who free ride and otherwise violate group norms.

This study, of course, manipulated arginine vasopressin levels to see their effect on behavior, making it impossible to determine if genetic differences were responsible. However, other studies have shown that levels of this hormone are themselves influenced by genes, with people possessing a variety of mutations that impact its production.[42] Therefore, it is quite possible that people with certain variants of at least one gene involved in the production of arginine vasopressin develop more of the hormone, which in turn, affects their social behavior.

Could this be the genetic mechanism that explains why some people stop the free riders in their work groups but others don't? Perhaps, but we are a long way from research giving us that answer. For now, we just have evidence of some intriguing relationships between our genes and the production of arginine vasopressin and between that hormone and our behavior.

Communicating

The ability to communicate is an important human skill and one that is of great value in the workplace. A simple stroll through the business section of your local bookstore attests to the centrality of this issue. It's hard to find a topic more written about than the ability to communicate effectively. Whether you need to talk to subordinates, supervisors, peers, suppliers, or customers, if you work in an organization, you need to communicate.

Scientists have recently discovered that your ability to do this depends, in part, on the versions of certain genes that you inherited from your parents, specifically the genes for testosterone production. As we saw in earlier chapters, genetic factors account for 80 percent of the difference across men in the base rate of production of this hormone.[43]

Researchers have found that fetal testosterone levels, in turn, affect brain development. The more of this hormone that a baby receives while in the womb, the more the right side of its brain develops and the less the left side—the one with the language and communication centers—grows. Female babies, which are exposed to less fetal testosterone than male babies, develop language and communication centers that are packed with 11 percent more neurons. Some researchers believe that the effect of testosterone on the development of the communication centers of the brain accounts for the better social skills that women tend to have.[44]

But the link between genetic differences in testosterone levels and the development of social skills isn't just seen in the difference between men and women; it's also observed in studies of just one gender. For instance, studies have shown that levels of fetal testosterone are related to later empathy scores.[45] That is, individuals exposed to more testosterone when developing in their mothers' wombs tend to become less empathetic later in life. Studies also show that testosterone levels are inversely related to a person's interest in talking and socializing.[46] Simply speaking, people whose bodies produce a lot of testosterone like to talk less. In sum, scientists have provided intriguing evidence to suggest that genetic differences in testosterone levels account for the variation among us in our communication skills, skills that are central to work in modern organizations.

Born Competitors

Working in organizations demands both competition and cooperation. On the one hand, the business world is competitive. Companies fight for customers, applicants compete for jobs, and employees battle for promotions. So to succeed in the business world, you need to be an effective competitor. As Ray Kroc, "the founder of McDonald's, once said of competition in the fast food industry: 'this is rat eat rat, dog eat dog. I'll kill 'em and I'm going to kill 'em before they kill me.' "[47]

But, in business, you also need to be a good cooperator. To be successful, employees need to work together in teams, and companies need to form alliances with their suppliers and customers.

As you no doubt realize from your own work environment, some people are better at the competitive side of work, while others excel at the cooperative dimension. Take, for example, two coworkers at one company, Leah and Simon. Simon is a hypercompetitive person. All his life, he has viewed the situations he was in through a competitive lens. From the earliest days of kindergarten, when he challenged himself to write more neatly than the other kids sitting at the same table in his classroom, to his work as an engineer at a major multinational corporation, Simon has focused on being better than the people around him. Perhaps because of his hypercompetitive nature, collaborating has always been difficult for Simon. From his first days of school until today, he has never much wanted to cooperate, seeing such efforts as an opportunity for others to gain advantage over him.

Leah is the opposite of Simon. She has never been very competitive. From her earliest days, Leah has always tried to work with others rather than against them. In grade school, she had a hard time with individual sports because she never felt comfortable trying to beat her friends in a race or a tennis match. And at work, she has gravitated to team assignments, disliking the competitive nature of performance appraisals and promotions at her company.

What makes some employees like Simon and others like Leah? While the characteristics of the work itself and the incentives that people are given by their employers certainly play a part, some people are born with a genetic predisposition to be more competitive than others. Studies show that much of the difference between people in the desire for dominance is innate, with the specific amount a function of the group studied and the way that the characteristic is measured. This desire for dominance also plays out in how people work in groups and lead others, with one study showing that genetic factors account for 21 percent of the difference between people in a preference for a dominance-oriented approach to leadership.[48]

We don't know for sure how our DNA impacts our desire to compete with and dominate others, but evidence from research on the serotonin system, and the genes that regulate it, provide some clues. The body's serotonin levels are influenced by genes that provide instructions for the production of serotonin receptors and transporters. These same genes also predispose people to competition or cooperation.[49]

For instance, researchers have shown that people with one version of the serotonin receptor gene HTR1B,[50] (which I will call the "aggression" gene) are more aggressive than people with a different variant of the same gene.[51]

Another source of difference in competitiveness might be genetically influenced variation in levels of testosterone production. People with high testosterone levels are more competitive and less cooperative than those with lower levels of this hormone,[52] seeking to exact revenge and to punish others to a greater extent.[53] So those individuals with a particular genetic variation might end up producing more than the average amount of testosterone, which, in turn, makes them more likely than others to be aggressive and competitive.

Genes and Managing Change

Some people describe the business world with the aphorism "the only constant is change itself." This saying highlights the fact that managing change is an important part of organizational life. Companies launch new products, hire new employees, start new strategic initiatives, lay people off, go out of business, and alter themselves in innumerable ways every day. Employees need to cope with these changes and perform their jobs, despite the shifting sands on which they stand.

Because managing change is so important, many companies spend lots of money on consultants to help their employees become more accepting of organizational metamorphosis. The premise of most of these consultants is that businesses can make their employees better at handling change by altering approaches to management, the structure of work units, or communication patterns. All of this consulting work is predicated on the assumption that the characteristics of organizations account for much of what makes people accept or reject change. But is this assumption really true?

Figuring out the answer to this question is important. If people are resistant to or uncomfortable with change because of something about the organization, then efforts to alter the work environment make a lot of sense. But if the reason lies in something about the people themselves, then the consultants' approach will do little.

This is where an understanding of genetics is important. Studies reveal that just under half, 45 percent, of the difference between people in their scores on the change scale of a major psychological test called the Personality Research Form is genetic.[54] Moreover, research has revealed genetic effects on the frequency with which people make changes, and the size of the modifications that they make.[55]

Because a large portion of the difference in people's ability to manage change is genetic, efforts by companies to improve their employees' responses to organizational transformation by enhancing communications, restructuring, or altering the characteristics of the workplace won't be as effective as the consultants would like them to be. These adjustments can't do anything to alter the genetic portion of variance in people's ability to handle change.

Born Negotiators

How well you negotiate is another important aspect of your management style. Bargaining is a big part of the work world. Companies negotiate contracts with their suppliers and customers, employees negotiate their salaries, and team members negotiate how they will work together. So differences between people in their ability to bargain has important ramification for their work lives.

So what makes some people better negotiators than others? You might be surprised to learn that it is being intraverted, disagreeable, and prone to displays of anger. Studies show that people who get mad easily bargain more effectively, perhaps because their outbursts of anger keep their counterparts off balance.[56] Agreeable and extraverted people tend to negotiate poorly, perhaps because their efforts to cooperate and share information undermine their performance.[57]

As you no doubt remember from earlier chapters, your genes influence your odds of being agreeable, extraverted, and demonstrative, with studies showing that as much as half of the difference between people in the first two traits, and 28 percent of the variance in the latter, is genetic.[58] In sum, while no one is truly a "born negotiator," some people are predisposed to be better at this activity than others. So the next time you plan to bargain over a raise or anything else, you might want to consider whether you are genetically inclined to be successful at it or at least better than the person on the other side of the table.

How Your Genes Affect Your Management Style

Clearly, there is a lot of evidence that your genes influence many aspects of your management style, from your self-direction to your tolerance for change to your level of competitiveness. So now, perhaps, you believe that genes play some role in the way you manage yourself and others. But how? How does our DNA influence these differences among us?

To date, we have evidence for three mechanisms: through instructions for the production of neurotransmitters, by coding for the production of hormones, and by predisposing us to develop the personality traits associated with certain approaches to management. Let's look first at neurotransmitters.

The Role of Neurotransmitters

Your neurotransmitter genes impact several aspects of your management style. For instance, your adrenaline and serotonin genes affect your level of self-direction. A number of serotonin system genes also influence how impulsive and planning-oriented you are, as well as your persistence and your tendency to seek social approval. Several dopamine system genes affect your need for social approval, persistence, and impulsiveness. And your MAO genes impact both your desire to plan and your persistence.[59]

Let's look at the example of the effect of serotonin system genes on the tendency to seek social approval to see how this process might work. People receive different versions of these genes from their parents. Some of the variants predispose people to a more negative reaction to stimuli than others. For instance, if interpersonal disagreement leads us to feel uncomfortable, then those with the "greater response" versions of the genes will experience a more adverse reaction than those with the other variants. As a result, they will take more pains to avoid conflict with others and develop a management style that tends to seek approbation from superiors and subordinates.

The Role of Hormones

The genes that provide instructions for the development of hormones also impact our management styles. Take, for example, those for testosterone production. This hormone influences how competitive we are and it's not hard to see how.

As with all hormones, testosterone has physiological effects. For instance, it increases energy levels and the production of red blood cells. So it is not surprising that people low in testosterone feel sluggish. In fact, people with a genetic predisposition toward high levels of this hormone may even be physically stronger and more vigorous than others.

The way that testosterone affects the body may also influence behavior. In particular, testosterone may increase aggressiveness. High-
testosterone men tend to score higher than those low in this hormone on
psychological tests that measure competitiveness and dominance,[60] and
men and women who receive testosterone supplements become more
aggressive and competitive, both physically and verbally.[61]

This aggressiveness might carry over to work life. High-testosterone
men and women might be more competitive at the office, just as they are
in other settings. Because this hormone increases the desire to dominate
others, it is plausible that high-testosterone people tend toward less
cooperative approaches to management.

Through Personality

Your genes might influence your approach to management through
their effects on your personality. As we saw in earlier chapters, certain
genetic variants are associated with the development of particular personality traits. Having those characteristics, in turn, predisposes people
to adopt certain management styles. Take, for example, locus of control,
which measures your belief that the events in your life occur largely
because of your actions. People with an internal locus of control believe
that they are responsible for what happens in their lives, while people
with an external locus of control think that outside forces account for
those events. So a person with an internal locus of control might believe
that his efforts to master the new accounting system at the office led to
his promotion, while a person with an external locus of control might
think that such efforts had little to do with it.

Your genes have a large effect on whether you have an internal or an
external locus of control.[62] Some people, it appears, are just born with a
greater tendency to believe that what happens to them is a function of
what they say and do.

Research shows that whether you have an internal or an external
locus of control affects your management style. People with an internal
locus of control tend to take a more hands-on approach to management
because they think that they can influence the context in which they find
themselves. For instance, they relish turnaround situations because they
have a strong belief in their ability to change the direction of floundering
organizations. In addition, they tend to be better at managing organization
politics than people low in locus of control because they believe that their
political maneuverings influence outcomes.[63]

Your genes also affect your persistence through their effects on the personality traits of neuroticism, conscientiousness, and self-esteem. As we have seen in earlier chapters, genetic differences predispose some people to develop these characteristics more than others. The genetic predispositions toward certain personality traits, in turn, affect the odds of being tenacious.[64] For instance, people with high self-esteem are more dogged than others because their self-confidence leads them to believe that they can overcome obstacles and makes them resilient in the face of setbacks.[65] Neurotics, on the other hand, tend not to be very persistent. Those high in anxiety tend to respond poorly to negative feedback from customers, supervisors, and others, and give up in the face of obstacles.[66] Conscientious people tend to be highly tenacious because conscientiousness helps them to plan for, and achieve, goals. Highly conscientious people also appear to be wired to continue working on a problem until it is solved.[67]

In fact, because they don't like to fail, conscientious people often persist so much that they escalate commitment. As a result, we see these folks continuing with failed courses of action—trying to salvage a bad strategy, retrain a poor hire, pursue a job that they will never get—much more than other people. Thus, a tendency to escalate commitment is partially inborn, with some people getting the versions of genes that predispose them to conscientiousness, which makes it more difficult for them to give up when things aren't working.

Similar patterns can be seen with change management. Studies show that individuals who are open to experience tend to be more positively disposed to change and tend to be more tolerant of ambiguity than other people.[68] Thus, it could be that genes account for some of the difference in the ability to manage organizational transformation through their effect on differences in the predisposition to be open to experience.

Gene-Environment Correlations in Management

The tendency of your genes to increase your odds of being in situations that support your innate predispositions can be seen in aspects of supervisory style. People, it seems, choose jobs that let them manage in ways consistent with their DNA. Take, for example, employment settings in which people have a lot of authority over how their work and work environment are set up and where they get to choose what tasks to do and how to do them. Approximately 21 percent of the difference in whether people have these types of jobs is genetic, suggesting that individuals with an innate predisposition toward planning and control tend to select jobs that give them the opportunity to engage in those activities.[69]

Conclusions

Your genes influence your management style. Studies show that your desire for control, penchant for rules, tendency to plan, need for social approval, approach to power and politics, degree of persistence, level of self-direction, degree of comfort with change, negotiation style, willingness to communicate, and level of competitiveness all have a genetic component.

Of course, no gene *guarantees* that you will be comfortable with change, be a great negotiator, or be highly self-directed. After all, genes don't *determine* anything about management style; they just influence it. You can easily be comfortable with change, negotiate effectively, and work well without supervision whether you have the relevant genetic predispositions or not. The odds are just greater for the genetically inclined than for the rest of us.

While we don't know for sure how genes go from providing instructions for the production of enzymes to influencing management style, scientists have suggested three likely paths. First, your genes affect your production of neurotransmitters, and these chemicals influence your physiological response to certain activities. Second, your DNA influences your body's production of hormones, which, in turn, influence your behavior. Third, the versions of the genes that you inherited from your parents affect the odds that you develop certain personality traits, and these characteristics influence the probability that you will manage in one way and not another.

Having described how genes impact management style, I now turn to their effect on leadership, the subject of the next chapter.

7

Born Leaders? How Your Genes Influence Your Approach to Leadership

Leona was determined to be a great leader. Even as a child, she paid a great deal of attention to who was heading up different groups and what those people did. When her peers acted like leaders, she would copy them in the hopes that she, too, would become a leader.

In college she begun to read books on leadership, a practice that she has continued. She was always clipping articles like "5 Key Traits of Great Leaders"; "The Hidden Qualities of Great Leaders"; "The Three Ways of Great Leaders"; and "Five Marks of a Great Leader," highlighting the key points and reciting them back to herself.

Later, when she had graduated from school and had gone to work, she made a habit of seeking out leadership training courses at the local university. And in job assignments, she'd try to find any possible opportunity to be in charge of something—a task force, a work group, a project.

To Leona's chagrin, she wasn't a very good leader. She didn't get to head many groups in grade school or high school because her friends and classmates just wouldn't follow her. At work, things weren't much better. In 360 degree assessments at her company, her subordinates regularly would point out the mistakes that she made in leading them. Because she was a poor leader, her bosses were reluctant to put her in charge of projects or groups. While her performance appraisals continually pointed out her value to the organization as an individual contributor, they clearly noted that she had a problem directing others, despite the effort she put into trying to do it well.

Leona didn't understand the problem. She tried all the things that the articles said were keys to effective leadership: moral courage, judgment, a sense of priority, humor, vision, passion, discipline, persistence, and team building. But, her efforts weren't as successful as she would have liked.

While following the recommendations in the articles she read didn't make her a worse leader, it didn't make her into an effective one, either.

   Looking at her friend Susan frustrated Leona even more. Susan never tried to be in charge. She never read anything about leadership, and couldn't identify the five key attributes that leaders had, even when armed with a crib sheet from the local university's business school. Yet people followed Susan all of the time. And she was constantly being asked to run different groups and projects.

Why is Susan such a good leader when she doesn't try to lead and Leona such a poor leader when she works so hard at it? We like to think that leadership—the ability to influence other people to work toward the achievement of a goal[1]—is something anyone can learn. In fact, we want to believe that everyone is *equally likely* to be a leader. The only difference between who takes charge and who doesn't, we tend to think, is how much people work at it.[2] But that's not true.

   Whether you become a leader or not isn't simply a choice that you make. And it isn't just the result of how your parents raised you or what you learned in school. It comes, at least in part, from what you were born with, your DNA. While your genes aren't destiny—you can take charge even if you aren't blessed with the genetics that make doing so more likely—the odds are not as good for you as they are for someone who has the right genes for leadership.

   Don't believe me? Take a look at the evidence.

The Genetic Basis of Leadership

Numerous studies have revealed that genes affect a variety of leadership dimensions. Your DNA influences your attitudes toward leadership, your ability to head up a group, your willingness to take on a leadership role, and even what kind of boss you become. Let's examine the support for each of these assertions, starting with attitudes toward leadership.

Attitudes Toward Leadership

Do you have a positive or a negative view toward directing others? Do you aspire to be a leader, or is it something that you don't care for, or even dislike? However you answer these questions, your genes are partially responsible. Some portion of your attitude toward leadership is genetic. In fact, from studies of identical and fraternal twins, we know that genetics accounts for about 40 percent of the difference between people in what they think of leadership.[3] The same genetic predispositions that accounted for our ancestors' interest in heading up the hunting party or running the clan, it seems, are still at work today, affecting our lives in modern organizations.

Leadership Potential

Not only do your genes affect your interest in being in charge, they impact your leadership potential, or the degree to which you possess the skills and characteristics necessary to head up a group. While leadership potential can be assessed in a variety of ways, many researchers have used a test called the California Personality Inventory (CPI) to measure it. The accuracy of this instrument has been shown in numerous studies of people from many different countries and across a variety of work settings, from the military to the private sector.

Studies using the CPI show that genetics has a substantial effect on leadership potential. For instance, one study of twins raised in separate families showed that almost half, 49 percent, of the difference between people on this dimension is genetic. Amazingly, the study showed that pairs of identical twins raised by different parents had the same leadership potential 47 percent of the time, while for fraternal twins raised together the score was the same in only 18 percent of the cases.[4] In short, some of us were born with an innate set of skills that makes us good candidates for directing a group of people toward a goal, whether the group is hunting wooly mammoths or installing a new company-benefits service center.

Achievement of Leadership Roles

Remarkably, several studies show that our genes influence whether or not we *achieve* leadership positions in the organizations in which we work. That is, your DNA—the chemicals that provide instructions for the production of enzymes—influences whether or not you move up to a supervisory position at your company. For instance, one study examined the effect of genes on the number of levels up the organizational hierarchy that men had moved, from the guys at the bottom, who manage no one, to the president at the top, who's in charge of everyone. Approximately 30 percent of the difference in how high the men had moved was explained by their genes.[5] Another study, this one of women, found very similar results; 32 percent of the variance among women in the achievement of leadership roles was found to be genetic.[6]

It might seem counterintuitive to some that our genes can influence the *actual* positions we reach in organizations. After all, no one is born with a gene for being a CEO or a genetic marker for moving five levels up the organizational hierarchy. (Such things don't even exist.) So it would appear at first glance that genetic factors couldn't account for the achievement of leadership roles in organizations.

But they do. And, as it turns out, it's not that difficult to envision how. People are born with different genetic endowments. For any given gene, you have one version or another. As we have seen in the previous chapters, some of these variants affect the odds that you will behave a certain way—planning versus not planning, taking risks versus playing it safe, leading others or following them, and so on. Because people tend to engage in behaviors that they are good at, those with the versions of genes that predispose them to develop leadership potential are more likely to gravitate toward leadership roles. Being in these positions allows them to further develop the skills they need to be in charge and helps them to move higher up in the organization. As a result, people with a genetic predisposition toward leadership end up not only with higher odds of being judged to have leadership potential, but also a greater tendency to be found in leadership roles. In short, genetics affects more than just the desire to become the CEO of a company; it also affects the chances of actually being one.

Leadership Styles

Leaders don't all act the same way. Some build consensus, while others command. Some are charismatic, while others are functional, using rewards to get people to work toward a common goal. For instance, Jack Welch, the legendary CEO of General Electric, was known for his ability to listen and take in information provided to him by all his subordinates. By contrast, "Chainsaw Al" Dunlap was a dictatorial leader who terrorized his subordinates.[7]

These differences in leadership style are important because some approaches are more valuable than others in certain situations. For instance, many experts believe that charismatic leaders are particularly valuable in crises, which may be why Barack Obama was elected president of the United States during an economic maelstrom. (But that is another story.)

Experts on leadership have found that one of the most important differences in leadership style lies in the contrast between transactional and transformational leaders. Transactional leadership is based on an agreement between the leader and his or her followers. The one in charge provides the others with pay, promotion, favorable job appraisals, and so on in return for their effort and compliance. For instance, the leader might say, "Meet this quota and you will get a raise" or "Do what I say and you will get a promotion." With a transactional leader, followers act in accordance with the wishes of the boss to receive the reward and to avoid whatever punishment—demotion, firing, financial penalties, and so on—that the chief imposes for failing to do so.[8]

Transformational leadership is different. It is not based on an agreement between the boss and subordinates, but on the leader's inspiration. Transformational leaders motivate their followers with a vision for the future. For instance, a transformational boss might be the entrepreneur who says, "Join me and together we will reinvent the auto industry with green technology." With a transformational leader, followers provide effort and compliance, not because they get something in return, but because they believe in the boss and his or her goals and objectives.[9]

I have gone into this discussion of the difference between these two approaches to leadership for a reason. Whether someone adopts a transformational or a transactional leadership style is partially genetic. In fact, by studying twins, one set of researchers found that approximately 59 percent of the variance across people in the display of transformational leadership and 48 percent of the difference in the use of transactional leadership comes from genetic factors.[10] In another study, scientists found very close to the same results: 57 percent of the variation between people in the demonstration of transformational leadership and 47 percent of the difference in the display of transactional leadership is genetic.[11]

How Our Genes Affect Leadership

The evidence of genetic effects on leadership, whether focused on attitudes, potential, role achievement, or style, is powerful. Clearly, we are not, as many HR consultants would have us believe, blank slates that trainers can transform into great bosses with equal probability of success. Rather, each of us is born with different genetic predispositions that affect how likely we are to become the boss and what type of leader we will be. This pattern raises a fundamental question: how does our DNA influence differences among us in leadership?

To be honest, no one knows for sure. We don't yet have direct evidence of the mechanisms through which this process works. But we have enough indirect evidence for scientists to suggest several paths. In general, researchers believe that genes affect leadership by increasing the predisposition to develop certain personality traits, temperaments, and cognitive abilities. For instance, one study found that 17 percent of the difference in the odds of becoming a leader comes from genetic influences on just our personalities and cognitive abilities.[12]

Let's take a closer look at how this process works.

Through Personality

Much research has shown that your genes influence whether you become a leader by affecting your personality. In the words of one set of authors, "It appears, at least in part, that individuals are born with genetic predispositions to emerge as leaders, and these genetic predispositions are captured fairly well by their personality...."[13]

The OCEAN personality traits impact both interest in leadership and leadership ability. For example, one massive study that combined the results of over 100 different research efforts found that extraversion, openness to experience, conscientiousness, and lack of agreeableness all increase the odds that a person will become a leader, and both extraversion and openness to experience raise the probability that an individual will be an *effective* leader.[14]

Moreover, these findings aren't based on a bunch of experiments conducted on college sophomores who pretend to be bosses to get extra credit in their psychology classes. These patterns have been found in a variety of real-world organizations, from businesses to nonprofits to the military.[15] Regardless of the type of organization in which people have been observed, researchers have found a solid relationship between certain personality traits and leadership.

As we saw in earlier chapters, half of the difference between people in the OCEAN personality traits is genetic.[16] More important, certain versions of neurotransmitter genes have been linked to these traits.[17] So it's easy to see how your genes can affect your personality, which in turn can influence you as a leader.

Other personality traits also influence your ability to lead. Those who take charge, we know from numerous scientific studies, tend to be more sociable, confident, forceful, persuasive, and achievement-oriented than other people.[18] Of course, self-confidence, sociability, forcefulness, persuasiveness, and a desire to achieve aren't developed at random. They are, in part, genetic.

Take self-confidence as an example. Many studies show that self-assured people are more likely than others to direct groups. After all, belief in oneself is necessary to inspire others.[19] It also helps to manage those who are skeptical or even hostile, by mitigating the need to seek their approval.[20] Moreover, self-confidence leads people to believe their skills and abilities are useful to the organizations they belong to, something that helps them to rise to the top of those entities.

As several studies have shown, our genes affect our self-confidence, accounting for more than one-third of the difference between us on this dimension.[21] Moreover, researchers have actually created genetically modified monkey leaders by manipulating the production of the neurotransmitters that contribute to self-confidence. Scientists caused the monkeys to move up or down the organizational hierarchy by genetically engineering them to have higher or lower serotonin and dopamine levels, which, in turn, affected the primates' self-confidence.[22] In short, it appears that some people are born with versions of genes that increase their predisposition to be self-confident, which, in turn, enhances their odds of becoming leaders.

Social Potency

Still don't believe that your genes influence your tendency to become a leader by affecting the development of your personality? Then consider another dimension: social potency, or how persuasive people are. Great leaders often seem very convincing when you listen to them speak because they are usually socially potent. Leading people involves getting them to act toward a common goal, which often demands persuasiveness. After all, it's difficult to get others to do what you want them to do if you can't convince them to do it.[23]

Social potency is partially genetic, with studies showing that DNA accounts for more than half of the difference between people.[24] Research shows that identical twins have much more similar social potency scores than fraternal twins, even if they are raised in different households. Moreover, studies demonstrate that the social potency score of one identical twin predicts that of the other at a later point in time.[25]

More important, we have evidence that links the impact of genes on social potency to the influence of DNA on leadership. Researchers have found that 24 percent of the genetic effect on leadership comes from the *same* genes that affect social potency. Put differently, the researchers' findings mean the same genes that influence your odds of being persuasive and influential also make you more likely to have run projects, planned special events, or led something, such as a department or work group.[26] While we don't know yet which variants of which genes contribute to social potency, this research suggests that they are the same ones that make people more likely to take on leadership roles.

Not Leading

Not all dimensions of personality predispose people to become leaders. Some increase the odds that individuals won't take charge. These traits also have a genetic component. For example, we know that being anxious and depressed reduces the odds that a person will become a leader, and, if such an individual does take charge, he or she won't be very good at it. Because anxiety and depression have a genetic component, it's easy to see how DNA accounts for part of the tendency *not* to lead others through the development of certain personality traits.

Narcissism

Not all personality characteristics are desirable, nor are all dimensions of leadership favorable. Some people take charge because they have traits that predispose them to become the kinds of leaders we'd be better off not having. And these aspects of personality also have a genetic component.

A good example of this is narcissism, which is the tendency toward self-love, self-admiration, and an overestimation of one's value. Narcissists like to become leaders. They bask in the adulation of others and think that only they have the skills and abilities to be in charge. Unfortunately, research shows that narcissists perform poorly as leaders, perhaps because having a selfish focus hinders efforts to bring others together to work toward a common goal.[27] Take, for instance, Nobel laureate William Shockley, whose creation of Shockley Semiconductor launched the microchip industry. His narcissism made him unable to accept his employees' ideas and drove away the brilliant people he had hired.[28] Dubbed the "traitorous eight," these men left Shockley to found Fairchild Semiconductor, from which such famous companies as Intel and Teledyne were later born.

Studies show that a substantial portion of narcissism is genetic—45 percent as assessed by the California Personality Inventory and between 42 and 49 percent as measured by the Dimensional Assessment of Personality Pathology.[29] Amazingly, one study showed that one identical twin's narcissism predicted the other's 53 percent of the time in pairs that were raised in completely different families. By contrast, fraternal twins raised in the same homes by the same parents were equally narcissistic only 11 percent of the time.[30] In short, your genes influence the development of personality dimensions that make you a bad leader, just as they impact the traits that make you a good one.

Types of Leaders

Genetically influenced personality traits also affect the *type* of leader that you will become. Suppose you are born with particular variants of the following genes: "impulsiveness" (DRD2), "novelty-seeking" (DRD4), "harm-avoidance" (CNRA4), "sleep" (ADORA2A), "worrier" (COMT), and "persistence" (HTR2A). Studies suggest that you might be more likely to be conscientious, persistent, and self-directed than a person without those gene variants.[31] Similarly, suppose you have certain versions of the "impulsiveness" (DRD2), "novelty-seeking" (DRD4), and "antisocial" (MAOA) genes.[32] Your odds of being high in extraversion might be greater than those of other people.[33] What if you have certain variants of the following genes: "activity" (DAT1), "adrenaline" (PNMT), "harm-avoidance" (CNRA4), "sex hormone" (CYP19), "cooperativeness" (GABRA6), and "getting along" (OXYR)?[34] Research suggests that your chances of developing an agreeable and cooperative personality might be larger than those of people with different versions of the genes. (Keep in mind that the effect of each of these genes might be small, and that the studies suggesting their influence have not been extensively replicated.)

These gene combinations also might affect the kind of boss you become because your personality influences the likelihood you'll adopt different leadership styles. For instance, people higher in conscientiousness and extraversion are more likely to empower others, while those lower in these traits tend to favor command and control.[35] Thus, based on what we know about the genetic sources of personality characteristics, we have some idea of the source of the preference for different leadership styles. Versions of the "impulsiveness" (DRD2), "novelty-seeking" (DRD4), "harm-avoidance" (CNRA4), "sleep" (ADORA2A), "concern" (HTR2C), "persistence" (HTR2A), "worrier" (COMT), "transcendence"

(SLC18A1), and "antisocial" (MAOA) genes might influence your chances of being extraverted and conscientious, which in turn might affect your odds of being an empowerment, as opposed to a command-and-control, type of leader.

Moreover, research shows that the genetic part of the tendency to become a transformational leader also increases the chances that you will be conscientious, extraverted, and open to experience, while the genetic portion of the predisposition to become a transactional leader also raises the odds that you will be non-conscientious, intraverted, and disagreeable.[36] The common genetic source of both leadership style and personality suggests that the same genes affect both. That is, people with certain versions of the "impulsiveness" (DRD2), "novelty-seeking" (DRD4), "concern" (HTR2C), "activity" (DAT1), "adrenaline" (PNMT), "cooperativeness" (GABRA6), "getting along" (OXYR), "sex hormone" (CYP19), "harm-avoidance" (CNRA4), "sleep" (ADORA2A), "persistence" (HTR2A), "worrier" (COMT), "transcendence" (SLC18A1), and "antisocial" (MAOA) genes might be more likely to get others to follow them by offering a vision of the future, while those with other variants of the same genes might be more likely to lead by cutting deals. If we think back to the civil rights movement of the 1960s and the leadership of that effort, one might hypothesize that the visionary Martin Luther King Jr., with his dream of the little white boy and little black boy, had a genetic predisposition to lead in a different way than President Lyndon Johnson, with his history of Senate deal making.

Through Temperament

Another way genes affect leadership is by influencing our predisposition to develop certain temperaments. Most transformational leaders tend to be optimistic, the-glass-is-half-full kinds of people. When the going gets tough, these kinds of leaders get going.

People with positive temperaments attract followers because they paint a vision for the future that is both positive and attainable.[37] For example, Winston Churchill, in the darkest days of World War II, rallied the British with his optimism, ensuring them that, despite the bleak circumstances they faced, they would defeat the Nazis.

According to Jack Welch, the legendary former CEO of General Electric, leaders need to be optimists because leadership involves infecting other people with hope.[38] A positive outlook improves productivity, increases morale, and enhances performance. It gets people thinking that they can achieve better outcomes. This, in turn, provides them with the energy and commitment to obtain those results.[39]

In contrast, pessimistic people paint a negative picture of the future. Their dark outlook reduces their willingness to try new things or to even attempt to solve problems. The-glass-is-half-empty types don't improve morale or rally others, making it difficult for them to improve productivity or spur people to accomplish difficult tasks.

As we saw in chapter 3, numerous studies show that half of the difference in whether people are optimistic or pessimistic is genetic.[40] Moreover, several genes that govern neurotransmitter function affect our temperaments.[41] Perhaps, people endowed with the versions of serotonin, dopamine, and monoamine genes associated with having a rosy outlook are also more likely to become leaders, and are more effective at leadership, than other people. After all, researchers have provided evidence for both the path from genes to optimism and from optimism to leadership.

Through Intelligence and Cognitive Abilities

Perhaps you have thought your boss is a terrible leader because, as all of your coworkers agree, he is an idiot. At lunch, at least once a week, you and your colleagues discuss the parallels between his leadership style and that of TV's most famous boss, Michael Scott of Dunder Mifflin. In virtually all discussions, your group agrees that, like Michael Scott, your boss's lack of intelligence is responsible for his administrative blunders. Once or twice, someone in the group has wondered if your boss's stupidity-induced lack of leadership is innate. Preposterous? Maybe not.

Our genes affect our leadership skills in part through their influence on our intelligence. As we have seen in previous chapters, researchers have found strong evidence for a genetic effect on a wide variety of cognitive abilities. At least 40 percent of the difference between people in general cognitive ability[42] and 75 percent of difference in IQ scores comes from our DNA.[43]

The genetic effect on intelligence and cognitive skills is intriguing because both of these affect leadership.[44] A study that combined the results of 151 different investigations of leadership and intelligence found that smarter people are more likely to become bosses.[45] Brainier people also have a greater tendency to view themselves as leaders, as well as to hold leadership positions in businesses, the military, religious groups, and a variety of other organizations. Because people with the "right" versions of certain genes tend to be smarter than other people, and smarter people are more likely to be leaders, it is likely that some people are born with the versions of genes that both increase their mental ability and their tendency to be interested in, and good at, leadership.

Through Selection into Leadership-Favorable Situations

While some of how your genes affect your leadership interests and skills might occur through genetic predispositions to develop favorable personality traits or temperaments, another part probably occurs through your tendency to choose situations that reinforce your genetic predispositions. For instance, suppose you have two job options open to you. One of those positions is more favorable to becoming a boss because it offers more mentoring, the chance to participate in a leadership training program, and the opportunity to head up a team. People who have this job are more likely to become leaders than individuals who have the other one.

At first glance, it appears that your odds of becoming a leader depend on which position you get assigned to. But the characteristics of your job aren't just passed out randomly as part of the organization's annual employment lottery. Instead, they are affected by your efforts to get certain positions and avoid others. If you want to become a leader— and tend to be good at running things—you will probably angle for a job that funnels people toward leadership roles. You might do this by showing your supervisor you have the right skills and attitudes for the position or by getting other people to recommend you. On the other hand, if you don't want to be a leader and tend not to be good at being in charge, you will probably seek another job.

Whether you are conscious of it or not, your DNA is going to affect which job you try to get. If your genes predispose you to develop the right personality, temperament, and cognitive skills to be a boss, you are going to be more likely to angle for the leadership-opportunity-rich position. In fact, studies show that our genes influence whether or not we find ourselves in work situations that are favorable to leadership development. For example, one investigation of businesswomen found that about 31 percent of the difference in the tendency to have the kinds of work experiences that facilitate achieving a leadership role—such as having a mentor, participating in training and development programs, and facing job challenges—is genetic.[46]

How does this happen? How do your genes affect the odds you will have a job that is favorable to leadership development? One possibility is the mechanism just described. Employees with a greater genetic predisposition for running the show find leadership-development-rich situations more attractive than do other people and so are more likely to put themselves in those settings.[47]

Supervisors also put subordinates who are genetically predisposed toward leadership in situations that facilitate the development of relevant skills because they sense that their employees have an innate gift for directing others. That is, people with a genetic predisposition toward leadership give off signals of that tendency, which others respond to.

The genetic predispositions to develop the personality traits, temperaments, or cognitive abilities that make some people more likely to find themselves in leadership-rich situations don't just exert their influence at a single moment in your life. Rather, they take you down a corridor of choices toward a leadership track over the course of your life. Take, for example, a person who has the versions of the genes that predispose him to be both dominant and sociable. People with these personality characteristics tend to enjoy being in situations that facilitate the development of leadership skills. In school, they might like being class president, head cheerleader, or project-team leader, more than kids without these traits.[48] As a result, they develop more positive attitudes than other kids toward being in charge and constantly put themselves in situations that enhance the growth of their leadership talent.[49] In school, they may go out for team captain, run for class president, or start a new club. At work, they may volunteer to direct a team tasked with a difficult assignment, or they may choose a job that pays a lower salary, but offers the opportunity to participate in a leadership development program. Over time, the odds that these people will become leaders increase because their genetic predispositions led them to continuously select leadership-favorable situations in which to hone their skills.

Much of the time that we think people are *learning* to become leaders they really aren't. People who are born with the versions of genes that increase their odds of becoming the boss are just more likely to find themselves in leadership-rich situations as they respond to their genetic predispositions. For instance, some people might be slightly advantaged at leadership because of their endowment of DNA. Because these individuals are predisposed to be better at directing groups, they tend to enjoy being in charge more than others. Over time, they choose more and more challenging situations in which to display their leadership skills, giving the illusion that they are becoming better leaders with experience. But they aren't. They're just travelling down a corridor that they were genetically predisposed to go through. As one author explained, "If you are a born leader, you will seek out experiences that help you develop. You will feel energized when things go well in their development, as when your parents support you. Born leaders often remember the energizing feeling when they were at their mother's knee, assuming that their mother was the one who instilled it, when their mother simply reinforced something that was already there."[50] Thus, "if you are born with raw leadership ability, your early experiences will serve to help you understand it, exercise it, come to terms with it, and 'fine tune' it. But your early experiences don't make you a leader—you are born that way."[51]

A similar pattern exists when we think about our self-assurance as leaders. Just because we become more comfortable in leadership roles as we undertake more of them doesn't mean that our confidence in our leadership skills is learned. As one author explains,

> When a successful leader is young, he often feels trepidation in front of more senior people, or when confronted with difficult situations, yet later he becomes more confident. So it must be learned, right? The confusion here is whether you can develop into a confident leader, not whether you're able to inspire confidence from the day you were born. (Did Napoleon command anyone the day he was born?) The ability to *develop into* a leader over time is what's innate.[52]

Through Interaction with Environmental Factors

While this chapter has addressed a key issue for understanding our work-related behavior—the role that our genes play in our beliefs toward, and skills at, leadership—it's important to realize that the tendency to take charge is far from genetically predetermined. In fact, most researchers believe that the development of both positive attitudes toward, and favorable capabilities at, leadership is explicitly the result of the interaction between our genes and the situations in which we find ourselves. Although our genes are responsible in part for our presence in those situations (which makes figuring this out difficult), we nonetheless have solid evidence of this interaction. For instance, one study found that experiences as a young adult influence whether an innate predisposition to take charge manifests itself in adulthood. People with a genetic inclination to lead, but no chance to act on that predisposition in childhood, are less likely to become leaders than those who have the same genetic tendency, but who also have the opportunity to try out leadership roles at school or in their families.[53]

One set of researchers found that genetic predispositions interact with the characteristics of the situations we are in to influence our achievement of leadership roles. People who have the versions of genes that predispose them to become leaders are less likely to do so if their teenage years are spent in nurturing environments. If the kids with favorable variants of the key genes grew up with parents who were not very supportive, then they were more likely to reach leadership positions than people with similar genetic tendencies who were raised in more nurturing families.[54]

The study also found that the genetic tendency to take charge appears to interact with the occurrence of a major negative event during one's teenage years, such as the loss of family wealth, death of a parent, or illness of a sibling, to increase the odds that a person will become an adult leader. It seems that overcoming hardship as a young adult helps those who are genetically predisposed to lead to do so later in life.[55]

Conclusions

The heading of this chapter had a question mark in it for a reason. None of us is truly a "born leader." Your DNA does nothing to guarantee that you will become a boss, any more than it precludes you from directing a group. On the other hand, leadership does have a large genetic component. Our genes influence our attitudes toward leadership, our leadership abilities, our willingness to adopt leadership roles, and even the kinds of leaders we become.

While researchers don't yet have a complete understanding of how our genes influence us as leaders, they have provided enough evidence to sketch out some of the likely mechanisms. Our DNA affects our predispositions to develop certain personality traits, temperaments, and cognitive abilities, and these tendencies, in turn, impact how we feel about being in charge, as well as our leadership skills.

But genes don't just exert their influence through our personalities, temperaments, and cognitive abilities; they also affect our tendency to find ourselves in leadership-friendly settings. Having certain genetic predispositions leads us to choose the most beneficial situations for leadership, as well as to be selected by others for those settings, repeatedly throughout our lives. As a result, those of us with leadership-friendly genetic endowments benefit from more often finding ourselves in environments that support the development of leadership attitudes and abilities.

Of course, no one is genetically predetermined to be a boss. In fact, many scientists believe that people with innate tendencies toward leadership are more likely than other people to become leaders *only* if they experience the kind of events that trigger those predispositions to become active.

Having made the case that your genes affect the odds that you will become a leader, I turn now to a discussion of how they impact your chances of becoming the next Leonardo DaVinci, or at least how they influence your creativity and innovativeness, which is the subject of the next chapter.

8

Creative Genius? Your Genetic Predisposition for Creativity and Innovation

Jim worked in product development at a major consumer electronics company. His job involved a great deal of creative activity. He designed new products and worked with marketing personnel on the strategy to roll them out. He even came up with new ways to develop prototypes of new products when he found the existing tools lacking.

Jim really enjoyed product development. He liked interacting with creative people and found working in an environment in which things were always changing exhilarating.

Jim had always leaned in this direction. As a young child, he often invented new approaches to the games he played. For example, instead of playing baseball with the other kids, he would try to get them to use new rules that he had created for the sport.

His kindergarten teacher referred to him as the kid who wanted to "color outside of the lines;" and Jim thought that his teacher was probably right. He would much rather come up with a new design than color in something that someone else had drawn.

Jim was a very good artist and had gravitated to creative courses in college. He majored in engineering design because he really liked going to the labs and making prototypes. So when it was time for him to graduate, he went looking for a job in product development, where he could be creative. And he tried to get that position at the most innovative company he could find.

Many companies would like more Jims. Creativity and innovation are important parts of organizational life, and crucial to the success of many businesses. Moreover, the pace of change in many industries has accelerated dramatically in recent years, making a capacity for innovation a prerequisite for employment in numerous sectors of the economy. Employees who can come up with novel ideas may be increasingly in demand as companies focus more on the development of new technology and entrepreneurial activity.[1]

So it is no surprise that many companies look for creativity in their prospective employees. These businesses conduct psychological tests to assess how inventive their potential hires are. They explore the work histories of possible employees to find examples of innovation. And they use interviews to search for evidence of an imaginative mind-set.

All of this effort points to the importance of figuring out the source of creativity and innovation. Billions, if not trillions, of words have been written purporting to identify the key that unlocks human ingenuity. Of course, there is no way that I can review the reams of paper, gallons of ink, and tons of silicon that have been devoted to this topic, so I'm not even going to try. Instead, I'm going to just bring up a single point. The vast majority of what has been written assumes that everyone is equally likely to come up with novel ideas. We are, in the eyes of most experts, blank slates that can be transformed into imaginative and inventive individuals if only we are trained correctly and put into the right work environments. Baloney!

While I won't argue that the right work environment or training are *irrelevant* for making people more creative and innovative, I will point out that we aren't blank slates when it comes to these activities. Some of us are born lucky in this regard (or unlucky, depending on your perspective). We have a genetic predisposition to be inventive and ingenious. In short, the answer to the question "what makes people like Jim more creative than other people?" is their genes. At least in part.

The Genetics of Creativity and Innovation

Born innovator. It has a nice ring to it. And lots of people use the phrase. But it's not just an expression. It reflects an underlying reality. Studies of the creative thinking of identical and fraternal twins raised apart demonstrate that innovativeness has a substantial genetic component, with as much as 55 percent of the difference on standard tests of creativity being accounted for by our genes. In one study, half of the pairs of identical twins raised in separate households, often many miles away from one another, had the same scores on measures of creative temperament, while fraternal twins raised together had corresponding numbers only 12 percent of the time.[2]

Creative thinking, of course, is not the only dimension on which innovativeness is measured. Some observers focus on imaginativeness. Studies show that between 34 and 40 percent of the difference between people in vividness of their imagination and between 49 and 52 percent of the variance in their intellectual curiosity and openness to new ideas are explained by our genes.[3]

Studies also show that the genetic effects on imaginativeness and intellectual curiosity are different from those that influence the trait of openness to experience, the aspect of personality to which these characteristics are most closely related. One study showed that only 29 percent of the genetic effect on imaginativeness is captured by innate differences in overall openness to experience.[4] Stated differently, this means different genetic factors influence how imaginative and open to experience you are. So you might have the versions of genes that predispose you to be more imaginative than your cubicle mate, even though you are less open to trying new and exotic foods or travelling to foreign countries.

We often think of creativity as falling into different domains. For example, we think of the imaginativeness of painters, sculptors, dancers, and so forth, as one type of creativity (artistic creativity) and the inventiveness of engineers, biologists, chemists, and other scientists, as another kind (scientific creativity). Research shows that both kinds have a genetic component. Specifically, between 22 and 36 percent of the difference between people in scientific and artistic creativity comes from our DNA.[5]

Of course, aspects of the environment in which you work, such as the incentives that your employer gives you and the company's organizational structure and rules, also influence your ingenuity. Companies that don't reward innovativeness tend to get less of it from their employees. Bureaucratic and hierarchical organizational structures also tend to stifle employees' inventiveness.

As it turns out, however, your employer's incentives, structure, and rules are also affected by your DNA. As chapter 2 explained, your genes impact the environments you are in, something that researchers call gene-environment correlations. The genetic influence on the context in which you work emerges because you choose your employer, and do so at least in part on the basis of the features that the organization has. And your genes influence your preference for those characteristics over others.

Several studies indicate that our genes affect the importance we place on having a creative work environment—one in which we have the freedom to think up our own solutions and chart our own course. For instance, one set of researchers asked identical and fraternal twins about the value to them of working in that type of organization. The results showed a much greater similarity between the answers of pairs of identical twins than between pairs of their fraternal counterparts.[6] Stated differently, our genes influence our creativity in part through gene-environment correlations. Genetic differences lead some people to prefer to work in companies in which they can be creative, whereas others favor different employment settings.

The behavioral geneticists are not the only ones who have found evidence of an innate component to innovativeness. Molecular geneticists have gotten into the act as well, identifying specific genes that are related to being creative. While the molecular genetics results need to be qualified because they have not been extensively replicated and because the effect of any single gene is small, the findings are nonetheless instructive. In one study, researchers showed that the "impulsiveness" gene (DRD2) was associated primarily with verbal creativity—how creative a person is at describing something. Another gene, TPH1,[7] which provides instructions for the production of tryptophan hydroxylase 1, an enzyme that affects the pace of synthesis of serotonin, was related primarily with numerical creativity—how creative a person is with patterns of numbers. Together, these two genes account for 9 percent of the difference between people in creativity.[8]

(I will call TPH1 the "risk-taking" gene. But please note that this is not the only gene to affect risk taking, and taking chances isn't the only behavior that this gene affects. The name is just a mnemonic device to help you to remember one of the gene's many functions.)

These two genes are very unlikely to be the only ones that affect our creativity. Many researchers believe that numerous genes influence how innovative we are, and that those genes work together in complex ways. Some researchers even believe that the influence of many genes must be combined to affect creativity, and that the right versions of all of these genes need to be present before we get any impact at all.[9] This may be why so few people are highly creative. To be very innovative, you probably have to have a very rare combination of the right versions of many different genes.

How Genes Affect Creativity

How do your genes make you more or less creative than other people? After all, there's no Leonardo gene that will give you DaVinci-like inventiveness. As is the case for many aspects of work-related behavior, the path from specific genes to creativity is much more indirect. Although research is far from complete, scientists have traced out some of the plausible paths. The evidence collected to date suggests four routes: through hormones, cognitive abilities, personality, and temperament.

The Path through Hormones

Studies of the genes associated with creativity suggest that genetic effects start with the DNA that provides instructions for the production of hormones. Different people get different versions of these genes, causing some individuals to produce more of the hormones than others. As a result, even though the levels of these body chemicals fluctuate, depending on the time of day or what we are doing, the average around which they move differs across people.

Having different instructions for the production of hormones affects innovativeness because some of these body chemicals influence creative aspects of behavior. For instance, there are different versions of the "Alzheimer's"gene (APOE). People with one version of the gene have higher average levels of an adrenal steroid called dehydroepiandrosterone (DHEA) than people with another variant.[10] What makes this gene intriguing is the fact that DHEA levels are associated with how creatively people react to criticism. Those with less of the steroid are the most innovative in the face of a critique.[11] Thus, research suggests that people might be predisposed, because of their DNA, to produce more or less DHEA, and the levels of this steroid might affect how innovatively they respond to negative feedback.

Now consider another hormone—testosterone. As was discussed in earlier chapters, genetics accounts for most of the difference between people in their base the level of testosterone. Some versions of the testosterone genes lead the body to produce a lot of this hormone, while others lead it to generate much less.

Scientists have amassed a surprising amount of evidence that testosterone levels are related to creativity. They have found, for example, that giving postmenopausal women testosterone treatments increases their level of divergent thinking, while giving them estrogen raises their level of convergent thought.[12] They have also found that differences among people in musical creativity are related to variation in base testosterone levels.[13]

Scientists believe that testosterone might influence creativity through its impact on cognitive functioning. Testosterone affects many aspects of mental activity, including both attention and memory. Because innovativeness involves these cognitive processes, testosterone genes may impact creativity through their effects on different dimensions of mental functioning.

Born Smart and Creative

Our genes also influence our creativity through another path, one that begins with effects on the enzymes that produce neurotransmitters. Our genes, we know, influence the development of a number of key brain chemicals, including dopamine, serotonin, and monoamine oxidase, which affect how our brains function. People with certain versions of several neurotransmitter genes produce more serotonin and dopamine transporters and receptors and less of the chemicals that decompose them.

The different variants of these genes act like settings on a photocopy machine. For instance, people who have the versions of the serotonin transporter genes that say "make 20 copies of a molecule" instead of the versions that say "make 10" have more of these transporters in their systems at any point in time. Because they have more transporters to remove the serotonin, these individuals have less of the chemical lingering in their brains, reducing their predisposition toward impulsiveness and anxiety.[14]

Having more of certain neurotransmitters might enhance creativity through the effect of these brain chemicals on cognitive ability. Take dopamine as an example. This neurotransmitter is concentrated in the parts of the brain that are involved in memory, mental effort, mathematics, and complex planning. Moreover, dopamine has been implicated in reasoning, analysis, planning, prediction, and motor reaction time.[15] Creativity involves these and other cognitive processes that dopamine also affects.

Therefore, it is quite plausible for the genes that provide instructions for the production of neurotransmitters to influence your creativity by impacting your cognitive skills and abilities.

Through Personality

Your genes also influence your creativity through their effect on your personality. We have a wealth of evidence that people with certain psychological attributes are more innovative than others. Take, for example, openness to experience. People high in this trait have been found to be more creative than other people, particularly in science and art.[16]

Personality traits, as we saw in earlier chapters, aren't randomly given to people. They are partially a function of genetics. In the case of neuroticism, for instance, studies show that more than half of the difference between people is genetic.[17] Consistent with the stereotype of the tortured artist, anxious people tend to be more creative than those who are more emotionally stable.[18] Moreover, manic depression, which has a strong genetic component, is more common among innovative thinkers in business and the arts.[19] Thus, genetic differences could predispose some people to be more neurotic than others, which, in turn, makes them more likely to be creative.

Neurotics may be more creative than other people because of genetic differences in instructions for the production of neurotransmitters, such as serotonin. Some of the drugs used to treat extreme anxiety affect the production of this brain chemical, suggesting a biochemical link between serotonin and anxiety. Moreover, people with certain versions of serotonin genes are more neurotic than people with other variants. Therefore, the versions of the serotonin genes that you inherited from your parents might predispose you toward greater anxiety, a proclivity which might also direct your mental activity in more creative ways.

But neuroticism isn't the only trait through which your genes affect your personality. Openness to experience is another. Studies show that more than half of the difference between people in this personality dimension is innate.[20] Thus, genetic variation could predispose some people to be more open to experience than others, which, in turn, would make them more likely to be creative.

Conscientiousness is a third personality trait through which genes influence creativity. In contrast to the greater innovativeness of neurotics, research shows that conscientious people tend to be less creative than others, especially artistically.[21] Experts believe that highly conscientiousness people tend to be very organized and structured, which makes thinking outside the box more difficult for them.[22] This doesn't mean that everyone who is conscientious is uncreative. But it does indicate that, if you take a group of people—employees at your company, children at your local elementary school, your neighbors, or any other group you can think of—those who are highly conscientious will tend to show lower average levels of creativity than those who are not.

The lesser innovativeness of the highly conscientious might be partially a result of genetic differences. Research shows that more than 40 percent of the variation between people in this personality trait is genetic.[23] It appears that some of us were lucky (or unlucky) enough to be born with versions of genes that predispose us to be conscientious. This propensity, in turn, increases our odds of being good at some things, like planning and collecting disconfirming information, but makes us less likely to be creative and innovative.

The ways that our genes influence our creativity through our personalities are not limited to the OCEAN traits of openness to experience, conscientiousness, extraversion, agreeableness, and neuroticism. They also affect our creativity by predisposing us to be novelty seeking.

As we saw in earlier chapters, researchers studying twins and adopted children have found that more than half of the variance across people in novelty seeking (and the closely related concept of sensation seeking) is genetic.[24] Moreover, molecular geneticists have found versions of several genes to be associated with this dimension of personality, including variants of the "worrier" gene (COMT), the "substance dependence" (GABRB1) gene, the "risk-taking" (TPH1) gene,[25] the "sensation-seeking" gene (DRD1), the "impulsiveness" gene (DRD2), the "novelty-seeking" gene (DRD4), and the "activity" gene (SLC6A3).[26] (I am calling GABRB1, which provides instructions for the production of receptors that speed transmission of messages across synapses in the brain, the "substance-dependence" gene because it has been associated with alcohol dependence. I am naming DRD1, which codes for the production of dopamine receptors, the "sensation-seeking" gene because of its association with that personality trait.)

In the case of the "novelty-seeking" gene (DRD4), scientists believe that people with certain versions release less dopamine in response to external stimuli, like having a good meal or completing a project. Because dopamine makes people feel good, if we have less of it for some reason, we try to get more of it. This means that those individuals whose bodies release only a little dopamine in response to an external trigger seek out greater stimuli so they, too, can get a large release of this brain chemical and the good feeling that comes along with it.[27] Often, these people become novelty seeking in their quest for strong enough triggers to get their dopamine "rush."

The effect of differences in the "novelty-seeking" gene (DRD4) on behavior can be substantial. Studies have shown that the long variant of this gene alone accounts for 4 percent of the variance in how novelty-seeking people are.[28] You are likely to develop a different personality if you happen to be born with the long instead of the short version of this gene.

What does this have to do with creativity? A lot, actually. Novelty seekers tend to be more innovative than other people. Studies show that psychological test scores for novelty and sensation seeking are positively correlated with a variety of measures of creativity and divergent thinking.[29] Seekers of sensation and novelty are more interested in new ideas than other people. They also view novel situations more positively, are more susceptible to boredom, and are more averse to routine work.[30] Researchers have even found that sensation and novelty-seeking individuals are better than other people at coming up with new solutions to problems.[31] As one author explained, "Sensation seekers tend to be original and innovative in open-ended problem solving, whereas low sensation seekers tend to be too rigid and unimaginative."[32]

Your genes also influence how innovative you are by affecting your locus of control. As we saw in earlier chapters, locus of control is a belief that what happens to you is under your own power, as opposed to being externally determined.[33] Individuals with external locus of control tend to be less creative than other people because their tendency to attribute what happens to them to external forces—the sense that they can't affect outcomes through their actions—reduces their motivation to come up with novel solutions to problems.[34]

Whether you have an internal or external locus of control is, in part, genetic. Studies show that as much as 55 percent of the difference between people in this trait comes from their DNA.[35] In short, some of us appear to have versions of genes that predispose us to develop an internal locus of control, which, in turn, increases our odds of being creative.

The personality trait that has, perhaps, received the most attention for its association with creativity is psychoticism. That may be because it is a controversial trait, having, as it does, some negative connotations. Psychoticism, the psychologists tell us, involves the tendency to have a mild version of the characteristics possessed by psychotics: recklessness, lack of common sense, paranoia, and inappropriate social expression.[36]

While tending to display these undesirable characteristics, people high in psychoticism also tend to be very innovative. A long list of studies has documented the role that psychoticism has played in the creativity of great artists.[37] Moreover, people who score high on psychological tests of psychoticism also tend to score high on measures of creativity.[38] And those judged to be high in psychoticism are more likely than other people to be found in creative professions, like art, music, and writing.[39] In short, the way that many observers have portrayed innovative artists—possessing a tendency to engage in inappropriate social behavior and displaying a carelessness that borders on the foolish—appears to have scientific merit.

The association between psychoticism and creativity is intriguing because this personality trait is at least partially genetic. A statistical analysis that combined the results of 15 different studies showed that roughly half of the variance between people in psychoticism comes from their genes.[40] Moreover, some researchers believe that genetic differences in the production of the neurotransmitters serotonin and dopamine affect cognitive function in a way that contributes to both psychoticism and creativity.[41] Thus, it is plausible that some of us are born with versions of our genes—mutations, perhaps—that make us predisposed to psychoticism. This predilection, in turn, makes those high in the trait less well suited for much of the work of modern organizations, but offers a corresponding boost to creativity that might compensate for these disadvantages.

Temperament

A final way that your genes influence your creativity is through their effect on your temperament. Individuals who have a more positive outlook on the world—those who view the glass as half full as opposed to half empty—are more creative than those with a more negative worldview.[42] Why? It appears that being happy and positive makes people more flexible and open to new ideas, facilitating their efforts to come up with novel solutions to problems.[43]

As we saw in chapter 2, some individuals are simply born with more positive dispositions than others. Numerous studies show that much of the difference between people in their outlook on life is genetic.[44] Moreover, specific genes, most notably those that influence the workings of chemicals in our brains, affect how positive or negative our temperaments are.[45] So it is plausible to think that people endowed with certain versions of the genes that provide instructions for the creation of serotonin, dopamine, and monoamine oxidase are more likely than others to have favorable dispositions, and, consequently, greater odds of being creative.

Conclusion

Some folks are more innovative than others. In part, they are born that way. Studies of twins have shown that genetics accounts for a significant share of the difference between people in creativity; and individuals endowed with certain versions of neurotransmitter genes are more creative than those without them.

Of course, no version of a gene *guarantees* that you will be creative or innovative. Genes don't *determine* these attributes. Many people will be highly innovative even if they don't have the "right" versions of the genes associated with creativity. But genes do matter; your odds of being creative and innovative are greater if you have a favorable genetic predisposition.

While we are still in the early days of understanding how our genes influence our innovativeness, we have some idea of how this happens. Our genes affect the levels of hormones that our bodies produce, and some of these hormones influence how our brains function, resulting in, among other things, greater or lesser creativity. In addition, our genes predispose us to develop certain mental abilities, personality traits, and temperaments. These proclivities, in turn, contribute to our innovativeness.

Having outlined the way in which your genes affect how creative and innovative you are, I turn now to exploring how they influence your tendency to engage in entrepreneurial activity, the subject of the next chapter.

9

Born Entrepreneurs? How Your Genes Affect Your Tendency to Start Companies

John, it seems, had always wanted to be an entrepreneur. Even as a child, he would save his Halloween candy, while other kids ate theirs. Then, when his friends had none left, John would sell them his at a tidy profit.

As a teenager, John always had some sort of business, whether it was mowing lawns or babysitting little kids. When people asked him what he wanted to be when he grew up, he always replied, "an entrepreneur."

So it was no surprise to anyone when, shortly after graduating from college, John started his own company. While many people who found businesses aren't very successful, John was. His venture survived and grew. A few years later, he sold it to a major company. He then turned around and started another business.

At his 10th college reunion, John was asked to serve on a panel to talk to the students about being an entrepreneur. When the moderator asked him when he first became interested in striking out on his own, he replied, "I've always wanted to run my own company. I guess I was just born interested."

A venture capitalist who had invested in John's second company was asked to comment on why he thought John was successful as an entrepreneur. The VC replied, "He's a natural at running a business. He's just one of those people with a God-given talent for being an entrepreneur. I can't put my finger on what it is exactly. It's just that he seems to know intuitively the right decisions to make."

You might have heard John's story before. Or it might be your own. Either way, we all have heard about people who have always wanted to be entrepreneurs and who seem to be naturals at it. Is it possible that

John and other people like him were born with a predisposition to run their own businesses?

The idea is not preposterous. Researchers have long known that individuals whose moms and dads are entrepreneurs are much more likely than other people to start their own businesses. The academics have just attributed that pattern to the parents' efforts to teach their children about entrepreneurship, either directly or indirectly.

But could people like John become entrepreneurs because of something inborn? Could the relationship between parent and child entrepreneurs be a function of genes rather than learning?[1] As this chapter will show, the answer appears to be yes.

Some Part of Entrepreneurship Is Genetic

Research shows that part of the difference in the tendency to become an entrepreneur comes from our DNA. This is true whether we think of entrepreneurs as people who are self-employed, who have started companies, who own their own businesses, or who have been involved in the firm start-up process. One study examined the role of genetics in explaining who goes into business for themselves. The results provide strong evidence for an innate component to entrepreneurship, regardless of how the researchers defined it. The authors found that genetics accounted for the following effects:

- 48 percent of the difference in the tendency to be self-employed
- 39 percent of the variance in the number of years self-employed
- 37 percent of the variation in the tendency to be owner-operator of a business
- 37 percent of the difference in the number of businesses owned and operated
- 41 percent of the variance in having started a business
- 42 percent of the variation in the number of businesses started
- 41 percent of the difference in having engaging in the start-up process
- 42 percent of the variation in the number of start-up efforts undertaken.[2]

Even after taking into consideration the effects of age, gender, income, education, marital status, race, and immigrant status, genetic effects on the tendency to be an entrepreneur remained high. In short, all measures of entrepreneurship examined by the researchers showed a solid genetic influence, even after other potential explanations were accounted for.

However, the influence of DNA on the tendency to start a business might not be the same for both sexes. The research described above had a disproportionately female sample. So it's possible that the genetic patterns exist for women and not men.

Gender differences in genetic effects might exist because other factors are much stronger determinants of the decision to start a company for men than for women. If women tend not to found companies, even if they are in situations that motivate men to do so, then the effect of environmental factors on men's start-up decisions might be strong, while, for women, they might be weak. For instance, males might be more likely to respond to the experience of having a job in a small company by increasing their odds of striking out on their own, while this experience might not trigger entrepreneurial tendencies in females. The end result is little genetic effect on the tendency of men to become entrepreneurs, but a strong genetic effect on the chances of women doing so.

This pattern is essentially what a recent study by a team of researchers led by Zhen Zhang at Arizona State University found. The researchers looked at a more balanced sample of men and women than previous researchers, and found a strong influence of DNA on the tendency to start businesses for women, but not for men.[3] However, other researchers have found a similar genetic effect on the probability of becoming self-employed for both genders.[4] So, perhaps, genetic factors do affect the entrepreneurial inclinations of both men and women after all.

All of the studies described above focused on the process of starting or running a business. But a lot of research shows that people tend to found companies to pursue business opportunities they have identified. That raises an important question: do genetic factors affect the tendency of individuals to become entrepreneurs because they influence the odds that people will identify opportunities for new companies, or because they affect the probability that some other aspect of the entrepreneurial process will occur? Researchers have proposed that genetic factors are particularly likely to impact opportunity identification because that activity is primarily cognitive; it depends a lot on how people think. Because thinking is affected by brain function, it's easier to understand how genes coding for enzymes might impact the odds that someone will recognize a business opportunity than to see how those same genes might affect the likelihood that someone will, say, get the money that they need to start a company.

To get at this question, one set of researchers looked at whether coming up with an idea for a new business and starting a company are influenced by the same genetic factors. They found that approximately 53 percent of the correlation between those two activities is the result of common genetic factors.[5] This suggests that our DNA might well be influencing the odds that we become entrepreneurs by affecting our ability to identify new business opportunities.

How Our Genes Influence Our Tendency to Start Businesses

How do our genes influence the tendency to become an entrepreneur? After all, there is no start-up gene, and no babies are born knowing how to write business plans or seek venture capital.[6] So genetic effects on entrepreneurial endeavors must be indirect. Research suggests several different mechanisms by which your genes exert their influence, including working through your activity level, cognitive skills, and personality. Let's take a look at some of these mechanisms.

Entrepreneurs with ADHD

People differ in something that researchers call their activity level. In essence, this attribute captures how much of a couch potato you are. At one end of the activity spectrum, people are kinetic, always doing many things at once and never sitting still, while, at the other end, they are sedentary, able to sit still and do nothing for long periods of time.

At the extreme kinetic end of the activity-level spectrum, people are said to be hyperactive. These individuals display excessive movement, restlessness and poor attention. They bore easily, tend to forget plans, and have trouble keeping their mind on reading materials or conversations. Hyperactive people usually are not organized in their tasks and often fail to complete them. They also tend to be impulsive, making snap decisions and taking actions before thinking things through.[7]

It turns out that whether we are sedentary or hyperactive is partially the result of our genetic endowment. Studies have shown that as much as 84 percent of the difference between people in normal activity level is explained by our genes.[8] And as much as 89 percent of the variance in whether people are diagnosed with attention deficit hyperactivity disorder (ADHD) comes from our DNA.[9]

Researchers believe that the genes that control dopamine, norepinephrine, and serotonin affect whether or not a person develops ADHD. Certain versions of genes that regulate the release of neurotransmitters from the adrenergic neurons, such as the adrenergic alpha-2A receptor gene (ADRA2A[10]), are more common in people with ADHD than in people without this disorder.[11] (I will call ADRA2A the "orderliness" gene because one version of this gene has been associated with higher scores on this dimension in personality tests.[12] But keep in mind that this name doesn't mean the gene is exclusively responsible for orderliness, the labeling is just a way to help you to remember one of the many functions of this gene.) In addition, people with certain versions of the "activity" gene (DAT1), "impulsiveness" gene (DRD2), and "novelty-seeking" gene (DRD4) are all more prevalent in people with ADHD than those without it.[13] In fact, researchers have found that the risk of being diagnosed with ADHD goes up significantly if you have certain variants of the "novelty-seeking" gene (DRD4).[14] And the predictive value of having a specific variant of the "impulsiveness" gene (DRD2) has been estimated to be 16 percent.[15] (All of these results demand further replication before we can draw firm conclusions from them, so you should not consider them definitive.)

The genes that control the serotonin system also appear to influence the likelihood of developing ADHD. Studies have found variants of several of the serotonin system genes, including versions of the "persistence" (HTR2A[16]) gene, to be more common in people with ADHD than in people without this disorder.[17]

Furthermore, the genes that produce the brain chemicals that break down dopamine and serotonin are also associated with having ADHD. For instance, studies have shown that versions of the "antisocial" gene (MAOA) and the "worrier" gene (COMT) are more common among those with ADHD than those without it. Similarly, the DDC[18] gene, which controls the transformation of the chemical DOPA to dopamine and L-5 hydroxytryptophan to serotonin (and which I will call the "attention deficit" gene) are more prevalent in individuals with ADHD than in other people.[19]

The effect of these different versions of neurotransmitter genes on the odds that people develop ADHD is important to this book because individuals with ADHD are overrepresented among entrepreneurs. Studies have shown that as many as 30 percent of those with this disorder end up running their own businesses (as compared to as few as 5 percent of people without it).[20] Research also shows that people with ADHD tend to be better at many of the tasks demanded of entrepreneurs, such as recognizing opportunities and taking risks.[21] As David Neeleman, the founder of the airline JetBlue, who has ADHD explains, "My ADD brain naturally searches for better ways of doing things. With the disorganization, procrastination, inability to focus, and all the other bad things that come with ADD, there also come creativity and the ability to take risks."[22] In short, your genes might influence your odds of becoming an entrepreneur by affecting the production of several brain chemicals in ways that predispose you to develop ADHD, a disorder that increases your chances of having an entrepreneurial career.

Smart Enough to Strike Out on Their Own

Your intelligence is another mechanism through which your genes might affect your tendency to become an entrepreneur. As we saw in earlier chapters, your genes clearly affect how smart you are. Twin and adoption studies show that genes influence all aspects of cognitive ability, including both verbal and mathematical skills.[23] Moreover, these studies show that the *same* genetic factors impact a variety of mental abilities, from inspection time to reading ability to IQ, suggesting a common biological source (perhaps lying in the dopamine system) for all of them.[24] Finally, research has found that certain versions of key genes, including the "impulsiveness" gene (DRD2), are associated with higher intelligence and greater cognitive ability.[25]

The genetic effect on cognitive ability is intriguing because smarter people are more likely to start businesses. In fact, researchers have found that the higher a child's intelligence test scores measured at age 12, the greater the odds that he or she will be self-employed in adulthood.[26] So it is quite plausible some people are more likely than others to become entrepreneurs because they were born with the variants of genes that increase their odds of being smart.

One set of genes of particular interest to researchers are those that influence the development of language disorders, such as dyslexia, because these disorders are disproportionately common among people who start their own companies. Not only are several famous entrepreneurs—including Richard Branson, head of the Virgin Group of companies; Charles Schwab, the discount brokerage entrepreneur; and Paul Orfalea, founder of Kinkos—known to be dyslexic, but also studies show that entrepreneurs are more than twice as likely as non-entrepreneurs to have this disorder.[27] For instance, one study found that 35 percent of U.S. entrepreneurs report being dyslexic, as compared to only 15 percent of the overall U.S. population. Some experts believe that dyslexia is common among those who start their own businesses because the job involves less reading and writing than professions such as management, law, engineering, or medicine.[28] As a result, dyslexia is less of a handicap for entrepreneurs than for lawyers and doctors.

Researchers have confirmed that between 25 and 50 percent of the difference between people in their tendency to have language disorders is genetic.[29] Moreover, scientists have identified variants of several genes (DYX1C1, KIAA0319, ROB01[30], DYX2, and DYX3), including those responsible for the development of nerve cells, that are more common among dyslexics than other people.[31] Thus, perhaps the genetic lottery influences some people's odds of becoming entrepreneurs by giving them versions of genes that increase the probability of being dyslexic.

OCEAN Personality Traits

Many researchers believe that it is through our personalities that our genes exert their greatest influence on our tendency to start businesses.[32] Psychologists have studied a variety of personality traits and their effects on the odds of becoming an entrepreneur, and now believe that the most important of these are the OCEAN personality dimensions. So let's look at how your genes affect your odds of starting a business through their effects on these and other traits.

Extraversion

Extraversion is a personality trait that captures how sociable, talkative, and outgoing you are.[33] Studies conducted in a number of different countries using a variety of psychological instruments and various methodologies show that genes account for as much as two-thirds of the difference between people in extraversion.[34] Furthermore, as previous chapters explained, researchers have found that individuals with certain versions of particular neurotransmitter genes, most notably the "impulsiveness" (DRD2) and "novelty-seeking" (DRD4) genes, are more likely than other people to be extraverted and to develop warm and close personal relationships.[35]

The fact that extraversion has a genetic component is interesting because several studies show that entrepreneurs are more extraverted than the rest of the population. A meta-analysis that combined the results of several different studies showed that extraverts have higher odds of running their own businesses than introverts;[36] and a study of a cohort of people who were born in Great Britain the same week in March 1958 showed that being more extraverted at age 11 increases the likelihood of becoming an entrepreneur in adulthood.[37]

Moreover, the same genetic factors that account for extraversion also account for differences between people in the tendency to start businesses. A study conducted by a research team from Arizona State University found that much of the genetic variation between women in the tendency to be entrepreneurs came from innate differences in extraversion,[38] while a study that I conducted with my colleagues Nicos Nicoloau, Tim Spector, and Lynn Cherkas showed that 62 percent of the correlation between extraversion and the tendency to start a business comes from the same genetic factors.[39] In short, we have compelling evidence that your genes affect your odds of becoming an entrepreneur by influencing your predisposition to be extraverted.

Neuroticism

Neuroticism is another partially inherited personality trait that influences entrepreneurship. Studies of people of a variety of ages, from many different countries, using varied methodologies, show that between 27 and 68 percent of the difference between people in neuroticism is genetic.[40] Moreover, a number of neurotransmitter genes affect how neurotic you are, including several serotonin and dopamine genes.[41] For some of these genes, the effects are substantial. For instance, one study showed that a version of a single serotonin gene accounts for between 3 and 4 percent of the difference between people in this personality trait.[42]

These genes also might affect whether or not you start a business because entrepreneurs need emotional stability and a high tolerance for stress to cope with the hard work, significant risks, social isolation, pressure, insecurity, and personal financial difficulties that come from running their own companies.[43] Moreover, experts believe that those in business for themselves cannot worry excessively and need to be resilient in the face of setbacks.[44] As Tom Harrison, author of the book *Instinct*, explains,

> Successful entrepreneurs just don't get overwhelmed by life's dark side. . . . Inheriting a high level of Neuroticism imposes a double jinx for thinking like an entrepreneur. It predisposes you

to experience life generally more negatively than others. Even worse, you tend to react more strongly and emotionally to that perceived negativity. For example, if a venture capitalist treats you badly, you'll experience that as a major blow as opposed to just another step in the process.[45]

Research shows that neuroticism affects the odds that people will start businesses. One study showed that individuals who became entrepreneurs after going to a post-layoff outplacement service were more emotionally stable than those who went back to traditional employment.[46] Another research effort indicated that business founders were less neurotic than company owners who inherited their businesses or had taken them over through marriage.[47] Moreover, a meta-analysis of a large number of studies indicates that neuroticism is more common among managers than entrepreneurs.[48] Finally, the score on a measure of anxiety acceptance and hostility—two dimensions of neuroticism—taken at age 11 predicts self-employment at age 33.[49] In short, while we have no direct evidence that our genes influence the predisposition to start businesses by affecting our level of emotional stability, indirect evidence shows a plausible path through which this genetic effect might occur.

Agreeableness

A third personality dimension is agreeableness. People with this characteristic tend to be cheerful, courteous, trusting, cooperative, kind, and altruistic.[50] A variety of studies conducted in different places with varied methodologies show that between 33 and 66 percent of the variance between people in this trait is genetic.[51] Moreover, individuals with certain variants of several neurotransmitter genes, particularly those for serotonin, are more agreeable than people with other versions.[52] In fact, a single serotonin-system gene accounts for 2 percent of the difference between people in agreeableness.[53]

The effect of our genes on agreeableness might explain differences between people in their tendency to start businesses. Agreeable people are less likely than others to become entrepreneurs because they are not as inclined to pursue their own self-interest or drive difficult bargains.[54] One study showed that people who started businesses after being laid off were more "tough minded" and more "suspecting" than those who went back to traditional employment.[55] Moreover, a meta-analysis of a number of different studies showed that, on average, entrepreneurs are less agreeable than managers.[56] In short, while we have no direct evidence that our genes influence the predisposition to found companies by impacting our level of agreeableness, indirect evidence shows a plausible path through which genetic effects could operate.

Conscientiousness

Another personality dimension is conscientiousness. People with this trait tend toward perseverance, persistence, thoroughness, responsibility, and dependability.[57] Some portion of conscientiousness is inborn, with studies indicating that the genetic share of this personality trait is as much as 61 percent, depending on the way it is measured.[58] As with the other aspects of personality, versions of several neurotransmitter genes are more common in conscientious people, and people with related personality traits, including the "impulsiveness" (DRD2), "novelty-seeking" (DRD4), "persistence" (HTR2A), and "sleep" (ADORA2A) genes. In addition, other genes that affect brain function also appear to influence conscientiousness, persistence, and related attributes, including the "worrier" gene (COMT), which affects attention, time estimation, and working memory.[59]

The effect of our genes on conscientiousness might account for differences between people in the tendency to start businesses, because entrepreneurs need to be organized and deliberate, and have to move forward despite the obstacles that they face.[60] Empirical research provides evidence of this idea; a meta-analysis showed that entrepreneurs are more conscientious than managers. In fact, that study indicated that entrepreneurs and managers differ more on conscientiousness than on any other OCEAN personality trait.[61] Perhaps that's why billionaire and multiple-venture founder Sam Wyly says about being an entrepreneur, "If you can't be creative, disciplined, persistent, and rationally optimistic in the face of repeated failure, you need to find a different line of work."[62] In short, while we have no direct evidence that our genes influence the predisposition to become an entrepreneur by affecting our level of conscientiousness, indirect evidence suggests that this is true.

Openness to Experience

A final dimension in the OCEAN model is openness to experience. People with this trait tend to be imaginative, creative, curious, and inventive.[63] Where you come out on this aspect of personality is largely in your DNA, with studies showing that genetics accounts for between 45 percent and 61 percent of the variance in this characteristic.[64] Moreover, researchers have found individuals with certain variants of neurotransmitter genes, most notably those of the "novelty-seeking" gene (DRD4), to be more open to experience than people with other versions of the genes.[65]

Genetic effects on openness to experience might account for the differences between people in the tendency to start businesses. After all, founding a company requires the creativity to come up with ideas about how to solve customer problems, to obtain resources, and to develop business strategies. A recent meta-analysis provides evidence for this idea, showing that entrepreneurs are, on average, more open to experience than managers.[66]

Moreover, several researchers have looked explicitly at whether genetic effects on openness to experience also account for differences between people in the likelihood of founding a company, and have discovered that they do. A study that I conducted with my colleagues Nicos Nicoloau, Tim Spector, and Lynn Cherkas showed that 85 percent of the correlation between openness to experience and the odds of being an entrepreneur comes from the same genetic sources.[67] In another study with my same UK colleagues, I found that 62 percent of the relationship between openness to experience and the tendency to identify new business opportunities emanates from common genetic factors.[68] Thus, we have some compelling evidence that the chances of starting a business are affected by the same genes that predispose people to be open to experience, suggesting that one reason people become entrepreneurs is because they are endowed with genetically influenced levels of a trait that is useful in the firm creation process.

Other Personality Traits

The OCEAN traits are not the only ones through which your genes influence your tendency to start a business. In fact, one study my colleagues and I conducted revealed that *most* of the genetic predisposition to become an entrepreneur does *not* operate through these personality dimensions. Rather, it works through some other mechanism.[69]

Locus of Control

One of these other paths could be through the trait of locus of control. This dimension of personality captures the degree to which people believe that they can influence outcomes through their own behavior.[70] Research has shown that locus of control has a genetic component, with between one-third and 55 percent of the difference in this trait being accounted for by our genes.[71]

Having an external locus of control decreases the odds of becoming an entrepreneur because those going into business for themselves need to believe they can change outcomes through their own efforts.[72] Many studies of people of different races, genders, and nationalities show that entrepreneurs have a more internal locus of control than other people.[73] In fact, some studies even show that tests of locus of control in children predict whether those individuals will be self-employed later in life.[74] Thus, while we have no direct evidence that our genes affect the predisposition to found companies by influencing our locus of control, indirect evidence indicates that such a process is quite plausible.

Self-Esteem

Your genes might also influence your tendency to start a business through their effect on your self-esteem. Research has confirmed the presence of a significant genetic component to this personality trait, with studies showing that between 29 and 49 percent of the difference between people in self-esteem comes from genetic factors.[75]

Genetic effects on self-esteem might impact your likelihood of founding a company because entrepreneurs need to have confidence in their abilities to achieve their goals, even if there is no certainty that they will, and even if others—investors, employees, customers—believe that they won't.[76] A wide variety of studies show that entrepreneurs have higher self-efficacy than managers, and that having high self-efficacy increases the odds that a person will start a business.[77] One study even indicated that people who looked at new venture opportunities and then decided to found a company were more self-confident than those who looked at start-up opportunities but chose not to pursue them.[78] And experiments to make people more self-assured increase the number of business opportunities that they see.[79] In short, while direct evidence of the influence of our genes on the predisposition to start businesses through their effect on self-esteem awaits future research, the indirect evidence suggests that this is a likely path.

Novelty Seeking

Your genes might influence your odds of starting a business through their effect on your tendency to be novelty seeking. Numerous twin studies conducted around the globe show that between 50 to 60 percent of the difference in this personality trait is genetic.[80] Moreover, molecular geneticists' research, conducted in the United States, Japan, and Israel, shows that people with certain versions of the dopamine and serotonin genes are more novelty seeking than other people. Even within families, the children with the longer form of the "novelty-seeking" gene (DRD4) have been found to score higher on tests of this personality trait than their siblings with the short form. (This within-family evidence rules out an accidental result that comes from ethnic differences.)[81]

The effect of the "novelty-seeking" gene (DRD4) is not trivial, either. Studies show that it accounts for 4 percent of the variance between people in the personality dimension of the same name. Because 40 percent of the variation between people in this trait comes from our DNA, this means that a single dopamine gene accounts for a sizable chunk of the genetic difference between people in the odds of having a novelty-seeking personality.[82]

Okay, so novelty seeking is partially genetic, but do the genes that predispose people to seek novelty also affect the tendency to start companies? The idea is plausible. Novelty seekers do a lot of things to unleash dopamine—go hang gliding, have unprotected sex, and eat exotic foods. Because starting a business involves taking moderate risks to do something new, novelty seekers might see this activity as meeting their needs for a dopamine release.[83]

To answer this question, my colleagues and I examined whether the same genetic factors that influence the odds of being sensation seeking also affect their likelihood of being entrepreneurs. (Sensation seeking and novelty seeking are closely related traits that are measured slightly differently and therefore were given different names by psychologists.) We found that between 11 and 19 percent of the variation between people in their probability of being entrepreneurs (depending on which measure we were looking at) was accounted for by the same genes that predispose people to be sensation seeking.[84] In short, we have direct evidence that your odds of becoming an entrepreneur are affected by whether or not your genetic endowment influences your tendency to seek out novelty.

Need for Autonomy

You might be more likely than someone else to go into business for yourself because your genes predispose you to need a lot of freedom. Need for autonomy is a personality trait that makes independence very important to a person. Studies show that your genes influence the value you place on autonomy and how autonomous you are.[85]

People high in need for autonomy have a disproportionate tendency to start businesses, perhaps because they want to set their own rules and hours, pick their own goals and plans, and make their own decisions, all of which entrepreneurship facilitates.[86] Surveys conducted by academic researchers show that entrepreneurs have a greater need for autonomy and a lesser willingness to conform to authority structures than other people.[87] Perhaps that's why successful entrepreneur Sam Wyly, who built Universal Computing, Sterling Software, Maverick Capital, Bonanza Steakhouse, Michaels Stores, and Green Mountain Energy, writes in his autobiography: "I was not at heart a big company man, I didn't want to be under anyone else's authority. I wanted to call the shots for myself."[88] In short, while we do not have direct evidence of the influence of our genes on the predisposition to start companies through their effect on our need for autonomy, indirect evidence supports this conclusion.

Risk-Taking Propensity

You might be more likely than other people to go into business for yourself because you have a genetic predisposition to be comfortable with risk. As you probably remember from earlier chapters, genes account for as much as 55 percent of the difference in the willingness to take chances.[89] Moreover, researchers have identified the first gene associated with risk taking. Risk seekers are more likely than risk avoiders to have a particular version of the "worrier" gene (COMT).[90]

A willingness to take chances increases the odds that you will start a business, because starting a business is risky.[91] You need to invest your money and take a variety of actions before you know if you will make a profit. In addition, the incomes of entrepreneurs are much more variable than the incomes of people who work for others, adding to the risk of being self-employed.[92] So it's not surprising that a wide variety of academic studies show that entrepreneurs are more risk tolerant than other people.[93] Moreover, research shows that cautiousness measured in one's twenties predicts being self-employed later in life.[94] In short, while we await direct evidence that our genes affect the odds that we will become entrepreneurs by influencing our risk-taking propensity, the indirect evidence suggests it.

Gene-Environment Correlations

So far, I have focused on the ways that your genes might affect your probability of becoming an entrepreneur by influencing your chances of having a favorable personality or activity level. While these effects are important, they aren't the only way in which your genes might operate. Your DNA might also increase your chances of going into business for yourself by increasing your odds of finding yourself in situations that encourage new company formation. In *Instinct,* Tom Harrison provides a good example of how gene-environment correlations affect the tendency to start a business:

> Let's say you have a genetic predisposition to seeking out novelty. Because it's in your genes, you'll tend to seek out situations in which novelty seeking thrives. Entrepreneurial endeavors might be one of them, but they could be anything that demands putting yourself in new and challenging situations. That means you're likely to get more experience with risk taking at an earlier age than someone without the 'novelty-seeking' gene. That experience makes you even more confident and comfortable with taking still more risks—and the more you enjoy that, the more likely you are to do it again. You select what you're already genetically programmed to enjoy and be good at. Being good at it makes you want to do it some more. And doing it more makes you even better at it."[95]

Gene-environment correlations don't just work through personality; they also operate through aptitude. For example, your genes might influence your chances of becoming an entrepreneur by increasing your skill at repairing mechanical devices. Having an innate talent for fixing things is likely to affect the choices that you make throughout your life. It's going to increase the odds that you'll, say, study to become an auto mechanic rather than a high school history teacher. What you learn in school affects the profession you choose—high school history teachers are much more likely to have studied history than car repair. So those with innate mechanical aptitude will have a higher probability of being auto mechanics than teachers. Because a much higher percentage of auto mechanics than teachers go into business for themselves, your genetic endowment of mechanical aptitude ultimately affects your odds of starting a company by increasing your chances of finding yourself in an entrepreneurship-favorable profession.

Your genes also could affect your odds of being an entrepreneur through a variety of other gene-environment correlations. Take, for example, the genetic predisposition to be interested in business described in chapter 3. As we saw there, your DNA influences whether you love commerce or want nothing to do with it. Because people often identify entrepreneurial opportunities from their knowledge of an industry or through conversations with customers, experience working in the business world increases your odds of starting a company.[96] Thus, your genes might affect your chances of becoming an entrepreneur by altering the probability that you find yourself in a job in which you gain business experience, as opposed to familiarity with something else.

There are, in fact, many different ways that your genes could influence your odds of becoming an entrepreneur through gene-environment correlations—too many, in fact, to innumerate here. But let me offer just a couple more examples. We have a lot of evidence that people who work in marketing jobs are more likely than those who labor in accounting and finance to start companies. Notwithstanding the very socially oriented accountants out there, on average, marketing demands stronger interpersonal skills than accounting. So people with a genetic predisposition to be highly social will be more likely to become marketers than accountants. Being in marketing jobs, in turn, will increase their odds of going into business for themselves.

As strange as it may sound, your DNA may even influence your odds of starting a business through gene-environment correlations with marriage. Studies show that much of the difference in whether or not people marry is genetic.[97] So your DNA affects your chances of having a spouse. Having a husband or wife, in turn, increases the probability that you will become an entrepreneur, perhaps because married couples can invest more money in launching businesses, have spousal health insurance to offset the loss of coverage from leaving an employer, and have trusted partners to help run companies.[98] In short, having a genetic predisposition to get hitched makes you more likely to find yourself in a family situation that allows you to jump on an entrepreneurial opportunity when one comes along.

Gene-Environment Interactions

Most observers believe that your genes interact with the situations you are in to influence your behavior. That is, people with a genetic predisposition to do something, whether that is to do drugs, have unprotected sex, vote, get married, or anything else, tend to engage in that activity only in the right situations. Having unprotected sex is a good example. You can have the world's greatest genetic tendency to have risky relations, but you still won't have them without a willing partner. So it's having a genetic predisposition to have unprotected sex *and* being in a situation where having such sex is possible that enables the behavior to occur.

The tendency to start a business follows a similar pattern, not because the oldest profession involves entrepreneurship, but because, like having unprotected sex, starting a business demands the interaction of a situational trigger and a genetic predisposition. Let me give you an example. Suppose you have the versions of the genes that increase your odds of seeking novelty. Being born with these genetic variants is insufficient to drive you to become an entrepreneur because you could pursue novelty in a lot of different ways. While you might start a business, you could also take up hang gliding, travel the world, or pursue a myriad of other new experiences. So your decision to start a business doesn't just come from having particular versions of certain genes, but from the interaction between those genetic variants *and* experiencing the right environmental triggers.

One stimulus to starting a company might simply be learning about a new business opportunity. If you have the genetic predisposition to seek novelty, you'll be more likely than others to pursue the opportunity in response to learning this information. But, if you have the predisposition to seek novelty and, instead of learning about a business opportunity, you come across a willing sex partner, well, you might engage in unprotected sex instead.

Of course, this is only one example. Many other gene-environment interactions might also affect your decision to go into business for yourself. For example, suppose you have the versions of the dopamine genes that help you to notice patterns in new information. While pattern recognition helps entrepreneurs to identify new business opportunities, seeing clues in data isn't sufficient for you to decide to start a company. After all, pattern recognition is important to scientists, detectives, and people in a host of other jobs. So your decision to found a new venture doesn't just come from noticing patterns in information, but also from the type of data you scan. If your job entails looking over economic statistics to select investments for a mutual fund, your genetic predisposition to see data patterns will probably help you to pick stocks more than it will lead you to start a company. And if you're a paleontologist, these pattern recognition skills might help you discover a new species of dinosaur, but they aren't likely to lead you to become an entrepreneur. However, if you're the head of marketing at a software company, genetic predispositions to pattern recognition might help you identify the next new, new thing in software. And that discovery might send you running down the street to the nearest venture capitalist, business plan in hand.

Conclusions

Your genes influence the odds that you will become an entrepreneur. This statement is true whether entrepreneurship means being self-employed, owning and operating a business, founding a company, or participating in the business start-up process.

The use of the word "odds" in the previous paragraph is deliberate. There is nothing in your genetic makeup that will *guarantee* you will become an entrepreneur and nothing that will *preclude* it. Even if you lack the versions of the genes associated with starting a business, you can always overcome your genetic predispositions. But, if you have the genetic variants that increase the probability of becoming an entrepreneur, the odds will be in your favor.

While genetics accounts for a lot of the difference between people in the likelihood of becoming a company founder, we are still in the early stages of figuring out how genes exert their influence. Research so far suggests that innate predispositions for a high activity level, greater intelligence, dyslexia, and the personality traits of self-esteem, novelty seeking, risk-taking propensity, disagreeableness, extraversion, emotional stability, openness to experience, and conscientiousness, increase the odds that a person will go into business for him- or herself. Moreover, your genes influence your chances of starting a company by impacting the likelihood that you will find yourself in entrepreneurship-favorable situations.

While your genes affect your chances of starting a company through their impact on your personality traits, cognitive abilities, and activity level, people with a genetic endowment favorable to entrepreneurship are more likely to found businesses in the right situations. For example, if you were raised in the Soviet Union in the 1930s, it wouldn't matter what your DNA showed, you wouldn't have been very likely to become self-employed.

Having described how your genes influence your odds of becoming an entrepreneur, I now turn to their effect on your performance at work, the subject of the next chapter.

10

Good Workers, Bad Workers: How Your Genes Influence Your Job Performance and Your Income

Albert was not the greatest of employees. He often came late to work, if he showed up at all. And when he did work, his effort was lackluster. His job appraisals reflected his poor performance, rarely showing above-average ratings on any dimension of his job. Albert's work history was consistent with this pattern. He had a series of low-paying, entry-level, low status jobs, and was frequently unemployed.

Albert went through a series of training programs, designed to help him do better at work. They were of some value, but he couldn't completely break out of his pattern of poor performance. In fact, Albert struggled all his life with the skills it takes to be a good employee. Even in childhood, he was often late, didn't try very hard, and never did particularly well at anything, from schoolwork to sports to music.

This pattern wasn't unusual in Albert's family. Except for his sister Teresa, who was a diligent student, worked hard, went to college, and became a nurse, all of the kids in the family showed similar behavioral patterns in childhood, and all ended up in dead-end, low-paying, low-status jobs, which they performed poorly. On the dimension of work performance, all of the kids, except Teresa, were just like their dad, and his dad before him.

However, one day Albert entered a different kind of training program. Instead of treating poor performers as if they were good at their jobs, the course started from the premise that Albert and his co-participants didn't have any decent work habits. Assuming that the attendees needed to be taught even the most basic job skills worked to improve Albert's performance. While he wasn't on the fast track to becoming a CEO, Albert was able to get and keep a job, which for him was a significant improvement.

Why was Albert such a loser at work? Were he and most of his brothers and sisters poor performers because their parents raised them badly? Did Albert come from a long line of dads that just didn't get child-rearing, and did it poorly? Or is something else at work?

Some researchers believe that something else *is* going on, and that something is encoded in Albert's DNA. Because of the genes he inherited from his parents, Albert might have been born with greater odds of being a loser at work. His genetic endowment might have left him with a higher chance of performing poorly in a series of low-paying, low-status, dead-end jobs, no matter how good his mom and dad were at parenting.

Moreover, Albert's genes might have interacted with the environment to influence his work outcomes. That's why, to get and keep a job, he required a different approach to training than what was effective with good workplace performers.

While no one is genetically *predestined* to be a lousy worker, genetics plays a role in work outcomes. Research shows that your genes impact your income, your occupational status, and your work performance. This chapter provides the evidence for DNA's effects and explains how your luck with the genetic lottery impacts these important outcomes. Let's begin with a look at genetic effects on income.

Born to Be Rich

How much money do you make? To a lot of people, this is an important question. They spend years getting an education and many hours at their jobs, trying to boost their pay. While not everyone cares about making money, more people strive for higher incomes than strive for lower ones, making us, as humans, interested in knowing how to earn more. (A quick Google search brings up millions of hits for the phrase "how to get rich.")

Guess what? There's one thing that most of the self-help books don't tell you about how to get rich. That's to be born with the right genes. Studies of identical and fraternal twins consistently show that identical twins have much more similar incomes than their fraternal counterparts.[1] From these twin studies, researchers have estimated that about 45 percent of the variation between adults in their annual incomes is the result of genetic factors.[2] Scientists have also found that about 40 percent of the variance between people in hourly wages,[3] and about 27 percent of the difference in personal earnings, comes from our DNA.[4]

Income and wealth are closely related. People who make a lot of money tend to have a high net worth, while people who make very little tend to have less. So, having read the previous paragraphs, it should not surprise you that your DNA also impacts your wealth. One study showed that about 30 percent of the difference in people's overall financial position is explained by genetic factors.[5] In short, having the right DNA boosts your wealth and income. (So, for those of you who like to blame your parents for your predicaments, here's another way to fault them for your failure to become rich.)

Now, keep in mind that I'm not saying that there is an income gene. Your genes influence your income and wealth indirectly. I'll describe more about the ways that researchers think this happens later in the chapter, but for now, let me point out that the effect could be as simple as the result of genetic predispositions for doing certain kinds of work. Even as I write this, in the wake of the financial crisis of 2008, hedge fund managers still earn more than elementary school teachers. So it could be that our genes influence our aptitudes in ways that lead us toward certain types of jobs and away from others. And those employment choices might account for the genetic differences in income. But, given the fascination that we humans have in how much money we make and have, genetic effects on wealth and income probably interest a lot of people, however our genes exert their influence.

Occupational Status

Not only do your genes affect your income and wealth, they also influence your occupational status. Occupational status is just a fancy sociological term that refers to how much people respect your job. Doctors, for example, have higher occupational prestige than trash collectors or cashiers in a grocery store, because most people think that the job of a doctor is more impressive than that of a sanitation engineer or cashier. Because some part of job status comes from what a position pays, a lot of the genetic effect on occupational cachet is the same as that on wealth and income. But not all of it. For instance, members of the clergy have high occupational status without making a lot of money; and the job of elementary school teacher is typically more respected than that of insurance salesman, but it usually pays less.

Chapter 3 explained that your genes affect your job choice. So if some positions are more prestigious than others, then your genes are going to influence your occupational status, too. While it shouldn't surprise you that your DNA affects the cachet of the job you pick, it might startle you to learn how much of an influence genes have. Researchers have found that 60 percent of the difference between people in their occupational status is genetic.[6]

In short, your DNA appears to affect your place in the status hierarchy. As with our animal ancestors, we are biologically wired to seek a particular place in the pecking order. While baboons do this on the basis of age, gender, and lineage, we add prestige of the job to the mix. But it's still the same thing.

Job Performance

Chapter 3 explained how your genes impact your choice of employment. Chapter 4 outlined how they influence your job satisfaction. And many other chapters discussed the effects of your DNA on your management style, approach to leadership, decision-making techniques, creativity, and entrepreneurship. But it turns out that your genes don't just impact your job choice, how satisfied you are with your work, or even how you do your job. They also influence how well you *perform* at it.

Research has revealed that genes affect several employment outcomes. One of these is job appraisals. Many organizations measure how well people do their jobs through performance ratings conducted by supervisors on their subordinates. As a result, scientists can get a picture of how genes affect work outcomes by looking at the differences between the scores of identical and fraternal twins on formal performance appraisals conducted by their employers. In one study, scientists focused on negative items, such as reprimands and dismissals. They found that 37 percent of the difference between people in something that the researchers called "censured job performance"—a measure that combined reprimands, probation, and performance-related firing—was genetic.[7]

It's easy to see how this genetic effect might work. Say you are less calm than other people because of a genetic difference that makes you emotionally volatile. This hot-bloodedness makes you more prone to lashing out at others when challenged. As a result, you have a tendency to scream back at your boss, pound the wall, or storm out of the room when criticized.[8] Frequently engaging in these behaviors probably increases the odds that your boss will tell you that your services are no longer needed. In short, having the versions of the genes that increase your predisposition to emotional volatility can account for more censured job performance.

The fact that censured job performance includes performance-related dismissal suggests that keeping a job might also have a genetic component. Indeed, chapter 4 explained that 36 percent of the difference between people in the frequency of employment changes is genetic.[9] While we have no way of knowing whether the genetic effect on shifting jobs lies in voluntary or involuntary turnover, unless the influence of DNA lies solely in voluntary separation, genetic factors influence the odds of getting fired.

Receiving a negative performance appraisal or even getting fired are relatively minor examples of bad work outcomes. While it might not be good to show up late to work so many times that your boss reprimands you for it at review time, you won't go to jail for being late for work. But what about taking part in really bad behavior, such as stealing or committing fraud? Do your genes affect odds of engaging in these outcomes as well? The answer is yes. Studies of both twins and adopted children, conducted in a variety of countries, show that some of the difference between people in the tendency to participate in criminal activity is genetic.[10] Moreover, the influence of genetic factors has been found for the kind of crimes that occur in the workplace, like theft and fraud, as well as other types of crime.[11]

(Your genes even affect the odds that you become the next Hannibal Lecter. Research shows that DNA accounts for as much of 81 percent of the difference between people in measures of psychopathology.[12] But that behavior is beyond the scope of this book, no matter what you say about your boss.)

What about the tendency to behave dishonestly in the workplace? Is that genetic too? The answer again appears to be yes. As we saw in chapter 6, psychologists have a term for the tendency to lie, act deceitfully, and manipulate others. It's called Machiavellianism. As I'm sure you are well aware, there are a lot of high-Mach individuals in the working world, ruthlessly maneuvering others to achieve their goals. Some famous examples include "Chainsaw Al" Dunlap, who drove his subordinates to book revenue that his company hadn't earned, and Andrew Fastow, whose manipulations of coworkers at Enron Corporation contributed to driving that giant company into bankruptcy.[13]

While all bad behavior in the workplace can't be attributed to "poor genes," some part of the tendency toward Machiavellianism is innate.

As chapter 6 explained, 31 percent of the difference between people in this characteristic is accounted for by genetic factors.[14] So, I'm sad to say, fraudulent, manipulative, and otherwise destructive organizational behavior is something that some people's DNA makes them more likely than others to engage in.

How Do Our Genes Influence Work-Related Outcomes?

I suspect that some of you are now wondering how your DNA affects your income and job outcomes. As is the case for many other aspects of work-related behavior discussed in this book, the effects are largely indirect and not completely understood. Nevertheless, we have some clues to suggest how our genes influence our work performance, income, occupational status, and tendency to engage in criminal activity. Many researchers believe that genetic effects operate primarily through appearance, intelligence, personality, temperament, and activity level. So we'll take a look at those mechanisms.

Attractive High Performers

Scientists have found some compelling evidence that your genes affect your job performance and income through their influence on your physical appearance. That's right; your genes increase your odds of getting a big paycheck by making you look good. And how this happens isn't so hard to see. As you no doubt already know, your genes impact what you look like—the color of your hair, eyes, and skin are all affected by your genes. So are your height and weight and muscle mass. In short, a clear and incontrovertible link exists between your genes and your appearance.

What you might not know is that your genetically influenced looks impact both your income and your performance at your job. A number of studies show that weight, height, and physical attractiveness all predict income.[15] Basically, taller, thinner, better-looking people make more money.

Attractive people also tend to get better performance reviews from their supervisors. Part of that's because they have higher self-esteem. Studies show that better-looking people tend to be more self-confident, which makes them work harder and do better on the job. But bosses also tend to evaluate physically attractive subordinates more positively than homely ones. It's just a function of how human beings are wired to think about physical appearance.

No matter how physical attractiveness affects job performance and income, there is a link there. Because good looks have a strong genetic component, it is quite plausible that one of the ways our genes affect our incomes and work performance is through our appearance. Think about it this way: having the variant of the gene for blond hair might be worth money to you.

Cashing in on Genes for Smarts

While some of the effect of genes on income and job performance probably operates through genetic differences in physical attractiveness, it's not likely that all of it does. Another plausible mechanism is through intelligence. Studies show that your cognitive ability predicts how high you are likely to rise in an organizational hierarchy and how prestigious your job is likely to be.[16] Moreover, smarter people tend to perform better at their jobs than those less intelligent than them. Researchers believe that their mental abilities allow them to better understand the different aspects of their jobs and to solve problems more effectively than other people.[17]

A variety of different measures of intelligence—IQ scores, assessments of spatial ability, and tests of perceptual accuracy (the ability to accurately recognize information)—all predict job performance.[18] We also know that individuals with a higher g perform better at work than other people, even when results are looked at as much as five years later, and that the relationship between general cognitive ability and outcomes is present whether the measure of performance is the quantity or quality of production, supervisor ratings, or other things.[19] In fact, one study showed that mental ability assessed in high school predicted occupational attainment 11 years later, and was a better indicator of the organizational level reached than anything else that the researchers looked at, while another study showed that general cognitive ability was the best predictor of job performance in a sample of military recruits.[20]

In fact, g has its greatest effect on work outcomes for people in supervisory positions, and becomes more influential as the complexity of job increases. Mental ability, it seems, matters more in settings where problem-solving skills are crucial.[21] However, general cognitive ability affects work performance even for jobs that don't require a lot of intellectual skills, such as working the assembly line.[22]

Cognitive ability also forecasts future wages. One study showed that math and reading test scores measured at age 10 predict the salaries people earn in adulthood,[23] while another study showed that these scores assessed at ages 7, 11, and 16 accounted for 20 percent of the difference in average adult earnings.[24]

As we saw in previous chapters, much of the variance between people in intelligence and cognitive abilities is accounted for by genetic factors. Moreover, innate sources are responsible for at least some of the difference between individuals in income and job performance. So a logical question to ask is whether the same genetic factors are responsible for the variation in both brains and work outcomes.

Research shows that the answer is yes. One study showed that the genes that influence intelligence also account for 21 percent of the difference between people on workplace-performance appraisals, across a wide variety of jobs. (If we add in the contribution made by the genes that influence personality, the portion of job performance explained by genetic factors rises to 30 percent, but more about the genetic effects that operate through personality in the next section.[25]) In short, the pattern is clear: your genes influence your intelligence, and through it, impact your work performance, and even your income.

Who You Know Matters

The old adage, "It's not what you know, it's whom you know" has merit when it comes to explaining performance in the work world. Knowing the right people influences your ability to get a job, whether you get promoted, and how much money you make. Researchers have found that people use their social networks to find jobs, get plum assignments and receive better performance appraisals.[26] As a result, the size of your social circle, the strength of your relationships to others, and how central you are to your network of contacts all impact how much money you earn.[27]

Recently, researchers have found that how many friends you have, how closely connected your buddies are, and how important you are to your social group, are all affected by your genetics.[28] Some people are simply born with an innate predisposition to have more friends and to be more central to their social network than others. This propensity might explain the greater incomes and higher positions that some people achieve. While researchers haven't yet identified the exact mechanism through which this process works, here's one possibility: People with a genetic predisposition to be at the center of large social networks might get better jobs, plum assignments, and superior performance appraisals, enhancing their income and helping them to move up the corporate ladder.

From Personality to Money

Another way that your genes influence your work performance, occupational status, and income is by predisposing you to develop favorable personality characteristics. One of these traits is self-efficacy. As we saw earlier, genetics explains more than one-third of the difference in people's level of self-confidence.[29] High levels of self-assurance, in turn, lead people to choose higher status occupations, perform better at their jobs, and earn greater incomes.[30] The earnings of men, in particular, seem to increase with their self-confidence. Self-esteem measured in one's teenage years predicts both wages and frequency of unemployment in adulthood.[31]

Your genes also influence your job performance and income by affecting how neurotic you are. As we saw in several previous chapters, your genes influence your emotional stability, in part through the instructions they provide for the development of key neurotransmitters. As a result, much of the difference in neuroticism has a genetic origin.[32]

Moreover, some observers think that a "bad" draw of serotonin and other neurotransmitter genes might reduce your odds of becoming wealthy. Research shows that the more neurotic men and women are the less money they earn.[33] Thus, having particular versions of certain genes might predispose people to emotional stability, which, in turn, makes them more likely to earn a high income.

Your genes influence your work performance by impacting your odds of being conscientious. Researchers have found that genes account for over three-fifths of the difference between people in this personality trait.[34] Conscientiousness, in turn, enhances job performance and income.[35] Diligent employees are more likely to show up at meetings on time, develop careful work plans, and ensure that their work is high quality.[36] They have higher job proficiency and are easier to train than other employees.[37] (While conscientious people do better at all types of jobs, the performance gap between highly conscientious people and those less so is greatest in jobs that are not carefully monitored and demand a great deal of problem solving, skills development, and change.[38])

You might have better job performance and earn a higher income than other people because you received the versions of the neurotransmitter genes that are found disproportionately in cooperative and agreeable people, including variants of the "persistence" (HTR2A) and "cooperativeness" (GABRA6) genes.[39] Disagreeable people tend to perform poorly at many jobs because they often have trouble taking direction, frequently oppose what others want them to do, and, more often than not, end up in conflict with those in authority—characteristics that studies show are, at least in part, genetic.[40]

Closely related to disagreeableness is the tendency to engage in deviant and delinquent behavior.[41] As I am sure you are aware, people who steal, undermine others, and act against the interests of their employers tend not to get the best employment evaluations. But, what you might not know is that deviance and delinquency—things like stealing resources, tanking the projects of coworkers, or otherwise acting counter to the company's best interests—are, in part, genetic.[42] Therefore, your genes also affect your job performance by predisposing you to engage in this type of undesirable behavior.

Another way that your genes affect your work performance is by predisposing you to be extraverted or intraverted. As previous chapters have shown, your genes influence where you come out on this personality trait through (among other things) the instructions they provide for the development of several neurotransmitters.[43] Your job performance, in turn, is impacted by your genetically influenced level of extraversion, with research showing that extraverts are more trainable, get better job appraisals, are less likely to be laid off or unemployed, and earn more money than introverts, particularly in jobs that demand a great deal of interaction with other people.[44]

You might get better performance appraisals from your boss and earn higher raises than your coworkers because your genes predispose you to be open to experience. As much as 61 percent of the difference across people in this trait is genetic, with the genes for the production of the brain chemical dopamine playing a role in its development.[45] Being open to experience, in turn, enhances job performance, perhaps by making people more accepting of different sources of information or approaches to problem solving.[46] In short, the version of the neurotransmitter genes that your parents gave you might influence both your job performance and your income by affecting your odds of becoming a self-confident, emotionally stable, conscientious, agreeable extravert who is open to new experiences.

Small Effects but Multiple Genes

It's true that researchers have found the size of the effect of any one gene on personality characteristics, such as agreeableness or conscientiousness, to be small, on the order of 2 percent. And traits aren't perfectly correlated with job performance, further reducing the influence of these genes when carried through to work outcomes. But multiple genes affect the predisposition to develop each dimension of personality, and several traits join together to impact job performance, augmenting the genetic effect. As a result, genes can exert a significant influence on important outcomes, such as how much you earn, even if any given gene has a small impact, and those effects occur indirectly.

Moreover, even the tiny edge that comes from one gene's influence on a single personality trait could have a very large effect on your income if compounded over time. To see how, take the example of salary negotiation. The version you have of a single neurotransmitter gene might affect how agreeable you are. If you get the variant that predisposes you to be disagreeable, some researchers believe that your odds of being a good negotiator will increase. (Studies show that agreeable people bargain poorly because they are too eager to compromise.) Your negotiation skills influence your starting salary when you join a company. So maybe your genetic draw will help you to bargain for 2 percent more money than the other employees hired along with you. Your incoming salary will affect your subsequent earnings because raises are often set as a percentage increase on current compensation. So your initial 2 percent advantage compounds, giving you substantially higher pay in later years than others in your cohort. In short, even the small influence of a single gene on just one personality trait can have a noticeable effect on your income over the course of your work life.[47]

Rich with Happiness

Your genes might enhance your job performance and income by increasing the odds that you develop a positive outlook on life. Numerous studies show that genetics affects temperament.[48] Some people are endowed with the "right" versions of dopamine and serotonin system genes (among others), giving them sunnier dispositions from birth.[49] This genetic effect on temperament impacts how much money you make. Recent research shows that the *same* genes that affect happiness also influence income and socioeconomic position.[50]

This genetic endowment also enhances on-the-job performance. People prefer optimists to pessimists, which leads them to give more support and assistance to coworkers with positive worldviews.[51] Moreover, people with a negative outlook on life tend to engage in more workplace deviance, which hinders their job performance. Finally, supervisors generally give better evaluations to subordinates with sunny dispositions, even if those with negative temperaments are equal performers, because most human beings prefer happy people to sad ones.[52] In short, your luck in getting the versions of genes that predispose you to a positive worldview will increase your performance on the job, and your income, in a variety of ways.[53]

Activity Level and Job Performance

Your genes affect your job performance and income by influencing your activity level. As we saw earlier, genetics accounts for as much as 89 percent of the variation across people in whether they are frenetic or sedentary.[54] Moreover, molecular geneticists have linked these differences in activity level to variation in the genes that influence the development of the dopamine system.[55]

So, indirectly, your genes impact work outcomes. For instance, studies show that adults with ADHD—a disorder very much influenced by genetics—have higher absenteeism and more lost workdays than those not afflicted. They also tend to choose lower social-status occupations and experience higher levels of unemployment than individuals without ADHD. Finally, hyperactive adults tend to make less than other people.[56] In short, those who get the versions of the neurotransmitter genes that predispose them to develop ADHD might earn less and have worse job performance than other people.

Through Gene-Environment Correlations

To make clear the explanation of how your genes influence your job performance and income, I have focused the discussion so far on how your DNA impacts your activity level, temperament, personality, and cognitive skills, and how these things affect your performance appraisals and compensation. While your genes influence job outcomes these ways, there is another important mechanism that I haven't touched on: gene-environment correlations.

As you probably recall from chapter 2, the term *gene-environment correlation* is just a fancy way to say that people with certain genetic variants are more likely to find themselves in particular situations than people with other versions of the same genes. Gene-environment correlations turn out to be quite important in accounting for differences between people in work outcomes, because certain genetic propensities may lead to the development of associated personal characteristics, which, in turn, may carry you down a path toward "better" job performance and higher income. For instance, people whose genes predispose them to be good at mathematics tend to take more math courses and are more likely to major in highly quantitative fields in college, giving them greater odds of ending up in high-paying, numbers-based, jobs, such as investment banking. While anyone can choose to be an investment banker, the people with the versions of the genes that code for strong math skills may be more likely to do so.[57] In short, your genes may affect your income if an innate gift increases your odds of heading down a path to a high-paying occupation.

Income isn't the only performance outcome that is impacted by gene-environment correlations. Occupational status is another. For example, you might have been born with the "right" versions of certain genes, which give you above-average intelligence. Your genetically influenced smarts can affect the prestige of your job by increasing your odds of choosing a high-status occupation, such as medicine. How this happens might look something like this: your genetic gift made reading very easy for you when you were a child. As a result, you got tremendous satisfaction from this activity and read a lot more than other children. Your love of the printed word made you a very good student in elementary school. Because you received good grades, your mom and dad let you go to an expensive summer camp at the science center, where you did advanced mathematics and science experiments. The camp program put you far ahead of your peers, and you ended up taking a lot of college classes in high school. Your secondary school experience, in turn, helped you to ace organic chemistry when you got to college. Your A+ in this course made it easier for you to get into a good medical school, which, of course, was necessary for you to become a doctor. So you ended up a physician, not through any direct effect of your genes on your occupational status, but through a series of choices you made that were triggered initially by your genetically influenced intelligence.

In contrast, your best friend from first grade was born with different versions of the genes that promote intelligence. As a result, she was of only average smarts. This genetic endowment meant that your friend didn't excel at any academic subjects. Because people prefer to spend time on what they do well, your pal spent as little time as possible on schoolwork. Instead, she focused on sports. At this, she excelled, because of the versions of several genes that *she* was born with. So, while you studied, she played tennis and soccer, and swam and rode bikes. When you went on to college after graduating from high school, she, instead, became a sports trainer at the local gym. Because most people think of doctors as having more prestigious jobs than sports trainers, you have higher occupational status than your best friend. In sum, the differences between your occupational status and your buddy's came about through gene-environment correlations; you each made a series of divergent choices over the course of your lives because you were born with different genetic predispositions.[58]

Through Gene-Environment Interactions

Recent research indicates that performance outcomes are often influenced by interactions between genes and the situations in which people find themselves. A good example concerns the type of nonviolent criminal acts, such as theft, that get people fired from their jobs. Delinquency has a genetic component; researchers have found that individuals who have certain versions of the "antisocial" (MAOA), "activity" (SLC6A3), and "impulsiveness" (DRD2) genes, are more likely than other people to engage in such behavior. But—and this is a very important "but" for understanding how genetics affects workplace outcomes—the negative influence of these gene variants are all mitigated by strong social support. For instance, researchers have found that teens with the "negative" versions of these genes who get more help in school, and from their parents and friends, don't engage in as much delinquency as teens with the same genetic variants, but who lack this assistance.[59] If the parallel holds in the workplace, people with certain gene variants might be more likely than others to engage in delinquent behaviors, but those negative outcomes might be mitigated by organizational efforts to provide strong social support to employees.

It's a Whole Lot More Complicated Than That

So far, I have described the effect of your genes on your work performance by focusing on one aspect of behavior at a time. However, that is just an artifact of exposition. In reality, many genes are operating at once, influencing personality traits, activity levels, temperament, cognitive skills, and a number of other factors, simultaneously. Moreover, these genes may not be working in concert, but instead might be exerting countervailing influences on your behavior. In some people, for instance, the different versions of the genes that affect conscientiousness and extraversion might cancel each other out, accelerating and breaking to yield no net impact on how you act, while in other people, they might be pulling in the same direction, enhancing or inhibiting certain behaviors.

Moreover, only some of the people genetically predisposed to develop the personality traits that increase the odds of positive work results will experience enhanced income or job performance. Many individuals will see no effect of their genes on these outcomes because they lack complementary genetically influenced characteristics. For instance, research shows that MBAs who are both highly intelligent *and* conscientious earn higher salaries, have a faster rate of pay increase, achieve speedier promotions, and garner more success at job searches than other MBAs.[60] Thus, for their genes to affect these performance outcomes, people need to have the "right" versions for *both* intelligence and conscientiousness.

And this is just a simple example because it involves the combination of only two dimensions—cognitive ability and a single personality trait. If you consider the multitude of individual characteristics that your genes impact, and take into account that several of them might need to be joined together to affect job performance, the degree of complexity in accounting for genetic effects jumps dramatically. And even this level of complication pales with what is introduced when we consider the number of different ways genes can combine to create predispositions for each of these attributes.

Finally, we need to consider that some of the effects of genes on performance outcomes, such as income and job appraisals, may be subject to threshold effects. Unless a mixture of genes influences all of our personality traits, temperament, cognitive skills, and activity level simultaneously and by a sufficient amount, the effect on behavior might be nonexistent. Absent a version of a single gene, for example, and the earnings effect one might expect is simply not there. In short, we know something about how our genes influence our job performance, income, and occupational status, but we're a long way from a world of Gattaca, in which employers can measure our likely work performance just by looking at our DNA.

Conclusions

Your genes influence how much money you earn and the prestige of your chosen occupation. They also affect how well you perform your job, including the odds that you will receive negative performance appraisals, clash with your superiors, or engage in delinquent workplace behavior.

So are you predestined to be paid little, get poor performance appraisals, and have trouble holding a job because of your DNA? Of course not. Genetics is about probabilities, not destiny. Even if you have the versions of every gene associated with a negative outcome on every dimension of workplace performance, from compensation to performance appraisals, you could still be the highest paid person and have the best job reviews of anyone in your company. Nevertheless, research shows that your odds of high performance in the workplace are improved by having favorable versions of several genes.

Your genetic composition might affect your job performance by influencing your appearance, cognitive abilities, personality traits, and activity level. However, while some of the effect of your genes on your work performance probably occurs through their impact on these attributes, much of their influence likely occurs through gene-environment correlations. That is, your genetic predispositions lead you to make a series of choices that put you in situations that are more or less favorable to job performance.

Your DNA might also affect your work outcomes in other complex ways, most notably through interactions between a broad set of genes that predispose you to develop different dimensions of personality, temperament, cognitive skills, and activity levels, and through the interplay of those genes and the environment.

Now that I have described how your genes affect your work performance, occupational status, and income, I turn to the message of the final chapter: what difference all of this makes.

11

Your Genes Matter! So What?

Sometime in the future, a company will come to the conclusion that it needs to change its hiring processes. It will decide to do away with interviews, which, as most human resource managers will tell you, aren't a very effective way to select employees. In place of meetings with prospective hires, the firm will turn to swabbing their mouths to identify their DNA. The business will contract out to a laboratory to measure the potential employees' genetic predispositions to prefer certain types of work, to make decisions in particular ways, to lead others, and to be entrepreneurial, among a host of other things. The company will use the result of the genetic tests to choose which employees to hire and, if they prove to be promising candidates, which department to put them into.

Is this example futuristic and apocryphal? Yes, of course. And the alert reader might notice that it is based loosely on the story told in the 1997 film *Gattaca*. But it illustrates an important point. While we aren't yet at the point where companies can use genetic information diagnostically, we might be in the near future. And as we make advances in genetics and begin to understand better how our genes influence many aspects of our workplace behavior, we will face a number of choices about what to do with what we have learned. Perhaps the largest of the issues facing us is whether organizations should be allowed to use genetic tests to select employees. But advancing genetic knowledge will raise other questions as well, including whether companies should be permitted to consider genetic information when making job assignments. More important, greater understanding of genetics will require companies to evaluate the effectiveness of many interventions used to enhance employee performance, such as incentive plans and approaches to training. While I take no position on whether people *should* be allowed to use genetic data in the different ways described, we need to understand the implications of our growing knowledge of genetics and its influence on work-related behavior.

Chapters 3 through 10 showed how our genes impact numerous aspects of our work lives, from our tendency to start businesses to our job satisfaction to our leadership abilities to our decision-making styles. These chapters summarized a great deal of evidence of how our genes influence our behavior at our jobs by affecting much about us— cognitive abilities, personalities, activity levels, temperaments, and even hormones. We have a good amount of information about how our genes interact with each other and with the situations in which we find our-selves to influence what we do in the workplace. Research shows how our tendency to opt into situations that favor our genetic strengths exerts subtle but powerful effects on many aspects of employment, from the jobs we choose to the roles we take in work teams. In short, our genes matter for explaining our work-related behavior.

But so what? What difference does it make to know that your genes influence your work life? As the introductory vignette to this chapter points out: it matters a lot. While human behavior is complex and is influenced by a wide variety of factors, genetics can provide insights into how people act. Understanding the role of your DNA in your job-related behavior can help to identify what aspects of employment you are likely to do well and what you are predisposed to do poorly, information that can help you to understand yourself. Moreover, genet-ics can provide you with knowledge of how to improve your skills and abilities so you can perform better at work.

An understanding of how DNA affects work-related behavior can also help companies to address many issues that our advancing knowledge of the biological basis of human behavior is beginn-ing to raise. For example, it can help businesses figure out whether their efforts to change employee behavior, such as instituting a new incentive plan, are likely to be effective. It can also aid firms by permitting more targeted approaches to influencing employee ac-tions, showing how to fit organizational structures, corporate cultures, and incentive plans to workers' genetic predispositions. In short, this chapter answers the "so what" question, exploring the major implica-tions for the work world that come from the knowledge that genetics matters.

The Fine Print

Before describing the implications of genetics for workplace behavior, I want to stress that the conclusions discussed in this chapter are speculative. We need more research before anyone can make concrete recommendations. Most of the studies of how genetics affects human action have been behavioral rather than molecular. Although twin and adoption studies have shown evidence of genetic predispositions to a wide variety of employment-related behaviors, they have not identified specific genes that influence those actions. And without knowing which genes are affecting what outcomes, the implications we can draw are limited.

Second, the science behind twin and adoption studies is solid, but it is not foolproof. Relatively few studies have been conducted on twins raised apart, leaving open the possibility that the common behavior of identical twins is influenced by a disproportionate tendency to imitate each other. Moreover, a few researchers have recently questioned whether identical twins really are genetic copies of each other. Scientists in Toronto, for example, found that the genes of identical twins did not *behave* exactly the same way even though the twins' DNA was identical. As a result, twin studies might be less accurate ways to identify genetic effects than previously thought.[1]

Third, our ability to draw strong implications for workplace behavior from molecular genetics may be even more limited. Research suggests that a very large number of genes influence job-related outcomes. The portion of behavior accounted for by any particular gene is small, in many cases, less than 2 percent. Few studies have demonstrated the effects of multiple genes on a given workplace outcome, and researchers don't yet know the combination of genetic variants that would account for a sizable portion of most job-related behaviors. Moreover, some of the findings for the effects of specific genes discussed in this book have not been replicated, and experiments that have been repeated have not always shown consistent results. As a result, the ability to predict workplace behavior based on knowledge of a person's genetic endowment remains limited at present.

Fourth, few studies have explored how genes interact with external factors to affect behavior, and virtually none have examined more than one gene at a time in interaction with the environment. In fact, for some aspects of workplace behavior, such as leadership, we have *no* studies of the way in which genes interact with situational factors to influence how people act. The absence of evidence of gene-environment interactions keeps us from drawing hard-and-fast conclusions about how genetics affects any job-related outcomes. In short, the points made below, while perhaps provocative and important, should also be considered tentative.

Will Companies Use Genetics-Based Tools to Select Employees?

Let's start with the most controversial implication that comes from knowledge that genes influence job-related behavior. As the earlier chapters of this book made clear, some people are predisposed to be better than others at decision making, leadership, creativity, innovation, entrepreneurship, persistence, and much else, because of the versions of genes they were born with. As some observers have pointed out, the most straightforward (and controversial) implication of this evidence is that companies would benefit from selecting genetically inclined people to engage in the workplace behaviors that the company seeks, be that entrepreneurship, intuitive decision making, transformational leadership, or anything else.

While I am not arguing that such an approach is socially desirable or even ethical, it may become viable in the future. And if genetic selection for job-related behavior becomes a reality, people need to be aware of what companies might do, if only to prohibit it. For instance, suppose an employer wanted a more creative workforce. Someday, it might be able to choose people with certain variants of the "impulsiveness" (DRD2) and "risk-taking" (TPH1) genes because individuals with those versions are predisposed to be more creative than other people.[2] What if a company wanted customer service representatives who were agreeable and conscientious? The employer might be able to select potential hires who had particular variants of the "novelty-seeking" (DRD4), "activity" (SLC6A3), "cooperativeness" (GABRA6), "adrenaline" (PNMT), "impulsiveness" (DRD2), "persistence" (HTR2A), "sleep" (ADORA2A), and "worrier" (COMT) genes, which are more common in agreeable and conscientious people.[3]

How about team players? In the future, genetic-based selection might be possible here as well, because our DNA influences how well we cooperate with others. Researchers have found that extroverts, individuals high in conscientiousness, and those who are agreeable and open to experience perform better on teams than other people. And many companies already choose employees that are likely to be good team players by looking at their scores on personality tests. But, as you no doubt realize by now, the odds that people have these four personality dimensions depend a great deal on their genetic makeup.[4] So companies might be able to find more team players by selecting those employees with the versions of genes that predispose them to develop certain personalities.

Some experts have suggested that companies might also want to select people who have a genetic predisposition for job satisfaction. Job dissatisfaction and turnover is costly to companies, accounting for billions of dollars in additional expenses and lost revenues. Thus, avoiding employees with a genetic propensity to be unhappy with work could be financially beneficial. As one author explains, "Genetic disposition is one factor that causes job satisfaction. Some people are just genetically programmed to be satisfied or dissatisfied with their lives. . . . One way for companies to deal with this may be to hire applicants with good 'job satisfaction' genes."[5]

Moreover, some scientists believe that genetic testing might prove to be a *better* way to find the right hires than other selection tools currently being used. Given the poor predictive power of many indicators used to choose employees today, such as college grades or job interviews, picking on the basis of genetic endowment might prove to be more effective.

Some human resource experts believe that many companies are implicitly conceding this point. They say that businesses are really searching indirectly for a genetic predisposition to be a good employee when they give prospective hires personality assessments or look at their college transcripts. As one author explains, "Sifting through thousands of employees to find the ones with the right traits is really a crude process of finding those with leadership genes."[6]

These researchers are stretching the argument a bit. The research that has found relationships between versions of particular genes and certain attitudes, traits, temperaments, skills, and behaviors has not been replicated enough times for us to be sure that the genes that researchers have identified are definitely the right ones. Moreover, typically, many genes affect the predisposition to any workplace outcome, and each gene alone tends to account for a small share of the difference between people in that behavior. But scientists are hard at work trying to isolate specific genes that are responsible for a sizable portion of the variance in job-related outcomes and to replicate their results enough times to have a high degree of confidence in them. While these researchers may amass nothing more than an ever-growing list of genetic variants that each account for a minuscule portion of the difference between people, it is also possible that, sometime in the not too distant future, scientists will have identified a set of genetic variants that they are confident together explain a substantial portion of some aspect of workplace behavior.

In a capitalistic economy like ours, where companies are all searching for a competitive edge, it wouldn't be long before someone took those discoveries and designed a test that allowed employers to identify people with a predisposition to engage in desired job-related outcomes. Therefore, even if the list of genes that affect workplace behavior hasn't been completed, let alone double- and triple-checked, and no one (legitimate) is marketing a tool for genetic selection of prospective employees, such lists and tools might be coming, and anyone who works for or hires others needs to be prepared for the implications that such developments would have.

Ethical Issues

Because we aren't that far away from the possibility that someone will come up with a genetic test, or tests, that can be used to identify predispositions to engage in workplace behaviors, we need to confront the ethical issues that this development would raise. These issues are profound, and I don't have the answers to them. So please don't shoot the messenger. I'm not taking a position one way or another. I'm merely outlining the implications so that you can consider them.

At the most basic level, scientific developments in genetics raise the question: should companies be allowed to use genetic tests in the process of selecting employees? Many, it seems, have come down against this prospect. In the United Kingdom, the Nuffield Council on Bioethics has concluded, "Employees should be selected and promoted on the basis of their ability to meet the requirements of the job.... Employers should not demand that an individual take a genetic test for a behavioral trait as a condition of employment."[7]

The U.S. Congress has also answered no to this question. In the recent genetic nondiscrimination bill, Congress made it illegal to use genetic information "to make hiring, firing, and other job placement decisions."[8] While the government's intent was to keep companies from making employment decisions based on information about prospective hires' genetic propensities to develop medical problems, this law also means that companies cannot choose people for a certain position because they have versions of genes that predispose them to do well at that job.

But, like many things dealt with definitively by politicians or non-profit agencies, there is another part of the story, which makes the ethical issue less simple than it appears at first glance. Congress in the United States and the Nuffield Council in the United Kingdom clearly addressed one side of the issue: companies should not be allowed to hire people on the basis of something that they have no control over and can't really change, because doing so would be inherently unfair.

But the desire to be fair means that companies might have to employ inferior selection criteria. If the human resource experts are right, and having the best people is a source of competitive advantage for corporate America, then precluding companies from using genetic data would hinder their performance (assuming, of course, that genetic information is a good predictor of workplace outcomes).

That's all well and good if American companies only compete locally. But, in the real world, American businesses need to contend with entities from all over the globe. What should we do if companies in other countries don't have the same compunction about genetic testing that we do? (Think Singapore here, whose founding president, Lee Kuan Yew, is a big believer in selective breeding and has encouraged well-educated, professional Singaporeans to have children together.) What if foreign businesses were willing to allow genetic testing to identify employees with desired work-related behaviors? Companies from those countries might develop a competitive edge over American businesses because they were better at identifying human resources and allocating them to jobs inside the organization. Then what should we do?

There is also the question of how "fair" other selection criteria are relative to genetic testing. Hiring managers often choose employees on the basis of physical attractiveness, even when good looks aren't a necessary criterion for the job. Numerous studies have shown the bias that people involved in the employment process have for physically attractive job candidates of the opposite sex.

But one's appearance is, in large part, outside of people's control, and is hard to change. After all, genetics plays a big role in what we look like. Allowing employers to pick employees on the basis of good looks permits them to reward prospective hires for having the right genes.

How is it fair to allow managers to make employment decisions on the basis of attributes that are largely genetic, but bar them from using selection tools that incorporate the genetic information itself?

And physical attractiveness isn't the only selection criterion companies are permitted to use that is largely beyond individual control, hard to change, and has a significant genetic component. Many employers use personality tests to identify potential hires and assign jobs, even though personality traits are very difficult for adults to change and have a large genetic component. Is it fair to allow employers to hire on the basis of these tests but not allow them to look at the genetic factors that predispose people to develop the very dimensions that the tests measure?

What about the issue of fairness that comes up if we do *not* allow companies to use genetic data to assign people to jobs or training? If employers aren't permitted to use hereditary information in this way, and they subsequently punish people for poor performance on the job, then we are implicitly allowing the companies to engage in genetic discrimination. To see what I mean, take the example of Frito-Lay, which provides its employees with financial rewards if they take courses to develop their leadership skills.[9] As we saw in chapter 7, a sizable portion of the difference between people in the ability to direct others comes from their DNA. This means that some people are genetically inclined to do better than others in leadership development classes. By giving bonuses for the completion of these courses, Frito-Lay is implicitly rewarding people for being born with versions of genes that predispose them to take charge of groups. This is no fairer than paying more to people lucky enough to be born attractive because, as research shows, good-looking people are more likely than unattractive people to become leaders.

There is also the issue of companies' responsibility to their employees. Would it be fair to prohibit employers from conducting genetic tests on their employees if the goal was to ensure that no one had a disorder that put him or other workers at risk of harm? This question is not far-fetched. We know that Huntington's disease, which is genetically *determined,* leads some people to engage in antisocial behavior. What if companies could minimize the risk that one of their hires would harm other employees or customers by identifying whether or not the people working for them had the genetic variant responsible for the disease?

Some believe that, under these circumstances, the benefit of genetic testing to the majority of workers would outweigh the cost to the tested employee. For instance, in the United Kingdom, the Nuffield Council reported that employers *could* genetically test their hires if the former believe that the latter might be suffering from a genetic disorder that would result in harm to the employee or others.[10]

Even if the medical nondiscrimination bill's goal is to keep companies from using genetic predispositions to deny employees medical insurance or require them to pay higher premiums, it has a downside. The inability to use genetic data to charge less to those not predisposed to medical problems would raise the cost of insurance for all employees. Faced with a lack of information about genetic predispositions, companies would have to charge high premiums to everyone to ensure that the payments were sufficient to cover the costs of insuring those more likely to develop the problems.[11]

Moreover, the failure to gather data on genetic predispositions increases the potential for what insurance folks call adverse selection. Knowing that the insurers would lack access to information to identify those who are genetically predisposed to develop medical problems, people with a greater likelihood of having these ailments would be more likely than others to apply for medical insurance. As a result, the group of insured people would be biased toward those with genetic predispositions to develop these disorders. To protect against the higher cost of insuring this greater "at-risk" group, insurers would be forced to raise their rates on everyone, hurting those without the genetic propensities.

The Effectiveness of Interventions

Even if we decide that the use of genetic information in employee selection is ethically unacceptable, understanding the role of DNA in work-related behavior is still important. Genetic analysis points out how much of the difference in people's actions is accounted for by situational factors and how much is explained by innate forces. The share of behavior that comes from each of these tells us whether organizations are spending too much time and money on issues such as incentives and training.

To understand how, it is best to think of what it means for something to be unaffected by DNA and compare that to the case where something is completely genetically determined. If genetics accounts for *all* of the differences between people, then nothing else affects their behavior. Not the way that their parents raised them or what they learned in school or the conditions at their jobs. Under a scenario in which outcomes are 100 percent the result of DNA, any changes that companies make to financial incentives, organizational structure, communication patterns, and training are a complete waste of time and money. These things will have no effect on employees' behavior; the only way to change genetically *determined* behavior would be to change the employees' genes.

From this extreme, it is easy to see that the proportion of the variance between people in their decision making, leadership, creativity, innovation, and so on that is accounted for by genetics influences the usefulness of efforts to change employee behavior through training, organizational restructuring, financial incentives, and the like. The more genetics is responsible for workplace outcomes, the less important these efforts will be. As a result, companies may be spending more time and money on these activities than is justified, given the limited effect that these initiatives can have.

Take, for example, leadership training programs. Many organizations are interested in increasing the number of leaders in their ranks, with some having the goal of turning everyone in the organization into one.[12] As a result, businesses collectively spend billions of dollars per year on leadership development. These efforts are predicated on the assumption that nongenetic factors account for most of the difference in the ability to direct others. So companies teach employees to foster debate, align goals, set deliverables, communicate, and whatever else is thought to make them into better bosses.

But these efforts don't work very well, because a major component of what it takes to be an effective leader is genetic.[13] If characteristics that are hardwired into people are important in determining whether or not they will take charge of a group, then efforts to train people to do so will not be very effective. The portion of the difference between individuals in leadership ability that is inborn can't be influenced by the educational efforts. So the initiatives do little more than fine-tune the skills of those who are genetically predisposed to be in charge.[14]

Leadership is not the only thing that companies spend money on in the hopes of changing employee performance; they also pay for efforts to enhance creativity. Many companies send their employees to seminars and bring in consultants to teach ways to be more innovative. Some companies are quite inventive in their efforts to make their staff more innovative. L'Oréal, for instance, hires advisors to teach its workers to write music and cook food as part of this effort.[15]

Despite the billions of dollars spent every year on creativity-enhancement programs, these efforts have not been as effective as senior managers and company shareholders would like. Knowledge of how our genes affect our innovativeness offers insight into why these programs often fail to achieve their goals. These initiatives are based on the assumption that nongenetic factors, such as employees' knowledge of brainstorming or the structure of the organizational hierarchy, account for all of the differences in people's creativity. However, genetic differences indicate that this assumption is untrue. A substantial portion of the variation in innovativeness is innate. In short, creativity-training programs might have limited effectiveness because genetic effects matter too much.

Genetics might also limit what organizations can do to influence their employees' happiness. Improving worker job satisfaction is an important part of what human resource departments do. As we saw in chapter 4, employee discontent has a substantial effect on both revenues and costs, making high employee satisfaction a goal of many businesses. To enhance worker happiness, companies run surveys, hire consultants, and make changes to their incentive plans, organization structures, and corporate cultures, as well as whatever else is thought to enhance job satisfaction.

However, many businesses are unable to make their employees as happy as they would like, and efforts to redesign jobs and change organization cultures often fail to improve worker satisfaction.[16] This poor performance should not be surprising to anyone who has read chapter 4 of this book. A fairly sizable chunk of job satisfaction is accounted for by our genes, and so is beyond the reach of company efforts to improve it. As a result, many corporate initiatives to improve people's jobs, pay them more money, make the workplace more comfortable, or enhance job flexibility do little more than temporarily boost workplace happiness. The gains are often fleeting because people's genetically influenced outlook on life typically brings them back to their baseline level of job satisfaction.[17] To overcome genetically based predispositions toward workplace happiness, standard approaches may be insufficient. Companies may need to make very large changes, ones much greater than those that they think they need.[18]

The Importance of Interaction Effects

Interactions between genetic predispositions and environmental stimuli probably account for much of the difference between people in workplace outcomes. These interactions mean that people with an innate tendency to some aspect of job-related activity, be it leadership or job satisfaction or intuitive decision making, will not engage in that behavior unless stimulated by the right external trigger. As a result, influencing what people do in organizations depends a lot on figuring out the correct stimulus for different outcomes. Thinking in terms of these interactions will help employers to choose the right triggers to get the results they are looking for, be it workplace performance, job satisfaction, or something else.

For instance, suppose that your company is interested in enhancing employee leadership. Research shows that the ability to direct others tends to emerge among people with the right genetic predispositions *if* those people experience situations in which they need to overcome obstacles. This information suggests the value of knowing both who in the organization is genetically predisposed to take charge *and* exposing those people to settings that trigger their leadership tendencies. This might mean gathering data about employees' genetic makeup and assigning those who possess leadership-favorable genetic variants to challenging jobs in which they need to overcome adversity.

Knowledge of how genetic predispositions interact with external forces to trigger work-related behaviors can also be important for policy makers. For instance, suppose you are a government official and you want to increase the number of people engaged in productive business activity, while simultaneously reducing the number of people committing crimes. Understanding interactions between genetic predispositions and environmental stimuli might help you.

People with variants of the "novelty-seeking" gene (DRD4) might be predisposed to engage in entrepreneurial activities. But individuals can respond to this genetic tendency by becoming legitimate entrepreneurs, or by turning into criminals. More important, what they end up as could depend a lot on the kind of environment they experience. As one observer explained quite clearly, "Consider a high novelty seeker born into urban poverty. His curiosity might be expressed in 'exploring' the neighborhood with a handgun. The same [attribute] in someone born into a wealthy family might lead to explorations of the commodities market."[19] From the perspective of public policy, the implication of this quotation is quite clear: knowledge of how genetic factors influence workplace behavior tells us what we need to do to increase the amount of socially beneficial business activity. We need to figure out how to stimulate the genetically predisposed to choose productive business activity rather than the unproductive kind.

Gene-Environment Correlations

Gene-environment correlations have important implications for managing workplace behavior. Because these associations mean that people with a particular genetic makeup disproportionately find themselves in situations that reinforce their innate predispositions, managers can't ask for volunteers if they want to do something that affects everyone in the organization. Those genetically predisposed to engage in the activity will be overrepresented among participants.

Take, for example, diversity programs or ethics training. People who have a genetically influenced propensity to be tolerant of others or to have strong ethics are disproportionately attracted to these programs. As a result, diversity and ethics training involve a great deal of preaching to the choir. To involve those not genetically predisposed to support these initiatives, companies need to make the activities mandatory.

The need for required participation isn't just limited to ethics or diversity programs. Any activity, be it sales, leadership, accounting, or whatever, will be overrepresented by those genetically predisposed to be good at it. The only way to avoid the effects of gene-environment correlations is to command people to participate.

"Targeted" Approaches

An understanding of genetics makes possible "targeted" approaches to enhancing desired workplace behavior. In recent years, researchers have used knowledge of genetics to develop such treatments for medical problems. These interventions are targeted because they only affect, or have a greater influence on, people with certain genetic variants. For instance, the drug Herceptin makes chemotherapy work better for women with breast cancer if the disease has a certain version of the gene for human epidermal growth factor receptor 2 (Her2/neu).[20]

Just as we have created targeted treatments for medical problems, we can develop focused interventions for work-related behaviors. This would entail coming up with specific incentive plans, management styles, changes to organizational structure, and so on that are designed to fit the genetic composition of particular employees. The value of targeted approaches is made clear by the example of leadership education. Many organizations want to encourage their employees to become leaders, but the typical approaches to training people to take charge are often ineffective for individuals predisposed to be neurotic. It seems that high levels of worry keep the training from working on these folks,[21] suggesting that effective leadership education for them needs to be different.[22] Perhaps, helping those genetically predisposed to neuroticism might depend on counteracting the worry that being the boss induces.

The benefit of understanding genetic effects for the development of targeted approaches to management is not limited to leadership. It could also help us to figure out the most effective way for people to make choices. We know from chapter 4 that our genes influence many aspects of decision making, from the amount of information that we collect to the type of data that we want to the way that we use facts to solve problems. It is quite likely that there is no "best" way for a person to select between alternatives; the best method probably depends on his or her genetic composition. Under a targeted approach to decision making, everyone would not be expected to follow the same path but would instead make choices in the way that best fits his or her genetic composition. People with certain versions of the "impulsiveness" (DRD2), "novelty-seeking" (DRD4), "persistence" (HTR2A), "sleep" (ADORA2A), and "worry" (COMT) genes, for example, might seek out disconfirming information. People with these genetic variants tend to be conscientious and persistent, and those high in these personality traits tend to collect data that challenges their preconceptions when making choices.

We also might take targeted approaches when we design incentives. Some research suggests that the "impulsiveness" (DRD2) and "novelty-seeking" (DRD4) genes might influence our sensitivity to rewards and praise.[23] Thus, acknowledging someone's contribution might be an effective motivating strategy for people with certain versions of the dopamine receptor genes, but not for those with other variants. Knowing which versions their employees have would help organizations figure out how to motivate their people more effectively. For some workers, having a public ceremony in which they are given an award for their performance might be a better way to get them to work harder than paying them a bonus.

Another example might be fitting the provision of feedback to people's genetic composition as a way to enhance job satisfaction and reduce absenteeism and turnover.[24] People with particular versions of the dopamine and serotonin receptor genes are inclined to have more positive temperaments than individuals with other variants of the genes.[25] A person's disposition, in turn, influences how he or she reacts to negative news and setbacks. People who have the versions of the neurotransmitter genes that predispose them to be happy may react better to hearing bad news than other individuals. Therefore, providing these people with negative information directly might be the right way to go, but it might be more effective to take a different approach with those individuals who have the other versions of these genes.[26]

Perhaps the most interesting way that targeted management might affect business concerns the marketing of products. Take, for example, advertising. Our genes influence the emotionality and rationality of our decision making. If some people are genetically predisposed to make less cerebral choices than others, then marketers could appeal to them with targeted ads that trigger emotional responses.

In addition, companies could segment their markets on the basis of their customers' genetic compositions. Insurance provides a good example of this idea. People buy this product to protect themselves against financial loss in the event of an adverse outcome, like a flood, a car accident, or the death of a spouse who provides the family income. We know that people's tolerance for risk affects how much insurance they buy, with those who are more willing to take chances purchasing much less than other people. Because genetic differences affect how risk tolerant people are, they might provide a basis on which companies can divide up the insurance market. Businesses might spend more time and money targeting customers with a genetic predisposition for risk intolerance because these people would be more likely than others to buy insurance.

Insurance companies might also design alternative versions of their products for people with different genetically influenced predispositions. For instance, companies might target high-deductable insurance to people with a genetic tendency for risk tolerance and low-deductable coverage to people with the opposite bias. While this insurance product idea is, admittedly, only science fiction today, the likely identification of specific genes associated with risk taking in coming years shows the potential for such product development activities.

Knowing Yourself

Most of us are pretty poor at self-evaluation. Studies show that we don't really know our own strengths and weaknesses, and are less accurate at judging what we are good at than other people are. Because we don't know ourselves very well, we often make bad decisions. Take for example, the person who thinks that she is good at managing risk and so takes a position that requires handling a lot of uncertainty, only to discover that she performs poorly at the job and is unhappy. Or the person who thinks he is a good team player and so finds a position that requires a lot of collaborative work, only to learn that he is much better as an individual performer than as a member of a team.

Clearly, knowing more about yourself will help you make better choices about occupations, employers, jobs, and work assignments. This is where genetics comes in. Understanding how your innate predispositions affect your work preferences might give you insight into why you are more interested in, say, the arts than you are in business. That information might give you the courage to finally leave your job in chemical sales—the one that you have never really liked—to try your hand at making feature films. It might even help you to explain to your spouse or your parents why you find your job unfulfilling and want to change your career.

Perhaps most important, knowing how your DNA influences your work behavior will help you to *overcome* your genetic predispositions. While you might think that the best way to surmount genetically influenced weaknesses is to ignore them, ironically, the opposite is true. At the most basic level, overcoming your predispositions means recognizing that the current is flowing in the opposite direction from where you are trying to go. Swimming against the stream requires more effort and more conscious action than going with the flow. So knowing what your genetic propensities are helps you to figure out how hard you need to work to accomplish your goals.

Take, for example, a person who is genetically predisposed to be shy. Like everyone else, she can become a very effective public speaker, just as capable, in fact, as the person who is genetically inclined to be gregarious. But becoming a good orator is more difficult for her than for someone with a genetic tendency to be outgoing. That's where information about this woman's innate biases is valuable. Knowing that she has to work twice as hard as other people to become a good public speaker tells her how to spend her time and effort. Perhaps she needs to join Toastmasters or hire a coach to achieve her goal.[27]

Similarly, knowledge of how your DNA affects the way in which you make choices can help you figure out how to overcome your decision-making biases. For instance, you might be genetically predisposed to engage in hindsight bias—the propensity to see things that happened in the past as more predictable than they actually were[28]—which makes you awful at picking stocks or developing corporate strategy. Or you might have a genetic tendency to be self-serving, always rewriting the outcome of the previous day's meetings and events to make yourself look better, which leads you to be a relatively poor team player. As the experts explain, knowing that you have a problem is the first step to fixing it. So you are more likely to overcome your hindsight and self-serving biases if you are aware that you have them than if you are oblivious to this fact.

Consider the comments made by Jason Zweig, author of the Intelligent Investor column at the *Wall Street Journal*. After visiting the imaging genetics lab of Ahmad Hariri at the University of Pittsburgh, where he had five of his risk- and reward-related genes analyzed, Zweig wrote a column on DNA and investing. He explained how knowledge of his genetic tendencies helped him to overcome his biases. He wrote,

> I don't panic in bear markets, and bull markets make me un-comfortable.... Those habits, I now understand for the first time, don't come naturally to me. I have been fighting my genes for years, and the reflective parts of my brain have been struggling to rein in my emotions for a lifetime.... From studying the writings and careers of Benjamin Graham and Warren Buffet, I learned to distrust the crowd and remember that future returns depend on today's prices.[29]

In short, being aware of your genetic predispositions will help you to compensate for them.

Figuring Out What You Do Well

While it might be true that you can do anything if you put your mind to it, you are not genetically predisposed to become a star in all domains. All of us have innate abilities, which make us better or worse at different activities.[30] The Academy Award–winning actress who makes millions of dollars a year portraying characters on the big screen might be terrible at math and lousy at managing her own money. The brilliant corporate strategist who leads a company to tremendous growth might be a poor public speaker. The Nobel Prize–winning physicist, whose breakthroughs have been called the most important since Einstein's, might be unable relate on a meaningful level with his two-year-old daughter.

Understanding our genetic predispositions can help us to decide what jobs we want to have. Sure, we can overcome our weaknesses if we want to (the previous section pointed that out), but we are likely to be more successful and happier if we focus on what we do well. So, if you are born with a genetic tendency to be physically weak, you might try to overcome that disadvantage by spending a lot of time weightlifting in the gym, or you might decide that a career as a professional mover isn't for you. Instead, you might want to become the CEO of the moving company; physical strength isn't going to make a lot of difference in your ability to do that job.

Should we use genetic information to guide people in their career choices? I don't know. Greater minds than mine need to provide advice before we know which way to go. But it is clear that your genes affect your skills and abilities. You might want to take that into consideration when picking your career.

Person-Job Fit

Experts on organizational behavior believe that matching people to the right positions and employers is important for work performance. Therefore, when deciding what jobs to put their hires into, good managers take the employees' skills, intelligence, attitudes, and personalities into account.[31] Because our genes affect these individual attributes, some researchers believe that genetic effects should also be considered when making job assignments. As one expert explains,

> Understanding how [personality] traits affect performance is important—not just for you personally, but for the people who work with you. Managers have to match employees to the right tasks in order to give them the best chance for success. Looking at inherited personality traits gives managers more powerful tools in making hiring and training decisions and getting the most from employees.[32]

Take, for example, the case of leadership. Studies show that transformational leaders are most successful at times of stress and uncertainty.[33] Therefore, a company experiencing tough economic times might be better off with a transformational leader. Because genes account for some of the difference between people in their leadership styles, this school of thought suggests that a company's board of directors might want to consider CEO candidates who are (genetically) predisposed to be transformational leaders when picking a boss to head a turnaround effort.

Person-job fit doesn't just involve finding the right people for specific jobs; it also involves identifying individuals who fit a company's culture. Some organizations are competitive, while others are collegial. Some are consensus-oriented, others more hierarchical. Some organizations have a frenetic work pace, while others are more laid-back. Whatever its corporate culture, a company is best off selecting employees whose work values align with its corporate philosophy.

Some observers argue that understanding the effect of genetics on job-related behavior might be helpful because work values are at least partially innate.[34] To find people who have the right beliefs for their organizational culture, employers need to determine prospective employees' values.[35] To do this, they often interview potential hires. Unfortunately, talking to people isn't a very accurate way of assessing attitudes because people don't always honestly report them. Because many individuals think that they can make their values conform to their employer's culture, prospective employees often fudge, or even lie, in interviews, hiding their true beliefs from their potential bosses. In practice, people's work values are less malleable than they think, because a portion of those attitudes is innate. As a result, the employees' insincerity results in a poor fit between their beliefs and the employers' culture. In response, some observers suggest that companies might be better off if they used information about prospective hires' genetic predispositions to hold certain work values when deciding whether the latter's attitudes are a good fit with their corporate cultures.[36] (This point might be a stretch based on current research results.)

You might think that the use of genetic predispositions to hold certain beliefs as a way to assign people to jobs is unethical; and society might well decide that it is. But before we rush to judgment, let's consider the benefits of using this information. Hiring employees with work values that don't fit an organization's culture reduces their job satisfaction and increases turnover, as the unhappy employees look for more compatible employers. Thus, failing to identify hires who are the right match for an organization's philosophy has a cost—employee dissatisfaction and a higher quit rate.

What's Not an Implication of Understanding the Role of Genetics on Work Life?

Throughout this book I have stressed that genes are not destiny. Having a genetic predisposition toward workplace behaviors does not mean that you are predestined to engage in them. Lots of people overcome their innate tendencies all of the time.

Moreover, knowledge of genetics in no way negates your free will. On the contrary, as I have pointed out repeatedly, understanding your genetic propensities helps you to overcome tendencies that disadvantage you and exploit those that benefit you. Ironically, knowledge of genetic effects actually *enhances* your free will because it provides additional information with which to act.

Last Word

Genetic factors influence people's job-related behavior in a variety of different ways. True, scholarship in this area is in its infancy, with scientists having identified only a small number of genes that affect how you act in the workplace. Moreover, most of these genes account for only small differences in behavior, suggesting that much more research needs to be done before we have a comprehensive understanding of the way your DNA impacts how you work. However, the evidence collected to date shows that your genes influence such disparate dimensions as leadership, job satisfaction, decision making, and entrepreneurship. The implications that emerge from knowledge of genetic effects on work behavior are profound, including changing how we think about the balance between selection and training, altering our expectations of the effectiveness of efforts to enhance job satisfaction and work performance, and spurring the development of targeted approaches to management.

Although this book laid out the role of genetics in organizational life, it can't change how you use this information to be more effective in the work world. That is up to you. I hope that knowledge of how your genes affect your behavior will help you to become a better employee or employer.

Notes

Chapter 1

1. http://usmilitary.about.com/cs/genjoin/a/pilotvision.htm
2. Bouchard, T., McGue, M., Hur, Y., and Horn, J. 1998. A genetic and environmental analysis of the California Psychological Inventory using adult twins reared apart and together. *European Journal of Personality*, 12: 307–320; Loehlin, J., and Gough, H. 1990. Genetic and environmental variation on the California Psychological Inventory vector scales. *Journal of Personality Assessment*, 54(3–4): 463–468.
3. Reinberg, S. 2008. Genes get out the vote. Downloaded from http://news.yahoo.com/s/hsn/20080701/hl_hsn/genesgetoutthevote
4. Ibid.
5. Garrett, D. 2009. *Brain and Behavior*, Los Angeles: Sage.
6. Roiser, J., Rogers, R., Cook, L., and Sahakian, B. 2006. The effect of polymorphism at the serotonin transporter gene on decision-making, memory and executive function in ecstasy users and controls. *Psychopharmacology*, 188: 213–227.
7. http://ghr.nlm.nih.gov/handbook/basics/gene
8. Wright, L. 1997. *Twins and What They Tell Us about Who We Are*, New York: John Wiley and Sons, p. 144.
9. I experienced this reaction firsthand. When I presented my first research paper examining genetic effects on the tendency of people to start businesses, I practically got attacked by a business professor at the University of Wisconsin who was upset about the very idea that one would look at the effect of genes on entrepreneurship. Believe me when I tell you that the normal reaction from colleagues to a research paper is indifference. I can assure you that I never had a response like this to any other topic that I have written about.
10. Zhang, J., and Wang, S, 2008. Bill on genetic bias advances. *Wall Street Journal*, A11.
11. http://en.wikipedia.org/wiki/Eugenics

12. Brizendine, L. 2006. *The Female Brain,* New York: Broadway Books, pp. 6, 159.

13. Plomin, R. 1994. *Genetics and Experience: The Interplay between Nature and Nurture,* Newbury Park, CA: Sage.

14. Olson, J., Vernon, P., Harris, J., and Jang, K. 2001. The heritability of attitudes: A study of twins. *Journal of Personality and Social Psychology,* 80(6): 845–860.

15. Beard, A., and Blaser, M. 2002. The ecology of height: The effect of microbial transmission on human height. *Perspectives in Biology and Medicine,* 45(9): 475–498.

16. Lindh, T., and Ohlsson, H. 1996. Self-employment and windfall gains: Evidence from the Swedish lottery, *Economic Journal,* 106(439): 1515–1526.

17. Kaplan, K. 2007. It's in the genes: We are evolving faster than ever. *Plain Dealer,* December 11: A7.

18. Plomin, R. 1999. Genetics and general cognitive ability. *Nature,* 402: C25–C29.

19. Caldu, X., and Dreher, J. 2007. Hormonal and genetic influences on processing reward and social information. *Annals of New York Academy of Sciences,* 118: 43–73, p. 61.

20. Harrison, T. 2005. *Instinct.* New York: Warner Business Books; Hamer, D., and Copeland, P. 1999. *Living with Our Genes,* New York: Anchor Books.

21. Hamer and Copeland, *Living with Our Genes.*

22. Harrison, *Instinct,* p. 9.

23. Gibson, B., and Sanbonmatsu, D. 2004. Dispositional optimism and gambling: The downside of optimism. *Personality and Social Psychology Bulletin,* 30: 149–160.

24. Arvey, R., Bouchard, T., Segal, N., and Abraham, L. 1989. Job satisfaction: Environmental and genetic components. *Journal of Applied Psychology,* 74(2): 187–192.

Chapter 2

1. Macur, J. 2008. Little ones get test for sports gene. *New York Times,* downloaded from http://www.nytimes.com/2008/11/30/sports/30genetics.html?_r=1&partner=permalink&exprod=permalink.

2. Hamer, D. 2004. *The God Gene,* New York: Doubleday.

3. Hamer, D., and Copeland, P. 1999. *Living with Our Genes,* New York: Anchor Books.

4. Ibid.

5. Ibid.

6. Arvey, R., and Bouchard, T. 1994. Genetics, twins, and organizational behavior. *Research in Organizational Behavior,* 16: 47–82.

7. Hamer and Copeland, *Living with Our Genes.*

8. Plomin, R., and Kosslyn, S. 2001. Genes, brain and cognition. *Nature Neuroscience,* 4(12): 1153–1155.

9. Ibid.

10. Hamer and Copeland, *Living with Our Genes.*

11. Zuckerman, M. 2005. *Psychobiology of Personality,* Cambridge, UK: Cambridge University Press.

12. Arvey and Bouchard, Genetics, twins, and organizational behavior.

13. Garrett, B. 2009. *Brain and Behavior,* Los Angeles: Sage.

14. Arvey and Bouchard, Genetics, twins, and organizational behavior.

15. Oakley, B. 2008. *Evil Genes,* New York: Prometheus Books.

16. Hamer and Copeland, *Living with Our Genes.*

17. Ibid.

18. Nauert, R. 2008. Brain imaging helps explain behavior. *Psych Central News,* August 7.

19. http://www.ornl.gov/sci/techresources/Human_Genome/faq/gene-number.shtml

20. Austin, M., Riniolo, T., and Porges, S. 2007. Borderline personality disorder and emotion regulation: Insights from the polyvagal theory. *Brain Cognition,* 65(1): 69–76.

21. Pinker, S. 2009. My genome, my self. *New York Times Magazine,* January 11: 24–31; 46; 50.

22. Rutter, M. 2006. *Genes and Behavior,* Oxford, UK: Blackwell.

23. Arvey and Bouchard, Genetics, twins, and organizational behavior.

24. Hamer and Copeland, *Living with Our Genes.*

25. Ilies, R., Arvey, R., and Bouchard, T. 2006. Darwinism, behavioral genetics, and organizational behavior: A review and agenda for future research. *Journal of Organizational Behavior,* 27: 121–141.

26. Zuckerman, *Psychobiology of Personality.*

27. Wright, W. 1999. *Born That Way,* New York: Routledge.

28. Carey, G. 2003. *Human Genetics for the Social Sciences,* Beverley Hills, CA: Sage; Jang, K., McCrae, R., Algleitner, A., Riemann, R., and Livesay, W. 1998. Heritability of facet-level traits in a cross-cultural twin sample: Support for a hierarchical model of personality. *Journal of Personality,* 74(6): 1556–1565; Rowe, D. 1994. *The Limits of Family Influence,* New York: The Guilford Press.

29. http://freewill.typepad.com/genetics/2005/03/leadership_abil.html

30. Raevuori, A., Dick, D., Keski-Rahkonen, A., Pulkkinen, L., Rose, R., Rissanen, A., Kaprio, K., Viken, R., and Silventoinen, K. 2007. Genetic and environmental factors affecting self-esteem from age 14 to 17: a longitudinal study of Finnish twins. *Psychological Medicine,* 37(11): 1625–1633; Kamakura, T., Ando, J., and Ono, Y. 2007. Genetic and environmental effects of stability and change in self-esteem during adolescence. *Personality and Individual Differences,* 42(1): 181–190; Neiss, M., Sedikides, C., and Stevenson, J. 2002. Self-esteem: a behavioural genetic perspective. *European Journal of Personality,* 16(5): 351–367.

31. Ellis, L., and Bonin, S. 2003. Genetics and occupation-related preferences. Evidence from adoptive and non-adoptive families. *Personality and Individual Differences,* 35: 929–937.

32. Caspi, A., McClay, J., Moffitt, T., Mill, J., Martin, J., Craid, I., Taylor, A., and Poulton, R. 2002. The role of the genotype in the cycle of violence in maltreated children. *Science,* 297(5582): 851–854.

33. There is also a technical problem. Twin studies divide the portion of the difference between people in behaviors into genetic and environmental factors, but include measurement error with the environmental effect. Therefore, if we are to compare the size of the genetic and environmental influences, we have to assume that researchers' estimate of the environmental effect isn't subject to too much measurement error.

34. Plomin, R. 1994. *Genetics and Experience: The Interplay between Nature and Nurture,* Thousand Oaks, CA: Sage; Plomin, R., and Neiderhiser, J. 1992. Genetics and experience. *Current Directions in Psychological Science,* 1(5): 160–163.

35. Shanahan et al., Environmental contingencies and genetic propensities.

36. Plomin, R., DeFries, J., McClearn, G., and McGuffin, P. 2001. *Behavioral Genetics,* New York: Worth Publishers.

37. Plomin and Neiderhiser, Genetics and experience.

38. Spector, T. 2003. *Your Genes Unzipped,* London: Robson Books.

39. Plomin et al., *Behavioral Genetics.*

40. Segal, N. 1999. New twin studies show ... The career of your dreams may be the career of your genes. *Psychology Today,* September/October, 54–70.

41. http://freewill.typepad.com/genetics/motivation_memory_and_the_brain/index.html

42. Dawkins, R. 1982. *The Extended Phenotype,* Oxford, UK: Oxford University Press.

43. Gray, J., and Thompson, P. Neurobiology of intelligence: Science and ethics. *Neuroscience,* 5: 471–482; Plomin et al., *Behavioral Genetics;* Plomin, R., and Spinath, F. 2002. Genetics and general cognitive ability (g). *TRENDS in Cognitive Science,* 6(4): 169–175.

44. Hamer and Copeland, *Living with Our Genes;* Bouchard, T. 1981. Familial studies of intelligence: A review. *Science,* 212: 1055–1059.

45. Gray and Thompson, Neurobiology of intelligence.

46. Comings, D., Gade-Andavolu, R., Gonzalez, N., Wu, S., Muhleman, D., Blake, H., Mann, M, Dietz, G., Saucier, G., and MacMurray, J. 2000. A multivariate analysis of 59 candidate genes in personality traits: The temperament and character inventory. *Clinical Genetics,* 58: 375–385.

47. Zuckerman, M. 2005. *Psychobiology of Personality,* Cambridge, UK: Cambridge University Press.

48. Comings, D., Saucier, G., and McMurray, J. 2002. Role of DRD2 and other dopamine genes in personality traits. In J. Benjamin and R. Ebstein (eds.), *Molecular Genetics and the Human Personality,* Washington, D.C.: American Psychiatric Publishing.

49. Noble, E. 1998. The D2 dopamine receptor gene: A review of association studies in alcoholism and phenotypes. *Alcohol,* 16: 33–45.

50. Zuckerman, M. 2005. *Psychobiology of Personality,* Cambridge, UK: Cambridge University Press.

51. Comings et al., Temperament and character inventory.

52. In studies of twins, non-additive effects can be seen when the ratio of the correlation between identical twins to the correlation between fraternal twins is more than 2:1.

53. Zuckerman, *Psychobiology of Personality.*

54. Plomin, R, Chipuer, H., and Loehlin, J. 1990. Behavioral genetics and personality. In L. Pervin (ed.), *Handbook of Personality: Theory and Research,* New York: The Guilford Press.

55. Strobel, A., Lesch, K., and Brocke, B. 2003. Dopamine D4 receptor gene polymorphism and novelty seeking: Evidence for a modulatory role of additional polymorphisms. *Paper Presented at the 11th Biennial Meeting of the International Society for the Study of Individual Differences,* Graz, Austria.

56. Reuter, M., Schmitz, A, Corr, P., and Hennig, J. 2005. Molecular genetics support Gray's personality theory: the interaction of COMT and DRD2 polymorphisms predicts the behavioural approach system. *International Journal of Neuropsychopharmacology,* 9: 155–166.

57. Benjamin, J., Ebstein, R., and Lesch, K. 1998. Genes for personality traits: Implications for psychopathology. *International Journal of Neuropsychopharmacology,* 1: 153–168; Reif, A., and Lesch, K. 2003. Towards a molecular architecture of personality. *Behavioral Brain Research,* 139: 1–20, p. 7.

58. Reif and Lesch, Molecular architecture of personality.

59. Sen, S., Villafuerte, S., Nesse, R., Soltenberg, S., Hopican, J., Gleiberman, L., Weder, A., and Burmeister, M. 2004. Serotonin transporter and GABA(A) Alpha 6 receptor variants are associated with neuroticism. *Biological Psychiatry,* 55: 244–249.

60. Reif and Lesch, Molecular architecture of personality.

61. Ibid.

62. Comings et al., D2 receptor gene in pathological gambling.

63. Ebstein, R., Benjamin, J., and Belmaker, R. 2002. Behavioral genetics, genomics, and personality. In R. Plomin, J. DeFries, I. Craig, and P. McGuffin (eds.), *Behavioral Genetics in the Postgenomic Era,* Washington, DC: American Psychological Association, 265–388. The overlapping effects of genes on individual differences is not limited to a few genes, but is present with a variety of genes, including DRD4, TPH1, PNMT, CNRA4, ADORA2A, CYP19, OXYR, and COMT genes (Comings et al., Temperament and character inventory).

64. http://www.answers.com/topic/behaviour-genetics

65. Technically, fraternal twins share 50 percent of their *segregating* genes, on average.

66. If pairs of identical twins experience more similar environments than pairs of fraternal twins—as would be the case if parents treat identical twins more similarly than fraternal twins—then the results of twin studies are suspect. However, much research has shown that pairs of identical twins face no more similar environments than pairs of fraternal twins. Nevertheless, throughout the book, I try to highlight studies of identical and fraternal twins raised apart, which ensure that this is the case.

67. This is a hypothetical example. I know of no research that shows zero genetic effect for the type of house people live in. However, future research might show that the choice of house materials has a genetic component, in which case I will need to get a different example.

68. Twin studies typically show more of a genetic effect than adoption studies. This could be because identical twins are treated more similarly than fraternal twins or because there are non-additive genetic effects. (See Zuckerman, M. 1995. Good and bad humors: Biochemical bases of personality and its disorders. *Psychological Science,* 6(6): 325–332.)

69. Betsworth, D., Bouchard, T., Cooper, C., Grotevant, H., Hansen, J., Scarr, S., and Weinberg, R. 1994. Genetic and environmental influences on vocational interests assessed using adoptive and biological families and twins reared apart and together. *Journal of Vocational Behavior,* 44: 263–278.

70. http://www.medterms.com/script/main/art.asp?articlekey=4166

71. http://genome.wellcome.ac.uk/doc_wtd020778.html

72. Sometimes researchers compare a group with a particular genetic variant with a group that lacks it to see if the variant is related to the presence of a certain attribute.

73. Hirschhorn, J., and Daly, M. 2005. Genome-wide association studies for common diseases and complex traits. *Nature Reviews,* 6(2): 95–108.

74. Hamer, *The God Gene.*

75. Bender, E. 2003. Animal behavior holds the key to treatment advances. *Psychiatric News,* 38(8): 40.

76. Begley, D. 2003. Good genes do count, but intelligence may come from complex interactions. *Wall Street Journal,* June 20.

77. Kendler, K., and Prescott, C. 2006. *Genes, Environment, and Psychopathology,* New York: Guilford Press.

Chapter 3

1. Segal, N. 2005. *Indivisible by Two,* Cambridge: Harvard University Press, pp. 22, 25.

2. Harrison, T. 2005. *Instinct,* New York: Warner Business Books.

3. Keller, L., Bouchard, T., Arvey, R., Segal, N., Dawes, R. 1992. Work values: Genetic and environmental influences. *Journal of Applied Psychology,* 77: 79–88; Bouchard, T., McGue, M., Hur, Y., and Horn, J. 1998. A genetic and environmental analysis of the California Psychological Inventory using adult twins reared apart and together. *European Journal of Personality,* 12: 307–320.

4. Bouchard et al., Twins reared apart and together.

5. Beer, J., Arnold, R., and Loehlin, J. 1998. Genetic and environmental influences on MMPI factor scales: Joint model fitting to twin and adoption data. *Journal of Personality and Social Psychology,* 74(3): 818–827.

6. Roberts, C., and Johansson, C. 1974. The inheritance of cognitive interest styles among twins. *Journal of Vocational Behavior,* 4(2): 237–243; Betsworth, D., Bouchard, T., Cooper, C., Grotevant, H., Hansen, J., Scarr, S., and Weinberg, R. 1994. Genetic and environmental influences on vocational interests assessed using adoptive and biological families and twins reared apart and together. *Journal of Vocational Behavior,* 44(3): 263–278; Moloney, D., Bouchard, T., and Segal, N. 1991. A genetic and environmental analysis of the vocational interests of monozygotic and dizygotic twins reared apart. *Journal of Vocational Behavior,* 39(1): 76–109.

7. Moloney et al., Vocational interests of twins reared apart.

8. Bouchard, T., Lykken, D., McGue, M., Segal, N., and Tellegen, A. 1990. Sources of human psychological differences: The Minnesota study of twins reared apart. *Science,* 250(4978): 223–250.

9. Carter, H. 1932. Twin similarities in occupational interests. *The Journal of Educational Psychology,* 23(9): 641–655.

10. Vandenberg, S., and Stafford, R. 1967. Hereditary influences on vocational preferences as shown by scores of twins on the Minnesota vocational interest inventory. *Journal of Applied Psychology,* 51(1): 17–19.

11. Moloney et al., Vocational interests of twins reared apart; Arvey, R., and Bouchard, T. 1994. Genetics, twins, and organizational behavior. *Research in Organizational Behavior,* 16: 47–82.

12. Segal, N. 1999. *Entwined Lives,* New York: Penguin Books; Wright, L. 1997. *Twins and What They Tell Us about Who We Are,* New York: John Wiley and Sons.

13. Grotevant, H., Scarr, S., and Weinberg, R. 1977. Patterns of interest similarity in adoptive and biological families. *Journal of Personality and Social Psychology,* 35(9): 667–676.

14. Lichtenstein, P., Pedersen, N., and McClearn, G. 1992. The origins of individual differences in occupational status and educational level. *Acta Sociologica,* 35(1): 13–31.

15. Ellis, L., and Bonin, S. 2003. Genetics and occupation-related preferences. Evidence from adoptive and non-adoptive families. *Personality and Individual Differences*, 35(4): 929–937.

16. Wright, *Twins and What They Tell Us*.

17. Betsworth, D., Bouchard, T., Cooper, C., Grotevant, H., Hansen, J., Scarr, S., and Weinberg, R. 1994. Genetic and environmental influences on vocational interests assessed using adoptive and biological families and twins reared apart and together. *Journal of Vocational Behavior*, 44(3): 263–278.

18. Bouchard et al., Twins reared apart and together; Betsworth et al., Influences on vocational interests.

19. Lykken, D., Bouchard, T., McGue, M., and Tellegen, A. 1993. Heritability of interests: A twin study. *Journal of Applied Psychology*, 78(4): 649–661.

20. Holland, J. 1985. *Making Vocational Choices: A Theory of Vocational Personalities and Work Environments*, Englewood Cliffs, N.J.: Prentice Hall.

21. Robbins, S., and Judge, T. 2009. *Organizational Behavior*, 13th edition. Upper Saddle River, NJ: Prentice-Hall.

22. Roberts, C., and Johansson, C. 1974. The inheritance of cognitive interest styles among twins. *Journal of Vocational Behavior*, 4(2): 237–243; Betsworth, D., Bouchard, T., Cooper, C., Grotevant, H., Hansen, J., Scarr, S., and Weinberg, R. 1994. Genetic and environmental influences on vocational interests assessed using adoptive and biological families and twins reared apart and together. *Journal of Vocational Behavior*, 44(3): 263–278; Moloney et al., Vocational interests of twins reared apart; and Bouchard, T., McGue, M., Hur, Y., and Horn, J. 1998. A genetic and environmental analysis of the California Psychological Inventory using adult twins reared apart and together. *European Journal of Personality*, 12(5): 307–320.

23. Kessler, R., Gilman, S., Thornton, L., and Kendler, K. 2004. Health, well-being, and social responsibility in the MIDUS twin and sibling subsamples. In O. Brim, C. Ryff, and R. Kessler (eds.), *How Healthy Are We? A National Study of Well Being at Midlife*, Chicago, IL: The University of Chicago Press, 124–152.

24. Barach, J. 2007. Are we genetically programmed to be generous? Hebrew University scientists say yes. *Eureka Alert*, December 6, downloaded from http://www.bfhu.org/images/download/080129%20Programmed%20to%20be%20Generous.pdf

25. Brinn, D. 2005. Israeli researchers discover gene for altruism. *Bulletin of Herzon Hospital*, January 23. Downloaded from www.herzoghospital.com. Readers should note that Ebstein has named a different gene the altruism gene from the one that I gave that moniker to.

26. George, J. 1992. The role of personality in organizational life: Issues and evidence. *Journal of Management*, 18(2): 185–213.

27. Loehlin, J. Neiderhiser, J., and Reiss, J. 2003. The behavior genetics of personality and the NEAD study. *Journal of Research in Personality*, 37(5): 373–387.

28. Kessler et al., Health, well-being, and social responsibility.

29. Jang, K., McCrae, R., Algleitner, A., Riemann, R., and Livesay, W. 1998. Heritability of facet-level traits in a cross-cultural twin sample: Support for a hierarchical model of personality. *Journal of Personality*, 74(6): 1556–1565; Jang, K., Livesay, W., and Vernon, P. 1996. Heritability of the big five personality dimensions and their facets: A twin study. *Journal of Personality*, 64(3): 577–591.

30. Ibid.

31. Schroeder, Alice. 2008. *Snowball*, New York: Bantam Books.

32. Bouchard et al., Minnesota study of twins reared apart, 223–228.

33. Betsworth et al., Influences on vocational interests.

34. Ibid.

35. Schoenfeldt, L, 1968. The hereditary components of the project TALENT two-day test battery. *Management and Evaluation in Guidance,* 1(2): 130–140.

36. Moloney et al., Vocational interests of twins reared apart.

37. Betsworth et al., Influences on vocational interests.

38. Ibid.

39. http://www.career-lifeskills.com/pdf/sas-300–101_jvis.pdf

40. Moloney et al., Vocational interests of twins reared apart.

41. http://www.merriam-webster.com/dictionary/merchandising

42. Moloney et al., Vocational interests of twins reared apart.

43. Betsworth et al., Influences on vocational interests.

44. http://www.career-lifeskills.com/pdf/sas-300–101_jvis.pdf

45. Moloney et al., Vocational interests of twins reared apart.

46. Dabbs, J. 1992. Testosterone and occupational achievement. *Social Forces,* 70(3): 813–824.

47. Pinker, S. 2008. *The Sexual Paradox: Men, Women, and the Real Gender Gap,* New York: Scribner.

48. From an evolutionary perspective, genetic effects on testosterone levels might have had reproductive benefits. By facilitating physical activity, testosterone might have helped men to hunt, thereby making them more attractive mates.

49. Dabbs, Testosterone and occupational achievement.

50. Schlain, L. 1998. *The Alphabet Versus the Goddess,* New York: Penguin Books.

51. Pinker, *The Sexual Paradox.*

52. Ibid.

53. Janowsky, J. 2006. Thinking with your gonads: Testosterone and cognition. *Trends in Cognitive Science,* 10(2): 77–82; Grant, G., and France, J. 2001. Dominance and testosterone in women. *Biological Psychology,* 58(1): 41–47; Caldu, X., and Dreher, J. 2007. Hormonal and genetic influences on processing reward and social information. *Annals of New York Academy of Sciences,* 1118: 43–73.

54. Browne, K. 2005. Women in science: Biological factors should not be ignored. *Cardozo Women's Law Journal,* 11(3): 509–528.

55. Udry, J. 2000. Biological limits of gender construction. *American Sociological Review,* 65(3): 553–557.

56. Pinker, *The Sexual Paradox;* Browne, Women in science; Garrett, B. 2009. *Brain and Behavior,* Los Angeles: Sage.

57. Baron, S., Wheelwright, S., Stott, C., Bolton, P., and Goodyer, I. 1997. Is there a link between engineering and autism? *Autism,* 1(1): 101–109.

58. Sacks, O. 2001. Henry Cavendish: An early case of Asperger's syndrome? *Neurology,* 57(7): 1347.

59. Pinker, *The Sexual Paradox.*

60. Baron et al., Engineering and autism?

61. Bouchard, T. 1994. Genes, environment, and personality. *Science,* 264 (5166): 1700–1701.

62. Bouchard et al., Twins reared apart and together; Bouchard, T., and McGue, M. 1990. Genetic and rearing environmental influences on adult personality: An analysis of twins reared apart. *Journal of Personality* 58(1): 263–282; Jang et al., Heritability of facet-level traits; Jang et al, Heritability of the big five

personality dimensions; Loehlin, J., and Nichols, J. 1976. *Heredity, Environment, and Personality*. Austin: University of Texas Press; Horn, J., Plomin, R., and Roseman, R. 1976. Heritability of personality traits in adult male twins. *Behavior Genetics*, 6(1):17–30; Tellegen, A., Bouchard, T.; Wilcox, K;, Segal, N; Lykken, D; and Roch, S. 1988. Personality similarity in twins reared apart and together. *Journal of Personality and Social Psychology*, 54(6): 1031–1039; Beer, J., Arnold, R., Loehlin, J. 1998. Genetic and environmental influences on MMPI factor scales: Joint model fitting to twin and adoption data. *Journal of Personality and Social Psychology*, 74(3): 818–827; Loehlin, J. 1992. *Genes and the Environment in Personality Development*, Newbury Park, CA: Sage Publications; Loehlin, J., McCrae, R., Costa, P., and John, O. 1998. Heritabilities of common and measure-specific components of the big five personality factors. *Journal of Research in Personality*, 32(4): 431–453; Carey, G. 2003. *Human Genetics for the Social Sciences*, Beverley Hills: Sage; Zuckerman, M. 2005. *Psychobiology of Personality*, Cambridge, UK: Cambridge University Press.

63. Strobel, A., Gutknecht, L., Roth, C., Reif, A., Mossner, R., Zeng, Y., Brocke, B., and Lesch, K. 2003. Allelic variation in 5-HT1A receptor expression is associated with anxiety and depression-related personality traits. *Journal of Neural Transmission*, 110(12): 1445–1453; Benjamin, J., Ebstein, R., and Lesch, K. 1998. Genes for personality traits: Implications for psychopathology. *International Journal of Neuropsychopharmacology*, 1(2): 153–168; Hamer, D., and Copeland, P. 1999. *Living with Our Genes*, New York: Anchor Books; Ebstein, R., Benjamin, J., and Belmaker, R. 2002. Behavioral genetics, genomics, and personality. In R. Plomin, J. DeFries, I. Craig, and P. McGuffin (eds.), *Behavioral Genetics in the Postgenomic Era*, Washington, DC: American Psychological Association, 265–388; Zuckerman, M., and Kuhlman, D. 2000. Personality and risk taking: Common biosocial factors. *Journal of Personality*, 68(6): 999–1029; Hamer, D., Greenberg, B., Sabol, S., and Murphy, D. 1999. Role of the serotonin transporter gene in temperament and character. *Journal of Personality Disorders*, 13(4): 312–328; Winterer, G., and Goldman, D., 2003. Genetics of prefrontal function. *Brain Research Reviews*, 43(1): 13–63; Comings, D., Gade-Andavolu, R., Gonzalez, N., Wu, S., Muhleman, D., Blake, H., Mann, M, Dietz, G., Saucier, C., and MacMurray, J. 2000. A multivariate analysis of 59 candidate genes in personality traits: The temperament and character inventory. *Clinical Genetics*, 58(5): 375–385; Lesch, K. 2002. Neuroticism and serotonin: A developmental genetic perspective. 2002. Behavioral genetics, genomics, and personality. In Plomin et al., *Behavioral Genetics in the Postgenomic Era*; Greenberg, B., Li, Q., Lucas, F., Hu, S., Sirota, L., Benjamin, J., Lesch, K., Hamer, D., and Murphy, D. 2000. Association between the serotonin transporter promoter polymorphism and personality traits in a primarily female population sample. *American Journal of Medical Genetics*, 96(2): 202–216; Hamer et al., Role of the serotonin transporter gene; Lesch, K., Bengel, D., Heils, A., Sabol, S., Greenberg, B., Petri, S., Benjamin, J., Muller, C., Hamer, D., and Murphy, D. 1996. Association of anxiety related trait with a polymorphism in the serotonin transporter gene regulation region. *Science*, 274(5292): 1527–1531.

64. Furnham, A., Petrides, K., Jackson, C., and Cotter, T. 2002. Do personality factors predict job satisfaction? *Personality and Individual Differences*, 33(8): 1325–1342. Extraverts are more sensitive to motivator factors, things like responsibility or opportunities for advancement.

65. Larson, L., Rottinghaus, P., and Borgen, F. 2002. Meta-analyses of big six interests and big five personality factors. *Journal of Vocational Behavior*, 61(2): 217–239.

66. Loehlin, *Genes and the Environment*; Bouchard, T., and Loehlin, J. 2001. Genes, evolution and personality. *Behavior Genetics*, 31(3): 243–273.

67. Comings, D., Gonzalez, N., Wu, S., Gade, R., Muhleman, D., Saucier, G., Johnson, P., Verde, R., Rosenthal, R., Lesieur, H., Rugle, L., Miller, W., and MacMurray, J. 1999. Studies of the 48 bp repeat polymorphism of the DRD4 gene in impulsive, compulsive, and addictive behaviors: Tourette syndrome, ADHD, pathological gambling, and substance abuse. *American Journal of Medical Genetics*, 88(4): 358–368.

68. Bouchard and McGue, Influences on adult personality; Jang, K., Livesay, W., and Vernon, P. 1996. Heritability of the big five personality dimensions and their facets: A twin study. *Journal of Personality*, 64(3): 577–591; Loehlin and Nichols, *Heredity, Environment, and Personality*; Tellegen, A., Bouchard, T., Wilcox, K., Segal, N., Lykken, D., and Roch, S. 1988. Personality similarity in twins reared apart and together. *Journal of Personality and Social Psychology*, 54(6): 1031–1039; Reimann, R. Angleitner, A., and Strelau, J. 1997. Sociability and positive emotionality: Genetic and environmental contributions to the covariation between different facets of extraversion. *Journal of Personality*, 65(3): 449–475; Loehlin, *Genes and the Environment*; Loehlin et al., Heritabilities of the big five personality factors; Eaves, L., and Eysenck, H. 1975. The nature of extraversion: A genetical analysis. *Journal of Personality and Social Psychology*, 32(1): 102–112; J., Riemann, R., Angleitner, A., Strelau, J. 1997. Genetic and environmental influences on personality: A study of twins reared together using the self- and peer report NEO-FFI scales. *Journal of Personality*, 65(3): 449–475.

69. Benjamin, J., Li, L., Patterson, C., Greenberg, B., Murphy, D., and Hamer, D. 1996. Population and familial association between the D4 dopamine receptor gene and measures of sensation seeking. *Nature Genetics*, 12: 81–84; Strobel, A., Wehr, A., Michel, A., and Brocke, B. 1999. Association between the dopamine D4 receptor (DRD4) exon III polymorphism and measures of novelty seeking in a German population. *Molecular Psychiatry*, 4(4): 378–384; Farde, L., and Gusavsson, J. 1997. D2 dopamine receptors and personality traits. *Nature*, 385(6617): 590.

70. Zuckerman, *Psychobiology of Personality*; Bouchard and Loehlin, Genes, evolution and personality; Zuckerman, M. 1995. Good and bad humors: Biochemical bases of personality and its disorders. *Psychological Science*, 6(6): 325–332; Bergeman, C., Chipuer, H., Plomin, R., Pedersen, N., McClearn, G., Nesselroade, J., Costa, P., and McCrae, R. 1993. Genetic and environmental effects on openness to experience, agreeableness, and conscientiousness: An adoption/twin study. *Journal of Personality*, 61(2): 159–176.

71. Comings et al., Analysis of 59 candidate genes in personality traits; Comings et al., Polymorphism of the DRD4 gene; Lesch et al., Anxiety related trait with a polymorphism; Reif, A., and Lesch, K. 2003. Towards a molecular architecture of personality. *Behavioral Brain Research*, 139(1): 1–20; Hamer et al., Role of the serotonin transporter gene.

72. Loehlin, J., McCrae, R., Costa, P., and John, O. 1998. Heritabilities of common and measure-specific components of the big five personality factors. *Journal of Research in Personality*, 32(4): 431–453.

73. Hamer and Copeland, *Living with Our Genes*, p. 58.

74. Kendler, K., Gardner, C., and Prescott, C. 1998. A population-based twin study of self-esteem and gender. *Psychological Medicine*, 28: 1403–1409.

75. Neiss, M., Sedikides, C., and Steveneson, J. 2002. Self-esteem: A behavioural genetic perspective. *European Journal of Personality*, 16(5): 351–367.

76. http://www.career-lifeskills.com/pdf/sas-300–101_jvis.pdf

77. Hamer and Copeland, *Living with Our Genes*.

78. Zuckerman and Kuhlman, Personality and risk taking.

79. Ibid.

80. Hamer and Copeland, *Living with Our Genes*, pp. 33–4.

81. Bouchard and Loehlin, Genes, evolution and personality.

82. Zernike, K. 2008. Never let them see you sweat. *New York Times*, November 30: WK 1; 4.

83. Plomin, R., Pedersen, N., McClearn, G., Nesselroade, J., and Bergeman, C. 1988. EAS temperaments during the last half of the life span: Twins reared apart and twins reared together. *Psychology and Aging*, 3(1): 43–50.

84. Riemann, R., Angleitner, A., Borkenau, P., and Eid, M. 1998. Genetic and environmental sources of consistency and variability in positive and negative mood. *European Journal of Personality*, 12(5): 345–364.

85. Tellegen et al., Personality similarity in twins; Eid, M., Reimann, R., Angleitner, A., Borkenau, P. 2003. Sociability and positive emotionality: Genetic and environmental contributions to the covariation between different facets of extraversion. 74(3): 319–346; Plomin, R., Scheier, M., Bergeman, C., Pedersen, N., Nesselroade, J., and McClearn, G. 1992. Optimism, pessimism, and mental health: A twin/adoption analysis. *Personality and Individual Differences*, 13(8): 921–930.

86. Lykken, D., and Tellegen, A. 1996. Happiness is a stochastic phenomenon. *Psychological Science*, 7(3): 186–189; Segal, *Entwined Lives*.

87. Hamer and Copeland, *Living with Our Genes*.

88. Reif and Lesch, Towards a molecular architecture of personality.

89. Zuckerman, M. 1994. *Behavioral Expressions and Biosocial Bases of Sensation Seeking*, Cambridge, UK: Cambridge University Press.

90. Zuckerman, M., Buschbaum, M., and Murphy, D. 1980. Sensation seeking and its biological correlates. *Psychological Bulletin*, 88(1): 187–214.

91. Schooler, C., Zahn, T., Murphy, D., and Buschbaum, M. 1978. Psychological correlates of monoamine oxidase activity in normals. *The Journal of Nervous and Mental Disease*, 166(3): 177–186.

92. Staw, B., and Cohen-Charash, Y. 2005. The dispositional approach to job satisfaction: more than a mirage, but not yet an oasis. *Journal of Organizational Behavior*, 26(1): 59–78.

93. Lichtenstein, P., and Pedersen, N. 1997. Does genetic variation for cognitive abilities account for genetic variance in educational achievement and occupational status? A study of twins reared apart and twins reared together. *Social Biology*, 44(1–2): 77–90.

94. Deary, I., Spinath, F., and Bates, T. 2006. Genetics of intelligence. *European Journal of Human Genetics*, 14: 690–700; McGue, M., and Bouchard, T. 1989. Genetic and environmental determinants of information processing and special mental abilities: A twin analysis. In Sternberg, R. (ed.), *Advances in the Psychology of Human Intelligence*, Hillsdale, NJ: Erlbaum, 7–45; Scarr, S. 1981. *Race, Social Class, and Individual Differences in I.Q.*, Hillsdale, NJ: Lawrence Erlbaum; Bouchard, T., and McGue, M. 1981. Familial studies of intelligence: A review. *Science*, 212(4498): 1055–1059; Carey, *Human Genetics for the Social Sciences*; Gray, J., and

Thompson, P. Neurobiology of intelligence: Science and ethics. *Neuroscience,* 5: 471–482; Wright, M., De Gues, E., Ando, J., Luciano, M., Posthuma, D., Ono, Y., Hansell, N., Baal, C., Hirashi, K., Hasegawa, T., Smith, G., Geffen, G., Geffen, L., Kanba, S., Miyake, A., Martin, N., and Boomsma, D. 2001. Genetics of cognition: Outline of a collaborative twin study. *Twin Research,* 4(1): 48–56; Rose, R., Harris, E., Christian, J., and Nance, W. 1979. Genetic variance in nonverbal intelligence: Data from the kinships of identical twins. *Science,* 205(4411): 1153–1155.

95. McGue and Bouchard, Information processing. In Sternberg, *Psychology of Human Intelligence;* Pedersen, N., Plomin, R., Nesselroade, J., and McClearn, G. 1992. A quantitative genetic analysis of cognitive abilities during the second half of the life span. *Psychological Science,* 3(6): 346–353; Nichols, R. 1978. Twin studies of ability, personality, and interests. *Homo,* 29: 158–173; Alarcon, M., Plomin, R., Fulker, D., Corley, R., and DeFries, J. 1998. Multivariate path analysis of specific cognitive abilities data at 12 years of age in the Colorado adoption project. *Behavior Genetics,* 28(4): 255–264; Flint, J. 1999. The genetic basis of cognition. *Brain,* 122(11): 2015–2031; Ando, J., Ono, Y., and Wright, M. 2001. Genetic structure of spatial and verbal working memory. *Behavior Genetics,* 31(6): 615–; Posthuma, D., de Geus, E., and Boomsma, D. 2002. Genetic contributions to anatomical, behavioral, and neurophysiological indices of cognition. In Plomin et al., *Behavioral Genetics in the Postgenomic Era,* 141–161; Hamer and Copeland, *Living with Our Genes;* Plomin, R., DeFries, J., McClearn, G., and McGuffin, P. 2001. *Behavioral Genetics,* New York: Worth Publishers; Winterer and Goldman, Genetics of prefrontal function.

96. Bouchard, T., and McGue, M. 2003. Genetic and environmental influences on human psychological differences. *Journal of Neurobiology,* 54 (1): 4–45.

97. Hamer and Copeland, *Living with Our Genes;* Keller, L., Arvey, R., Bouchard, T., Segal, N., and Davis, R. 1992. Work values: genetic and environmental influences. *Journal of Applied Psychology,* 77(1): 79–88; McGue, M., and Bouchard, T. 1998. Genetic and environmental influences on human behavioral differences. *Annual Review of Neuroscience,* 21: 1–24.

98. Bratko, D., 1996. Twin study of verbal and spatial abilities. *Personality and Individual Differences,* 21(4): 621–624; Benyamin, B., Wilson, V., Whalley, L., Visscher, P., and Deary, I. 2005. Large, consistent estimates of the heritability of cognitive ability in two entire populations of 11-year-old twins from Scottish mental surveys of 1932 and 1947. *Behavior Genetics,* 35(5): 525–534; Dunnette, M. 1976. Aptitudes, abilities, and skills. In M. Dunnette (ed.), *Handbook of Industrial and Organizational Psychology,* Chicago: Rand McNally, 476–483. Our genes might even control particular brain circuits, such as those that are used for doing math or singing in perfect pitch. (See Hamer and Copeland, *Living with Our Genes.*)

99. Plomin, R., and DeFries, J. 1998. The genetics of cognitive abilities and disabilities. *Scientific American,* 278(5): 62–71; Loehlin, J., and Nichols, J. 1976. *Heredity, Environment, and Personality,* Austin: University of Texas Press; Scarr, *Race, Social Class, and Individual Differences.*

100. McGue, M., Hirsch, B., and Lykken, D. 1993. Age and the self-perception of ability: A twin study analysis. *Psychology and Aging,* 8(1): 72–80.

101. McGuire, S., Manke, B., Saudino, K., Reiss, D., Hetherington, E., and Plomin, R. 1999. Perceived competence and self-worth during adolescence: A longitudinal behavioral genetic study. *Child Development,* 70(6): 1283–1296.

102. Schmidt, F., Ones, D., and Hunter, J. 1992. Personnel selection. *Annual Review of Psychology*, 43: 627–670.

103. Ganzach, Y. 2003. Intelligence, education, and facets of job satisfaction. *Work and Occupations*, 30(1): 97–122.

104. Ganzach, Y. 1998. Intelligence and job satisfaction. *Academy of Management Journal*, 41(5): 526–539.

105. Robbins, S., and Judge, T. 2009. *Organizational Behavior*, 13th edition. Upper Saddle River, NJ: Prentice-Hall.

106. Ibid.

107. Plomin, R., and DeFries, J. 1998. The genetics of cognitive abilities and disabilities. *Scientific American*, 278(5): 62–71; DeFries, J., and Gillis, J. 1993. Genetics of reading disability. In R. Plomin and G. McClearn (eds.), *Nature, Nurture and Psychology*, Washington, DC: American Psychological Association, 121–145.

108. Stromsworld, K. 2001. The heritability of language: A review and meta analysis of twin, adoption, and linkage studies. *Language*, 77(4): 647–723.

109. Plomin, R., and Walker, S. 2003. Genetics and educational psychology. *British Journal of Educational Psychology*, 73: 3–14; Morris, D., Robinson, L., Turic, D., Duke, M., Webb, V., Milham, C., Hopkin, E., Pound, K., Fernando, S., Easton, M., Hamshere, M., Williams, N., McGuffin, P., Stevenson, J., Krawczak, M., Owen, M., O'Donovan, M., and Williams, J. 2000. Family based association mapping provides evidence for a gene for reading disability on chromosome 15q. *Human Molecular Genetics*, 9(5): 843–848.

110. Flint, Genetic basis of cognition.

111. Stromsworld, Heritability of language.

112. Taylor, K., and Walter, J. 2003. Occupation choices of adults with and without symptoms of dyslexia. *Dyslexia*, 9(3): 177–185.

113. Lichtenstein, Pedersen, and McClearn, Individual differences.

114. Heath, A., Berg, K., Eaves, L., Solaas, H., Corey, L., Sundet, J., Magnus, P., and Nance, W. 1985. Education policy and the heritability of educational attainment. *Nature*, 314(6013): 734–736; Lichtenstein, Pedersen, and McClearn, Individual differences; Tambs, K., Sundet, M., Magnus, P., and Berg, F. 1989. Genetic and environmental contributions to the covariance between occupational status, educational attainment, and IQ: A study of twins, *Behavior Genetics*, 19(2): 209–222; Rowe, D. 1994. *The Limits of Family Influence*, New York: The Guilford Press; Behrman, J., Hrubec, Z., Taubman, P., and Wales, T. 1980. *Socioeconomic Success: A Study of the Effects of Genetic Endowments, Family Environment, and Schooling*, Amsterdam: North-Holland Publishing Company; Ashenfelter, O., and Krueger, A. 1994. Estimates of the economic return to schooling from a new sample of twins. *American Economic Review*, 84(5): 1157–1172; Behrman, J., and Taubman, P. 1989. Is schooling 'mostly in the genes?' *Journal of Political Economy* 97(6): 1425–1446; Petrill, S., and Wilkerson, B. 2000. Intelligence and achievement: A behavioral genetic perspective. *Educational Psychology Review*, 12 (2): 185–199. The numbers may even be higher. The twin studies on which these estimates are based may understate the genetic effect on education because the education of spouses is correlated at 0.60. (See Plomin et al., *Behavioral Genetics*.)

115. Petrill and Wilkerson, Intelligence and achievement; Wainwright, M., Wright, M., Geffen, G., Luciano, M., and Martin, N. 2005. The genetic basis of academic achievement on the Queensland core skills test and its shared genetic variance with IQ. *Behavior Genetics*, 35(2): 133–144; Bartels, M., Rietveld, M., Van

Baal, G., and Boomsma, D. 2002. Heritability of educational achievement in 12-year-olds and the overlap with cognitive ability. *Twin Research*, 5(6): 544–553; Carey, *Human Genetics*; Plomin, R. 1990. The role of inheritance in behavior. *Science*, 248(4952): 183–189; Wainwright, M., Wright, N., Luciano, M., Montgomery, G., Geffen, G., and Martin, N. 2006. A linkage study of academic skills defined by the Queensland core skills test. *Behavior Genetics*, 36(1): 56–64; Thompson, L., Detterman, D., and Plomin, R. 1991. Associations between cognitive abilities and scholastic achievement: Genetic overlap but environmental differences. *Psychological Science*, 2(3): 158–165; Plomin, R. 2002. General cognitive ability. In Plomin et al., *Behavioral Genetics in the Postgenomic Era*, 141–161.

116. Hamer and Copeland, *Living with Our Genes*.

117. Plomin and DeFries, Genetics of cognitive abilities.

118. Petrill and Wilkerson, Intelligence and achievement.

119. http://freewill.typepad.com/genetics/motivation_memory_and_the_brain/index.html.

120. Begley, D. 2003. Good genes do count, but intelligence may come from complex interactions. *Wall Street Journal*, June 20. Downloaded from http://www.mindfully.org/GE/2003/Intelligence-Good-Genes20jun03.htm

121. Segal, N. 1999. New twin studies show...The career of your dreams may be the career of your genes. *Psychology Today*, September/October, 54–70.

122. Olson, J., Vernon, P., Harris, J., and Jang, K. 2001. The heritability of attitudes: A study of twins. *Journal of Personality and Social Psychology*, 80(6): 845–860.

Chapter 4

1. These descriptions are composites and do not represent actual individuals.

2. Anonymous. 2001. Employee turnover costs in the U.S. *Manpower Argus*, January: 5.

3. Robbins, S., and Judge, T. 2009. *Organizational Behavior*, 13th edition. Upper Saddle River, NJ: Prentice-Hall.

4. Arvey, R., Bouchard, T., Segal, N., and Abraham, L. 1989. Job satisfaction: Environmental and genetic components. *Journal of Applied Psychology*, 74(2): 187–192.

5. Arvey, R., McCall, B., and Taubman, P. 1994. *Personality and Individual Differences*, 17: 21–33.

6. Hershberger, S., Lichtenstein, P., and Knox, S. 1994. Genetic and environmental influences on perceptions of organizational climate. *Journal of Applied Psychology*, 79(1): 24–33.

7. Ilies, R., Arvey, R., and Bouchard, T. 2006. Darwinism, behavioral genetics, and organizational behavior: A review and agenda for future research. *Journal of Organizational Behavior*, 27: 121–141.

8. Plomin, R. 1994. *Genetics and Experience: The Interplay between Nature and Nurture*. Thousand Oaks, CA: Sage.

9. Hershberger, S., Lichtenstein, P., and Knox, S. 1994. Genetic and environmental influences on perceptions of organizational climate. *Journal of Applied Psychology*, 79(1): 24–33.

10. Ibid.

11. Bouchard, T., Segal, N., Tellegen, A., McGue, M., Keyes, M., and Krueger, R. 2004. Genetic influence on social attitudes: Another challenge to psychology from behavior genetics. In L. DiLalla (ed.), *Behavior Genetics Principles*, Washington, D.C.: American Psychological Association; Pinker, S. 1995. *The Language Instinct*, New York: Harper Books.

12. Eaves, L., Heath, A., Martin, N., Maes, H., Neale, M., Kendler, K., Kirk, K., and Corey, L. 1999. Comparing the biological and cultural inheritance of personality and social attitudes in the Virginia 30,000 study of twins and their relatives. *Twin Research*, 2: 62–80; Bouchard, T., Segal, N., Tellegen, A., McGue, M., Keyes, M., and Krueger, R. 2003. Evidence for the construct validity and heritability of the Wilson-Patterson conservatism scale: a reared apart study of social attitudes. *Personality and Individual Differences*, 34: 959–969; DiLalla, L. 2004. Behavioral genetics: Background, current research, and goals for the future. In DiLalla, *Behavior Genetics*; McCourt, K., Bouchard, T., Lykken, D., Tellegen, A., and Keyes, M. 1999. Authoritarianism revisited: genetic and environmental influences examined in twins reared apart and together. *Personality and Individual Differences*, 27: 985–1014.

13. Eaves et al., Virginia 30,000 study; Bouchard, T., Segal, N., Tellegen, A., McGue, M., Keyes, M., and Krueger, R. 2003. Evidence for the construct validity and heritability of the Wilson-Patterson conservatism scale: a reared apart study of social attitudes. *Personality and Individual Differences*, 34: 959–969; DiLalla, Behavioral genetics; McCourt et al., Authoritarianism revisited.

14. Olson, J., Vernon, P., Harris, J., and Jang, K. 2001. The heritability of attitudes: A study of twins. *Journal of Personality and Social Psychology*, 80(6): 845–860.

15. Bouchard et al., Wilson-Patterson conservatism scale; Olson et al., Heritability of attitudes.

16. Keller, L., Bouchard, T., Arvey, R., Segal, N., Dawes, R. 1992. Work values: Genetic and environmental influences. *Journal of Applied Psychology*, 77(1): 79–88.

17. http://www.career-lifeskills.com/pdf/sas-300–101_jvis.pdf

18. Keller et al., Work values.

19. Arvey et al., Job satisfaction.

20. Ibid.

21. Ilies, Arvey, and Bouchard, Darwinism.

22. McCall, B., Cavanaugh, M., and Arvey, R. 1997. Genetic influences on job and occupational switching. *Journal of Vocational Behavior*, 50(1): 60–77.

23. Loehlin, J., Horn, J., and Ernst, J. 2007. Genetic and environmental influences on adult life outcomes: Evidence from the Texas adoption project. *Behavior Genetics*, 37(3): 463–476.

24. McCall et al. 1997. Job and occupational switching.

25. Burke, A. E., FitzRoy, F. R., Nolan, M.A. 2000. When less is more: Distinguishing between entrepreneurial choice and performance. *Oxford Bulletin of Economics and Statistics*, 62(5): 567–587.

26. Nicolaou, N., Shane, S., Cherkas, L., Hunkin, J., and Spector, T. 2008. Is the tendency to engage in entrepreneurship genetic? *Management Science*, 54(1): 167–179.

27. Robbins and Judge, *Organizational Behavior*.

28. Cropanzano, R., James, K., and Konovsky, M. 1993. Dispositional affectivity as a predictor of work attitudes and job performance. *Journal of Organizational Behavior,* 14(6): 595–606; George, J., and Jones, G. 1996. The experience of work and turnover intentions: Interactive effects of value attainment, job satisfaction, and positive mood. *Journal of Applied Psychology,* 81(3): 318–325.

29. Cropanzano, James, and Konovsky, M. Dispositional affectivity; Staw, B., Bell, N., and Clausen, J. 1986. The dispositional approach to job attitudes: A lifetime longitudinal test. *Administrative Science Quarterly,* 31(1): 56–77.

30. Plomin, *Genetics and Experience;* Hamer, D., and Copeland, P. 1999. *Living with Our Genes,* New York: Anchor Books; Plomin, R., Scheier, M., Bergeman, C., Pedersen, N., Nesselroade, J and McClearn, G. 1992. Optimism, pessimism, and mental health: A twin/adoption analysis. *Personality and Individual Differences,* 13: 921–930.

31. Zuckerman, M. 1994. *Behavioral Expressions and Biosocial Bases of Sensation Seeking.* Cambridge, UK: Cambridge University Press; Schooler, C., Zahn, T., Murphy, D., and Buschbaum, M. 1978. Psychological correlates of monoamine oxidase activity in normals. *The Journal of Nervous and Mental Disease,* 166(3): 177–; Zuckerman, M., Buschbaum, M., and Murphy, D. 1980. Sensation seeking and its biological correlates. *Psychological Bulletin,* 88(1): 187–214; Hamer and Copeland, *Living with Our Genes;* Reif, A., and Lesch, K. 2003. Towards a molecular architecture of personality. *Behavioral Brain Research,* 139(1): 1–20.

32. Ilies, R., and Judge, T. 2003. On the heritability of job satisfaction: The mediating role of personality. *Journal of Applied Psychology,* 88(4): 750–759.

33. Judge, T., Locke, E., and Durham, C. 1997. The dispositional causes of job satisfaction: A core evaluations approach. *Research in Organizational Behavior,* 19, 151–188.

34. Miller, J., and Rose, R. 1982. Familial resemblance in locus of control: A twin-family study of the internal-external scale, *Journal of Personality and Social Psychology,* 42: 535–540.

35. Neiss, M., Stevenson, J., Sedikides, C., Finkel, E., Kumashiro, M., and Rusbult, C. 2005. Executive self, self-esteem, and negative affectivity: Relations at the phenotypic and genotypical level. *Journal of Personality and Social Psychology,* 89(4): 593–606; Lesch, K. Bengel, D., Heils, S., Sabol, Z., Greenberg, B., Petri, J., Benjamin, C., Muller, C., Hamer, D., and Murphy, D. 1996. Association of anxiety-related traits with a polymorphism in the serotonin transporter gene regulatory region. *Science,* 274(5292): 1527–1531.

36. Bouchard, T., McGue, M., Hur, Y., and Horn, J. 1998. A genetic and environmental analysis of the California Psychological Inventory using adult twins reared apart and together. *European Journal of Personality,* 12(5): 307–320; Bouchard, T., and McGue, M. 1990. Genetic and rearing environmental influences on adult personality: An analysis of twins reared apart. *Journal of Personality* 58(1): 263–282; Jang, K., McCrae, R., Algleitner, A., Riemann, R., and Livesay, W. 1998. Heritability of facet-level traits in a cross-cultural twin sample: Support for a hierarchical model of personality. *Journal of Personality,* 74(6): 1556–1565; Jang, K., Livesay, W., and Vernon, P. 1996. Heritability of the big five personality dimensions and their facets: A twin study. *Journal of Personality,* 64 (3): 577–591; Loehlin, J., and Nichols, J. 1976. *Heredity, Environment, and Personality.* Austin: University of Texas Press; Horn, J., Plomin, R., and Roseman, R. 1976. Heritability of personality traits in adult male twins. *Behavior Genetics,* 6: 17–30; Tellegen, A., Bouchard, T.; Wilcox, K; Segal, N; Lykken, D; and Roch, S. 1988. Personality similarity in twins reared apart and together. *Journal of*

Personality and Social Psychology, 54(6): 1031–1039; Beer, J., Arnold, R., Loehlin, J. 1998. Genetic and Environmental Influences on MMPI Factor Scales: Joint Model Fitting to Twin and Adoption Data. *Journal of Personality and Social Psychology*, 74 (3): 818–827; Loehlin, J. 1992. *Genes and the Environment in Personality Development.* Newbury Park, CA: Sage Publications. Loehlin, J., McCrae, R., Costa, P., and John, O. 1998. Heritabilities of common and measure-specific components of the big five personality factors. *Journal of Research in Personality*, 32(4): 431–453; Carey, G. 2003. *Human Genetics for the Social Sciences*, Beverley Hills, CA: Sage; Zuckerman, M. 2005. *Psychobiology of Personality*, Cambridge, UK: Cambridge University Press.

37. Neiss, M., Sedikides, C., and Stevenson, J. 2006. Genetic influences on level and stability of self-esteem. *Self and Identity*, 5(3): 247–266.

38. Judge, T., Heller, D., and Mount, M. 2002. Five-factor model of personality and job satisfaction: A meta-analysis. *Journal of Applied Psychology*, 87(3): 530–541; Furnham, A., Petrides, K., Jackson, C., and Cotter, T. 2002. Do personality factors predict job satisfaction? *Personality and Individual Differences*, 33(8): 1325–1342.

39. Zuckerman, *Psychobiology of Personality;* Loehlin et al., Heritabilities of big five; Moloney, D., Bouchard, T., and Segal, N. 1991. A genetic and environmental analysis of the vocational interests of monozygotic and dizygotic twins reared apart. *Journal of Vocational Behavior*, 39(1): 76–109; Judge, T., Locke, E., Durham, C., and Kluger, A. 1998. Dispositional effects on job and life satisfaction: The role of core evaluations. *Journal of Applied Psychology*, 83(1): 17–34.

40. Strobel, A., Gutknecht, L., Roth, C., Reif, A., Mossner, R., Zeng, Y., Brocke, B., and Lesch, K. 2003. Allelic variation in 5-HT1A receptor expression is associated with anxiety and depression-related personality traits. *Journal of Neural Transmission*, 110(12): 1445–1453; Benjamin, J., Ebstein, R., and Lesch, K. 1998. Genes for personality traits: Implications for psychopathology. *International Journal of Neuropsychopharmacology*, 1(2): 153–168; Hamer and Copeland, *Living with Our Genes;* Ebstein, R., Benjamin, J., and Belmaker, R. 2002. Behavioral genetics, genomics, and personality. In R. Plomin, J. DeFries, I. Craig, and P. McGuffin (eds.), *Behavioral Genetics in the Postgenomic Era*, Washington, DC: American Psychological Association, 265–388; Zuckerman, M., and Kuhlman, D. 2000. Personality and risk taking: Common biosocial factors. *Journal of Personality*, 68(6): 999–1029; Hamer, D., Greenberg, B., Sabol, S., and Murphy, D. 1999. Role of the serotonin transporter gene in temperament and character. *Journal of Personality Disorders*, 13(4): 312–328; Winterer, G., and Goldman, D., 2003. Genetics of prefrontal function. *Brain Research Reviews*, 43(1): 13–63; Comings, D., Gade-Andavolu, R., Gonzalez, N., Wu, S., Muhleman, D., Blake, H., Mann, M, Dietz, G., Saucier, G., and MacMurray, J. 2000. A multivariate analysis of 59 candidate genes in personality traits: The temperament and character inventory. *Clinical Genetics*, 58(5): 375–385; Lesch, K. 2002. Neuroticism and serotonin: A developmental genetic perspective. 2002. Behavioral genetics, genomics, and personality. In Plomin et al., *Behavioral Genetics*, 389–423; Greenberg, B., Li, Q., Lucas, F., Hu, S., Sirota, L., Benjamin, J., Lesch, K., Hamer, D., and Murphy, D. 2000. Association between the serotonin transporter promoter polymorphism and personality traits in a primarily female population sample. *American Journal of Medical Genetics*, 96(2): 202–216; Hamer et al., Serotonin transporter gene; Lesch, K., Bengel, D., Heils, A., Sabol, S., Greenberg, B., Petri, S., Benjamin, J., Muller, C., Hamer, D., and Murphy, D. 1996. Association of anxiety related trait with a

polymorphism in the serotonin transporter gene regulation region. *Science*, 274 (5292): 1527–1531.

41. Ilies and Judge, Job satisfaction.

42. Tesser, A. 1993. The importance of heritability in psychological research: The case of attitudes. *Psychological Review*, 100(1): 129–142.

43. Zuckerman, *Behavioral Expressions*.

44. Furnham, A., Forde, L., and Ferrari, K. 1999. Personality and work motivation. *Personality and Individual Differences*, 26(6): 1035–1043.

45. Judge et al., Dispositional effects.

46. Deary, I., Spinath, F., and Bates, T. 2006. Genetics of intelligence. *European Journal of Human Genetics*, 14: 690–700; McGue, M., and Bouchard, T. 1989. Genetic and environmental determinants of information processing and special mental abilities: A twin analysis. In Sternberg, R. (ed.), *Advances in the Psychology of Human Intelligence*, Hillsdale, NJ: Lawrence Erlbaum, 7–45; Scarr, S. 1981. *Race, Social Class, and Individual Differences in I.Q.*, Hillsdale, NJ: Lawrence Erlbaum; Bouchard, T., and McGue, M. 1981. Familial studies of intelligence: A review. *Science* 212(4498): 1055–1059; Carey, *Human Genetics*; Gray, J., and Thompson, P. 2004. Neurobiology of intelligence: Science and ethics. *Neuroscience*, 5: 471–482; Wright, M., De Gues, E., Ando, J., Luciano, M., Posthuma, D., Ono, Y., Hansell, N., Baal, C., Hirashi, K., Hasegawa, T., Smith, G., Geffen, G., Geffen, L., Kanba, S., Miyake, A., Martin, N., and Boomsma, D. 2001. Genetics of cognition: Outline of a collaborative twin study. *Twin Research*, 4(1): 48–56; Rose, R., Harris, E., Christian, J., and Nance, W. 1979. Genetic variance in nonverbal intelligence: Data from the kinships of identical twins. *Science*, 205(4411): 1153–1155.

47. Ganzach, Y. 2003. Intelligence, education, and facets of job satisfaction. *Work and Occupations*, 30(1): 97–122.

48. Allen, J., and Van der Velden, R. 2001. Educational mismatches versus skill mismatches: effects on wages, job satisfaction, and on-the-job search. *Oxford Economic Papers*, 53(3): 434–452.

49. McGuire, S., Manke, B., Saudino, K., Reiss, D., Hetherington, E., and Plomin, R. 1999. Perceived competence and self-worth during adolescence: A longitudinal behavioral genetic study. *Child Development*, 70(6): 1283–1296; Plomin, R., and DeFries, J. 1998. The genetics of cognitive abilities and disabilities. *Scientific American*, 278(5): 62–71; Loehlin and Nichols, *Heredity, Environment, and Personality*; Scarr, S. 1981. *Race, Social Class, and Individual Differences in I.Q.* Hillsdale, NJ: Lawrence Erlbaum; McGue, M., Hirsch, B., and Lykken, D. 1993. Age and the self-perception of ability: A twin study analysis. *Psychology and Aging*, 8(1): 72–80.

50. Arvey, R., and Bouchard, T. 1994. Genetics, twins, and organizational behavior. *Research in Organizational Behavior*, 16: 47–82.

Chapter 5

1. Robbins, S., and Judge, T. 2009. *Organizational Behavior*, 13th edition. Upper Saddle River, NJ: Prentice-Hall.

2. Ibid.

3. Oakley, B. 2008. *Evil Genes*, New York: Prometheus Books.

4. Robbins and Judge, *Organizational Behavior*.

5. Wyly, S. 2008. *1,000 Dollars and an Idea*, New York: Newmarket Press, p. 244.

6. Bouchard, T., and Hur, J. 1998. Genetic and environmental influences on the continuous scales of the Myers-Briggs type indicator: An analysis based on twins reared apart. *Journal of Personality*, 66(2): 135–149.

7. McGuffin, P., Riley, B., and Plomin, R. 2001. Genomics and behavior: Towards behavioral genomics. *Science*, 291(5507): 1232–1249.

8. Gomes, L. 2008. Why we are powerless to resist grazing on endless web data. *Wall Street Journal*, March 12: B1.

9. Anohkin, A., Golsheykin, S., Grant, J., and Health, A. 2009. Heritability of risk taking in adolescence: A longitudinal twin study. *Twin Research and Human Genetics*, 12(4): 366–371.

10. Zyphur, M., Narayanan, J., Arvey, R., and Alexander, G. Forthcoming. The genetics of economic risk preferences. *Journal of Behavioral Decision Making*, p. 11.

11. Cessarini, D., Johannesson, M., Lichtenstein, P., Sandewall, O., and Wallace, B. 2009. Genetic variation in financial decision making. *Working paper*, Massachusetts Institute of Technology.

12. Caldu, X., and Dreher, J. 2007. Hormonal and genetic influences on processing reward and social information. *Annals of New York Academy of Sciences*, 1118: 43–73.

13. Comings, D., Rosenthal, R. J. Lesieur, H. R., Rugle, L. J. Muhleman, D. Chiu, C., Dietz, G., and Gade, R. 1996. A study of the dopamine receptor gene in pathological gambling. *Pharmacogenetics*, 6(3): 223–234.

14. Zweig, J. 2009. Is your investing personality in your DNA? *Wall Street Journal*, April 4–5: B1.

15. Kuhnen, C., and Chiao, J. 2009. Genetic determinants of financial risk taking. *PLoS ONE*, 4(2): e4362.

16. Dreber, A., Apicella, C., Eisenberg, D., Garcia, J., Zamore, R., Lum, J., and Campbell, B. 2009. The 7R polymorphism in the dopamine receptor D4 gene (DRD4) is associated with financial risk taking in men. *Evolution and Human Behavior*, 30(2): 85–92.

17. Kreek, M., Nielsen, D., Butelman, E., and LaForgen K. 2005. Genetic influences on impulsivity, risk taking, stress responsivity and vulnerability to drug abuse and addiction. *Nature Neuroscience*, 8(11): 1450–1457.

18. Shah, K., Eisen, S., and Xian, H. 2005. Genetic studies of pathological gambling: A review of methodology and analyses of data from the Vietnam era twin registry. *Journal of Gambling Studies*, 21(2): 179–203, pp. 193, 195.

19. Burton, R. 2008. *On Being Certain*, New York: St. Martin's Press.

20. Bouchard, T., and Loehlin, J. 2001. Genes, evolution and personality. *Behavior Genetics*, 31(3): 243–273.

21. Cesarini, D., Dawes, C., Johannesson, M., Lichtenstein, P., and Wallace, B. 2009. Genetic variation in preferences for giving and risk taking. *Quarterly Journal of Economics*, 124(2): 809–842.

22. Wallace, B., Cesarini, D., Lichtenstein, P., and Johannesson, M. 2007. Heritability of ultimatum game responder behavior. *Proceedings of the National Academy of Sciences*, 104 (40): 15631–15634.

23. Oakley, *Evil Genes*.

24. Winterer, G., and Goldman, D., 2003. Genetics of human prefrontal function. *Brain Research Reviews*, 43(1): 13–163; Zuckerman, M., and Kuhlman, D. 2000. Personality and risk taking: Common biosocial factors. *Journal of Personality*, 68(6): 999–1029.

25. Roiser, J., Rogers, R., Cook, L., and Sahakian, B. 2006. The effect of polymorphism at the serotonin transporter gene on decision-making, memory and executive function in ecstasy users and controls. *Psychopharmacology*, 188(2): 213–227.

26. Zuckerman and Kuhlman, Personality and risk taking.

27. Spector, T. 2003. *Your Genes Unzipped*, London: Robson Books.

28. Garrett, B. 2009. *Brain and Behavior*, Los Angeles: Sage.

29. Reif, A., and Lesch, K. 2003. Towards a molecular architecture of personality. *Behavioral Brain Research*, 139(1): 1–20; Comings, D., Gonzalez, N., Wu, S., Gade, R., Muhleman, D., Saucier, G., Johnson, P., Verde, R., Rosenthal, R., Lesieur, H., Rugle, L., Miller, W., and MacMurray, J. 1999. Studies of the 48 bp repeat polymorphism of the DRD4 gene in impulsive, compulsive, and addictive behaviors: Tourette syndrome, ADHD, pathological gambling, and substance abuse. *American Journal of Medical Genetics*, 88(4): 358–368; De Castrol, I., Torres, A., Saiz-Ruiz, J., and Fernadex-Piqueras, J. 1997. Genetic association study between pathological gambling and a functional DNA polymorphism at the D4 receptor gene. *Pharmacogenetics*, 7(5): 345–348.

30. Garrett, *Brain and Behavior*.

31. Zuckerman, M. 1994. *Behavioral Expressions and Biosocial Bases of Sensation Seeking*, Cambridge, UK: Cambridge University Press.

32. Blanco, C., Orensanz-Munoz, L., Blanco-Jerez, C., and Saiz-Ruiz, J. 1996. Pathological gambling and platelet MAO activity: A psychobiological study. *American Journal of Psychiatry*, 153(1): 119–121.

33. Pinker, S. 2008. *The Sexual Paradox: Men, Women, and the Real Gender Gap*, New York: Scribner; White, R., Thornhill, S., and Hampson, E. 2006. Entrepreneurs and evolutionary biology: The relationship between testosterone and new venture creation. *Organizational Behavior and Human Decision Processes*, 100(1): 21–34.

34. Caldu and Dreher, Reward and social information.

35. http://neuroeconomics.typepad.com/neuroeconomics/2003/09/what_is_the_ult.html; Burnham, T. 2007. High testosterone men reject low ultimatum game offers. *Proceedings of the Royal Society*, 274(1623): 2327–2330; Matsushita, R., Baldo, D., Martin, B., and Da Silva, S. 2007. The biological basis of expected utility anomalies. *MPRA Working Paper*, August 17.

36. Cattell, R., 1982. *The Inheritance of Personality and Ability*, New York: Academic Press.

37. Heinstrom, J. 2003. Five personality dimensions and their influence on information behavior. *Information Research*, 9(1), downloaded from http://informationr.net/ir/9-1/paper165.html.

38. Gorla, N., and Lam, Y. 2004. Who should work with whom? *Communications of the ACM*, 47(6): 79–82.

39. Yellen, R., Winniford, M., and Sanford, C. 1995. Extraversion and introversion in electronically-supported meetings. *Information and Management*, 28(1): 63–74.

40. Loehlin, J., McCrae, R., Costa, P., and John, O. 1998. Heritabilities of common and measure-specific components of the big five personality factors. *Journal of Research in Personality*, 32(4): 431–453.

41. Benjamin, J., Li, L., Patterson, C., Greenberg, B., Murphy, D., and Hamer, D. 1996. Population and familial association between the D4 dopamine receptor gene and measures of sensation seeking. *Nature Genetics*, 12: 81–84;

Strobel; A, Wehr, A, Michel, A, and Brocke, B. 1999. Association between the dopamine D4 receptor (DRD4) exon III polymorphism and measures of novelty seeking in a German population. *Molecular Psychiatry*, 4(4): 378–384; Zuckerman, M. 1983. A summing up with special sensitivity to the signals of reward in future research. In M. Zuckerman (ed.), *Biological Bases of Sensation Seeking, Impulsivity, and Anxiety*, Hillsdale, NJ: Lawrence Erlbaum, 249–260.

    42. Harrison, T. 2005. *Instinct*, New York: Warner Business Books.

    43. Heinstrom, Five personality dimensions.

    44. Viken, R., Rose, R., Kaprio, J., and Koskenvuo, M. 1994. A developmental genetic analysis of adult personality: Extraversion and neuroticism from 18 to 59 years of age. *Journal of Personality and Social Psychology*, 66(4): 722–730; Lesch, K. Bengel, D., Heils, S., Sabol, Z., Greenberg, B., Petri, J., Benjamin, C., Muller, C., Hamer, D., and Murphy, D. 1996. Association of anxiety-related traits with a polymorphism in the serotonin transporter gene regulatory region. *Science*, 274 (5292): 1527–1531; Hamer, D., Greenberg, B., Sabol, S., and Murphy, D. 1999. Role of the serotonin transporter gene in temperament and character. *Journal of Personality Disorders*, 13(4): 312–328; Benjamin, J., Ebstein, R., and Lesch, K. 1998. Genes for personality traits: Implications for psychopathology. *International Journal of Neuropsychopharmacology*, 1(2): 153–168; Comings, D., Gade-Andavolu, R., Gonzalez, N., Wu, S., Muhleman, D., Blake, H., Mann, M, Dietz, G., Saucier, G., and MacMurray, J. 2000. A multivariate analysis of 59 candidate genes in personality traits: The temperament and character inventory. *Clinical Genetics*, 58(5): 375–385; Ebstein, R., Benjamin, J., and Belmaker, R. 2002. Behavioral genetics, genomics, and personality. In R. Plomin, J. DeFries, I. Craig, and P. McGuffin (eds.), *Behavioral Genetics in the Postgenomic Era*, Washington, DC: American Psychological Association, 265–388; Zuckerman and Kuhlman, Personality and risk taking; Reif and Lesch, Molecular architecture of personality.

    45. Oakley, *Evil Genes*.

    46. Heinstrom, Five personality dimensions.

    47. Loehlin, J. 1992. *Genes and the Environment in Personality Development*, Newbury Park, CA: Sage Publications; Bouchard and Loehlin, Genes, evolution and personality; Comings et al., Repeat polymorphism.

    48. Loehlin, J. 1992. *Genes and the Environment in Personality Development*. Newbury Park, CA: Sage Publications; Bouchard, T., and Loehlin, J. 2001. Genes, evolution and personality. *Behavior Genetics*, 31(3): 243–273.

    49. Zuckerman, M. 1995. Good and bad humors: Biochemical bases of personality and its disorders. *Psychological Science*, 6(6): 325–332; Bergeman, C., Chipuer, H., Plomin, R., Pedersen, N., McClearn, G., Nesselroade, J., Costa, P., and McCrae, R. 1993. Genetic and environmental effects on openness to experience, agreeableness, and conscientiousness: An adoption/twin study. *Journal of Personality*, 61(2): 159–176; Zuckerman, M. 2005. *Psychobiology of Personality*, Cambridge, UK: Cambridge University Press; Bouchard and Loehlin, Genes, evolution and personality.

    50. Comings et al., 59 candidate genes; Comings et al., Repeat polymorphism; Lesch et al., Anxiety-related traits; Reif and Lesch, Molecular architecture of personality; Hamer et al., Serotonin transporter gene; Benjamin, Ebstein, and Lesch, Genes for personality traits; Jang, K., Livesley, W., Reimann, R., Vernon, P., Hu, S., Angleitner, A., Ando, J., Ono, Y., and Hamer, D. 2001. Covariance

structure of neuroticism and agreeableness: A twin and molecular genetic analysis of the role of the serotonin transporter gene. *Journal of Personality and Social Psychology*, 81(2): 295–304.

51. Heinstrom, Five personality dimensions.

52. Robbins and Judge, *Organizational Behavior*.

53. Bouchard, T., McGue, M., Hur, Y., and Horn, J. 1998. A genetic and environmental analysis of the California Psychological Inventory using adult twins reared apart and together. *European Journal of Personality*, 12(5): 307–320; Bouchard, T., and McGue, M. 1990. Genetic and rearing environmental influences on adult personality: An analysis of twins reared apart. *Journal of Personality* 58(1): 263–282; Jang, K., McCrae, R., Angleitner, A., Riemann, R., and Livesay, W. 1998. Heritability of facet-level traits in a cross-cultural twin sample: Support for a hierarchical model of personality. *Journal of Personality*, 74(6): 1556–1565; Jang, K., Livesay, W., and Vernon, P. 1996. Heritability of the big five personality dimensions and their facets: A twin study. *Journal of Personality*, 64 (3): 577–591; Loehlin, J., and Nichols, J. 1976. *Heredity, Environment, and Personality*, Austin: University of Texas Press; Horn, J., Plomin, R., and Roseman, R. 1976. Heritability of personality traits in adult male twins. *Behavior Genetics*, 6:17–30; Tellegen, A., Bouchard, T., Wilcox, K., Segal, N., Lykken, D, and Roch, S. 1988. Personality similarity in twins reared apart and together. *Journal of Personality and Social Psychology*, 54(6): 1031–1039; Beer, J., Arnold, R., Loehlin, J. 1998. Genetic and Environmental Influences on MMPI Factor Scales: Joint Model Fitting to Twin and Adoption Data. *Journal of Personality and Social Psychology*, 74(3): 818–827; Bergeman et al., Openness to experience.

54. Noble, E., Ozkaragoz, T., Ritchie, T., Zhang, X, Belin, T., and Sparkes, R. 1998. D_2 and D_4 dopamine receptor polymorphisms and personality. *American Journal of Medical Genetics*, 81(3): 257–267; Benjamin et al., Population and familial association; Comings et al., 59 candidate genes; Hamer et al., Serotonin transporter gene; Ebstein, Benjamin, and Belmaker, Behavioral genetics. In Plomin et al., *Behavioral Genetics*, 265–388; Plomin, R., and Caspi, A. 1998. DNA and Personality. *European Journal of Personality*, 12(5): 387–407; Reif and Lesch, Molecular architecture of personality; Hamer, D. 2004. *The God Gene*, New York: Doubleday; Ebstein, R., Segman, R., Benjamin, J., Osher, Y., Nemanov, L., and Belmaker, R. 1997. $5HT_{2C}$ serotonin receptor gene polymorphism associated with the human personality trait of reward dependence: Interaction with dopamine D4 receptor (D4DR) and dopamine D3 Receptor (D3DR) polymorphisms. *American Journal of Medical Genetics*, 74(1): 65–72.

55. Caldu and Dreher, Reward and social information; Rosenbloom, T. 2003. Risk evaluation and risky behavior of high and low sensation seekers. *Social Behavior and Personality*, 31(4): 375–386; Zuckerman and Kuhlman, Personality and risk taking; Schooler, C., Zahn, T., Murphy, D., and Buschbaum, M. 1978. Psychological correlates of monoamine oxidase activity in normals. *The Journal of Nervous and Mental Disease*, 166(3): 177–186; Noble et al., D_2 and D_4 dopamine; Ebstein, Benjamin, and Belmaker, Behavioral genetics. In Plomin et al., *Behavioral Genetics*.

56. Hamer, D., and Copeland, P. 1999. *Living with Our Genes*, New York: Anchor Books

57. Zuckerman, *Psychobiology of Personality*; Zuckerman, *Behavioral Expressions*.

58. Hamer and Copeland, *Living with Our Genes*, p. 48.

59. Baumeister, R., Campbell, J., Kreuger, J., and Vohs, K. 2003. Does high self-esteem cause better performance, interpersonal success, happiness, or healthier lifestyles? *Psychological Science in the Public Interest*, 4(1): 1–44.

60. Neiss, M., Sedikides, C., and Stevenson, J. 2006. Genetic influences on level and stability of self-esteem. *Self and Identity*, 5(3): 247–266.

61. Plomin, R. 1994. *Genetics and Experience: The Interplay between Nature and Nurture*, Thousand Oaks, CA: Sage; Hamer and Copeland, *Living with Our Genes*; Plomin, R., Scheier, M., Bergeman, C., Pedersen, N., Nesselroade, J., and McClearn, G. 1992. Optimism, pessimism, and mental health: A twin/adoption analysis. *Personality and Individual Differences*, 13(8): 921–930.

62. Zuckerman, *Behavioral Expressions*; Schooler et al., Psychological correlates; Zuckerman, M., Buschbaum, M., and Murphy, D. 1980. Sensation seeking and its biological correlates. *Psychological Bulletin*, 88(1): 187–214; Hamer and Copeland, *Living with Our Genes*; Reif and Lesch, Molecular architecture of personality.

63. Robbins and Judge, *Organizational Behavior*.

64. Ibid.

65. Ibid.

66. Staw, B., Bell, N., and Clausen, J. 1986. The dispositional approach to job attitudes: A lifetime longitudinal test. *Administrative Science Quarterly*, 31(1): 56–77.

67. Oakley, *Evil Genes*.

68. Gonzalez, C., Thomas, R., Vanyukov, P. 2005. The relationships between cognitive ability and dynamic decision making. *Intelligence*, 33(2): 169–186.

69. Plomin, R., and Spinath, F. 2004. Intelligence: genetics, genes, and genomics. *Journal of Personality and Social Psychology*, 86(1): 112–129.

70. McGue, M., and Bouchard, T. 1989. Genetic and environmental determinants of information processing and special mental abilities: A twin analysis. In R. Sternberg (ed.), *Advances in the Psychology of Human Intelligence*, Hillsdale, NJ: Lawrence Erlbaum, 5: 7–45; Pedersen, N., Plomin, R., Nesselroade, J., and McClearn, G. 1992. A quantitative genetic analysis of cognitive abilities during the second half of the life span. *Psychological Science*, 3(6): 346–353; Nichols, R. 1978. Twin studies of ability, personality, and interests. *Homo*, 29:158–173; Alarcon, M., Plomin, R., Fulker, D., Corley, R., and DeFries, J. 1998. Multivariate path analysis of specific cognitive abilities data at 12 years of age in the Colorado adoption project. *Behavior Genetics*, 28(4): 255–264; Flint, J. 1999. The genetic basis of cognition. *Brain*, 122(11): 2015–2031; Ando, J., Ono, Y., and Wright, M. 2001. Genetic structure of spatial and verbal working memory. *Behavior Genetics*, 31(6): 615–624; Posthuma, D., de Geus, E., and Boomsma, D. 2002. Genetic contributions to anatomical, behavioral, and neurophysiological indices of cognition. In R. Plomin, J. DeFries, I. Craig, and P. McGuffin (eds.), *Behavioral Genetics in the Postgenomic Era*, Washington, DC: American Psychological Association, 141–161; Wright, M., De Gues, E., Ando, J., Luciano, M., Posthuma, D., Ono, Y., Hansell, N., Baal, C., Hirashi, K., Hasegawa, T., Smith, G., Geffen, G., Geffen, L., Kanba, S., Miyake, A., Martin, N., and Boomsma, D. 2001. Genetics of cognition: Outline of a collaborative twin study. *Twin Research*, 4(1): 48–56; Hamer and Copeland, *Living with Our Genes*; Plomin, R., DeFries, J., McClearn, G., and McGuffin, P. 2001. *Behavioral Genetics*, New York: Worth Publishers; Winterer and Goldman, Human prefrontal function; McClearn, G., Johansson, B., Berg, S., Pedersen, N.,

Ahern, F. Petrill, S., and Plomin, R. 1997. Substantial genetic influence on cognitive abilities in twins 80 or more years old. *Science*, 276(5318): 1560–1563.

71. Wright et al., Genetics of cognition.

72. Finkel, D., Reynolds, C., McArdle, J., and Pedersen, N. 2005. The longitudinal relationship between processing speed and cognitive ability: Genetic and environmental influences. *Behavior Genetics*, 35(5): 535–550; Luciano, M., Wright, M., Smith, G., Geffen, G., Geffen, L., and Martin, N. 2002. Genetic covariance between processing speed and IQ. In R. Plomin, J. DeFries, I. Craig, and P. McGuffin (eds.), *Behavioral Genetics in the Post-genomic Era*, Washington, DC: American Psychological Association, 163–181; Plomin and Spinath, Intelligence.

73. Luciano, M., Wright, M., Geffen, G., Geffen, L., Smith, G., and Martin, N. 2004. A genetic investigation of the covariation among inspection time, choice reaction time, and IQ subtest scores. *Behavior Genetics*, 34(1): 41–50; Luciano, M., Wright, M., Smith, G., Geffen, G., Geffen, L., and Martin, N. 2001. Genetic covariance among measures of information processing speed, working memory and IQ. *Behavior Genetics*, 31(6): 581–592; Deary, I., Spinath, F., and Bates, T. 2006. Genetics of intelligence. *European Journal of Human Genetics*, 14: 690–700.

74. Gray, J., and Thompson, P. 2004. Neurobiology of intelligence: Science and ethics. *Neuroscience*, 5: 471–482; Thompson, P., Cannon, T., Narr, K., van Erp, Poutanen, V., Huttunen, M., Lonnqvist, J., Standertskjold, C., Kaprio, J., Khaledy, M., Dail, R., Zoumalan, C., and Toga, A. 2001. Genetic influences on brain structure. *Nature Neuroscience*, 4(12): 1253–1254; Winterer and Goldman, Human prefrontal function; Hansell, N., Wright, M., Luciano, M., Geffen, G., Geffen, L., and Martin, N. 2005. Genetic covariation between event-related potential (ERP) and behavioral non-ERP measures of working-memory, processing speed, and IQ. *Behavior Genetics*, 35(6): 695–706.

75. Garrett, *Brain and Behavior*; Baare, W., Hulshoff, H., Boomsma, D., Posthuma, D., de Gues, E., Schnack, H., van Haren, N., van Oel, C., and Kahn, R. 2001. Quantitative genetic modeling of variation in human brain morphology. *Cerebral Cortex*, 11(9): 816–824.

76. Plomin, R., and Kosslyn, S. 2001. Genes, brain and cognition. *Nature Neuroscience*, 4(12): 1153–1155; Gray and Thompson, Neurobiology of intelligence; Winterer and Goldman, Human prefrontal function.

77. Egan, M., Kojima, M., Callicott, J., Goldberg, T., Kolachana, B., Bertolino, A., Zaitsev, E., Gold, B., Goldman, D., Dean, M., Lu, B., and Weinberger, D. 2003. The BDNF Va166met polymorphism affects activity-dependent secretion of BDNF and human memory and hippocampal function. *Cell*, 112(2): 257–269; Plomin and Kosslyn, Genes, brain and cognition; Wright et al., Genetics of cognition.

78. Reuter, M., Peters, K., Schroeter, K., Koebke, W., Lenardon, D., Bloch, B., and Hennig, J. 2005. The influence of the dopaminergic system on cognitive function: A molecular genetic approach. *Behavioural Brain Research*, 164(1): 93–99.

79. Previc, F. 1999. Dopamine and the origins of human intelligence. *Brain and Cognition*, 41(3): 299–350.

80. Winterer and Goldman, Human prefrontal function.

81. http://www.encyclopedia.com/doc/1087-WisconsinCardSortingtest.html

82. Tsai, S., Tu, Y., Lin, C., Chen, T., Chen, S., and Hong, C. 2002. Dopamine D2 receptor and n-methyl- *d*-aspartate receptor 2B subunit genetic variants and intelligence. *Neuropsychobiology,* 45(3): 128–130.

83. The first gene marker for IQ? *Science,* 280(5364): 681; Plomin and Spinath, Intelligence.

84. Dick, D., Aliev, F., Kramer, J., Wang, J., Hiinrichs, A., Bertelsen, S., Kuperman, S., Schuckit, M., Nurnburger, J., Edenberg, H., Porjesz, B., Bergleiter, H., Hesselbrock, V., Goate, A., Bierut, L. 2007. Association of CHRM2 with IQ: Converging evidence for a gene influencing intelligence. *Behavior Genetics,* 37(2): 265–272; Deary, Spinath, and Bates, Genetics of intelligence.

85. Ibid.

86. Barbaux, S., Plomin, R., and Whitehead, A. 2000. Polymorphisms of genes controlling homocysteine/folate metabolism and cognitive function. *Neuroreport,* 11(5): 1133–1136, p. 1133.

87. Morley, K., and Montgomery, G. 2001. The genetics of cognitive processes: Candidate genes in humans and animals. *Behavior Genetics,* 31(6): 511–531.

Chapter 6

1. Bouchard, T., McGue, M., Hur, Y., and Horn, J. 1998. A genetic and environmental analysis of the California Psychological Inventory using adult twins reared apart and together. *European Journal of Personality,* 12(5): 307–320.

2. Bouchard, T., and McGue, M. 2003. Genetic and environmental influences on human psychological differences. *Journal of Neurobiology,* 54(1): 4–45.

3. Moloney, D., Bouchard, T., and Segal, N. 1991. A genetic and environmental analysis of the vocational interests of monozygotic and dizygotic twins reared apart. *Journal of Vocational Behavior,* 39(1): 76–109.

4. Zuckerman, M. 1994. *Behavioral Expressions and Biosocial Bases of Sensation Seeking,* Cambridge, UK: Cambridge University Press.

5. Lublin, J. 2009. A CEO gets a rare second act. *Wall Street Journal,* February 3: A1; A12.

6. Eaves, L., and Eysenck, H. 1975. The nature of extraversion: A genetical analysis. *Journal of Personality and Social Psychology,* 32(1); 102–112; Zuckerman, M. 2005. *Psychobiology of Personality,* Cambridge, UK: Cambridge University Press; Saudino, K., Gagne, J., Grant, J., Ibatoulina, A., Marytuina, T., and Ravich-Sherbo, I. 1999. Genetic and environmental influences on personality in adult Russian twins. *International Journal of Behavioral Development,* 23(2): 375–389; Pederson, N., Plomin, R., McClearn, G., and Friberg, L. 1988. Neuroticism, extraversion, and related traits in adult twins reared apart and reared together. *Journal of Personality and Social Psychology,* 55(6): 950–957; Loehlin, J. 1992. *Genes and the Environment in Personality Development,* Newbury Park, CA: Sage Publications; Jang, K., McCrae, R., Angleitner, A., Rieman, R., and Livesley, W. 1998. Heritability of facet-level traits in a cross-cultural twin sample: Support for a hierarchical model of personality. *Journal of Personality and Social Psychology,* 74(6): 1556–1565.

7. Johnson, W., and Kreuger, R. 2004. Genetic and environmental structure of adjectives describing the domains of the big five model of personality: A nationwide US twin study. *Journal of Research in Personality,* 38(5): 448–472.

8. Bouchard, T. 1993. Genetic and environmental influences on adult personality: Evaluating the evidence. In J. Hettema and I. Deary (eds.), *Foundations of Personality*, Dordrecht, Netherlands: Klewer, 15–44; Johnson, W., and Krueger, R. 2004. Genetic and environmental structure of adjectives describing the domains of the big five model of personality: A nationwide US twin study. *Journal of Research in Personality*, 38(5): 448–472; Carey, G. 2003. *Human Genetics for the Social Sciences*, Beverley Hills, CA: Sage.

9. Eaves, L., Heath, A., Martin, N., Maes, H., Neale, M., Kendler, K., Kirk, K., and Corey, L. 1999. Comparing the biological and cultural inheritance of personality and social attitudes in the Virginia 30,000 study of twins and their relatives. *Twin Research*, 2(2): 62–80.

10. Eaves, L., Eysenck, H., and Martin, N. 1989. *Genes, Culture, and Personality*, London: Academic Press.

11. https://psychobiology.wustl.edu/TCI/rewardDependence.html

12. Heiman, N., Stallings, M., Young, S., and Hewitt, J. 2004. Investigating the genetic and environmental structure of Cloninger's personality dimensions in adolescence. *Twin Research*, 7(5): 462–470.

13. This gene was previously known by the symbol AD2.

14. This gene was previously known by the symbol CYP19.

15. This gene was previously known by the symbol PENT.

16. Jang, K., Livesley, W., Reimann, R., Vernon, P., Hu, S., Angleitner, A., Ando, J., Ono, Y., and Hamer, D. 2001. Covariance structure of neuroticism and agreeableness: A twin and molecular genetic analysis of the role of the serotonin transporter gene. *Journal of Personality and Social Psychology*, 81(2): 295–304; Ebstein, R., Benjamin, J., and Belmaker, R. 2002. Behavioral genetics, genomics, and personality. In R. Plomin, J. DeFries, I. Craig, and P. McGuffin (eds.), *Behavioral Genetics in the Postgenomic Era*, Washington, DC: American Psychological Association, 265–388; Ebstein, R., Segman, R., Benjamin, J., Osher, Y., Nemanov, L., and Belmaker, R. 1997. 5HT$_{2C}$ serotonin receptor gene polymorphism associated with the human personality trait of reward dependence: Interaction with dopamine D4 receptor (D4DR) and dopamine D3 receptor (D3DR) polymorphisms. *American Journal of Medical Genetics*, 74(1): 65–72; Comings, D., Gade-Andavolu, R., Gonzalez, N., Wu, S., Muhleman, D., Blake, H., Mann, M, Dietz, G., Saucier, G., and MacMurray, J. 2000. A multivariate analysis of 59 candidate genes in personality traits: The temperament and character inventory. *Clinical Genetics*, 58(5): 375–385; Plomin, R., and Caspi, A. 1998. DNA and Personality. *European Journal of Personality*, 12(5): 387–407; Hamer, D., Greenberg, B., Sabol, S., and Murphy, D. 1999. Role of the serotonin transporter gene in temperament and character. *Journal of Personality Disorders*, 13(4): 312–328.

17. Robbins, S., and Judge, T. 2009. *Organizational Behavior*, 13th edition. Upper Saddle River, NJ: Prentice-Hall.

18. Brenner, Marie, 2002. The Enron Wars. *Vanity Fair*, April: 180–210, downloaded   from   *http://www.maryellenmark.com/text/magazines/vanityfair/ 925E-000–024.html*

19. Vernon, P., Villani, V., Vickers, L., and Harris, J. 2008. A behavioral genetic investigation of the Dark Triad and the Big 5. *Personality and Individual Differences*, 44(1): 445–452; Eaves et al., Virginia 30,000 study.

20. Oakley, B. 2008. *Evil Genes*, New York: Prometheus Books.

21. Olson, J., Vernon, P., Harris, J., and Jang, K. 2001. The heritability of attitudes: A study of twins. *Journal of Personality and Social Psychology*, 80(6): 845–860.

22. This gene was previously known by the symbol DAT1.

23. Reif, A., and Lesch, K. 2003. Towards a molecular architecture of personality. *Behavioral Brain Research,* 139(1): 1–20; Comings et al., 59 candidate genes; Hamer, D. 2004. *The God Gene,* New York: Doubleday; Ebstein et al., 5HT$_{2C}$ serotonin receptor gene; Noble, E., Ozkaragoz, T., Ritchie, T., Zhang, X, Belin, T., and Sparkes, R. 1998. D$_2$ and D$_4$ dopamine receptor polymorphisms and personality. *American Journal of Medical Genetics,* 81(3): 257–267; Plomin and Caspi, DNA and Personality.

24. Harrison, T. 2005. *Instinct,* New York: Warner Business Books, p. 94.

25. Nor would we necessarily want to. Being persistent has its good and bad sides. Spending years writing a novel that no one would ever read, the way Jack Nicholson did in *The Shining,* isn't very useful.

26. Roberts, C., and Johansson, C. 1974. The inheritance of cognitive interest styles among twins. *Journal of Vocational Behavior,* 4(2): 237–243; Betsworth, D., Bouchard, T., Cooper, C., Grotevant, H., Hansen, J., Scarr, S., and Weinberg, R. 1994. Genetic and environmental influences on vocational interests assessed using adoptive and biological families and twins reared apart and together. *Journal of Vocational Behavior,* 44(3): 263–278; Moloney, Bouchard, and Segal, Vocational interests.

27. This gene was previously known by the symbol ADORA2.

28. Hamer et al., Serotonin transporter gene; Ebstein, Benjamin, and Belmaker, Behavioral genetics. In R. Plomin, DeFries, and McGuffin, *Behavioral Genetics;* Comings et al., 59 candidate genes.

29. Robbins and Judge, *Organizational Behavior.*

30. Lublin, Rare second act, p. A12.

31. Bouchard et al., California Psychological Inventory; Loehlin, J., and Gough, H. 1990. Genetic and environmental variation on the California Psychological Inventory vector scales. *Journal of Personality Assessment,* 54(3–4): 463–468.

32. Jang, K., Livesley, W., and Vernon, P. 1998. A twin study of genetic and environmental contributions to gender differences in traits delineating personality disorder. *European Journal of Personality,* 12(5): 331–344; Jang, K., Livesley, W., Vernon, P., and Jackson, D. 1996. Heritability of personality disorder traits: A twin study. *Acta Psychiatrica Scandinavica,* 94(6): 438–444; Livesley, W., Jang, K., Vernon, P. 1988. Phenotypic and genetic structure of traits delineating personality disorder. *Archives of General Psychiatry,* 55(10): 941–948.

33. Plomin, R. 1994. *Genetics and Experience: The Interplay between Nature and Nurture,* Thousand Oaks, CA: Sage.

34. Schnittker, J. 2008. Happiness and success: Genes, families, and the psychological effects of socioeconomic position and social support. *American Journal of Sociology,* 114(S): S233-S259.

35. Zuckerman, *Psychobiology of Personality.*

36. Zuckerman, *Behavioral Expressions;* Schooler, C., Zahn, T., Murphy, D., and Buschbaum, M. 1978. Psychological correlates of monoamine oxidase activity in normals. *The Journal of Nervous and Mental Disease,* 166(3): 177–186; Zuckerman, M., Buschbaum, M., and Murphy, D. 1980. Sensation seeking and its biological correlates. *Psychological Bulletin,* 88(1): 187–214; Hamer, D., and Copeland, P. 1999. *Living with Our Genes,* New York: Anchor Books; Reif and Lesch, Molecular architecture of personality.

37. Pinker, S. 2008. *The Sexual Paradox: Men, Women, and the Real Gender Gap*, New York: Scribner.

38. Caldu, X., and Dreher, J. 2007. Hormonal and genetic influences on processing reward and social information. *Annals of New York Academy of Sciences*, 1118: 43–73.

39. Pinker, *The Sexual Paradox*.

40. Michelini, S., Urbanek, M., Dean, M., and Goldman, D. 2005. Polymorphism and genetic mapping of the human oxytocin receptor gene on chromosome 3. *American Journal of Medical Genetics*, 60(3): 183–187.

41. Stanton, A. 2007. Neural Substrates of Decision-Making in Economic Games, Ph.D. Dissertation, Clairmont Graduate School.

42. Christensem, J., Siggaard, C., Corydon T., DeSancti, T., Kovacs, L., Robertson G., Gregersen, N., and Rittig, S. 2003. Six novel mutations in the arginine vasopressin gene in 15 kindreds with autosomal dominant familial neurohypophyseal diabetes insipidus give further insight into the pathogenesis. *European Journal of Human Genetics*, 12: 44–51.

43. Dabbs, J. 1992. Testosterone and occupational achievement. *Social Forces*, 70(3): 813–824.

44. Brizendine, L. 2006. *The Female Brain*, New York: Broadway Books.

45. Pinker, *The Sexual Paradox*.

46. Ibid.

47. Auletta, K. 2001. *World War 3.0*, New York: Broadway Books, p. 122.

48. Roberts and Johansson, Cognitive interest styles; Betsworth et al., Influences on vocational interests; Moloney, Bouchard, and Segal, Vocational interests.

49. Hamer and Copeland, *Living with Our Genes*.

50. This gene was previously known by the symbols S12, 5-HT1B, HTR1D2, and 5-HT1DB.

51. Oakley, *Evil Genes*.

52. Dabbs, J., and Morris, R. 1990. Testosterone, social class, and antisocial behavior in a sample of 4,462 men. *Psychological Science*, 1(3): 209–211; Comings et al., 59 candidate genes; Hamer and Copeland, *Living with Our Genes*.

53. Pinker, *The Sexual Paradox*.

54. Johnson, A., Vernon, P., Harris, J., and Jang, K. 2004. A behavior genetic investigation of the relationship between leadership and personality. *Twin Research*, 7(1): 27–32.

55. Plomin, R., and Nesselroade, J. 1990. Behavioral genetics and personality change. *Journal of Personality*, 58(1): 191–220.

56. Robbins and Judge, *Organizational Behavior*.

57. Ibid.

58. Zuckerman, M. 1995. Good and bad humors: Biochemical bases of personality and its disorders. *Psychological Science*, 6(6): 325–332; Bergeman, C., Chipuer, H., Plomin, R., Pedersen, N., McClearn, G., Nesselroade, J., Costa, P., and McCrae, R. 1993. Genetic and environmental effects on openness to experience, agreeableness, and conscientiousness: An adoption/twin study. *Journal of Personality*, 61(2): 159–176; Zuckerman, *Psychobiology of Personality*; Bouchard, T., and Loehlin, J. 2001. Genes, evolution and personality. *Behavior Genetics*, 31(3): 243–273; Loehlin, J., McCrae, R., Costa, P., and John, O. 1998. Heritabilities of common and measure-specific components of the big five personality factors. *Journal of Research in Personality*, 32(4): 431–453; Buss, A., Plomin, R., and

Willerman, L. 1972. The inheritance of temperaments. *Journal of Personality*, 41(4): 513–524; Plomin, R., Pedersen, N., McClearn, G., Nesselroade, J., and Bergeman, C. 1988. EAS temperaments during the last half of the life span: Twins reared apart and twins reared together. *Psychology and Aging*, 3(1): 43–50.

59. Reif and Lesch, Molecular architecture of personality; Comings et al., 59 candidate genes; Hamer, *The God Gene*; Ebstein et al., 5HT$_{2C}$ serotonin receptor gene; Noble et al., D$_2$ and D$_4$ dopamine receptor; Plomin and Caspi, DNA and Personality; Jang et al., Neuroticism and agreeableness; Hamer et al., Serotonin transporter gene; Ebstein, Benjamin, and Belmaker, Behavioral genetics. In Plomin et al., *Behavioral Genetics*.

60. Zuckerman, M. 1983. A biological theory of sensation seeking. In M. Zuckerman (ed.), *Biological Bases of Sensation Seeking, Impulsivity, and Anxiety*, Hillsdale, NJ: Lawrence Erlbaum, 37–76.

61. Pinker, *The Sexual Paradox*; Grant, G., and France, J. 2001. Dominance and testosterone in women. *Biological Psychology*, 58(1): 41–47.

62. Miller, J. Z., Rose, R. J. 1982. Familial resemblance in locus of control: A twin-family study of the internal-external scale, *Journal of Personality and Social Psychology*, 42: 535–540; Pedersen, N. L., Gatz, M., Plomin, R., Nesselroade, J.R., McClearn, G.E. 1989. Individual differences in locus of control during the second half of the life span for identical and fraternal twins reared apart and reared together. *Journal of Gerontology*, 44(4): 100–105.

63. Robbins and Judge, *Organizational Behavior*.

64. Noble et al., D$_2$ and D$_4$ dopamine receptor.

65. Baumeister, R., Campbell, J., Kreuger, J., and Vohs, K. 2003. Does high self-esteem cause better performance, interpersonal success, happiness, or healthier lifestyles? *Psychological Science in the Public Interest*, 4(1): 1–44.

66. Harrison, *Instinct*.

67. Hamer and Copeland, *Living with Our Genes*.

68. Robbins and Judge, *Organizational Behavior*.

69. Schnittker, Happiness and success.

Chapter 7

1. Robbins, S., and Judge, T. 2009. *Organizational Behavior*, 13th edition. Upper Saddle River, NJ: Prentice Hall.

2. http://freewill.typepad.com/genetics/leaders_and_followers/index.html

3. Olson, J., Vernon, P., Harris, J., and Jang, K. 2001. The heritability of attitudes: A study of twins. *Journal of Personality and Social Psychology*, 80(6): 845–860.

4. Bouchard, T., McGue, M., Hur, Y., and Horn, J. 1998. A genetic and environmental analysis of the California Psychological Inventory using adult twins reared apart and together. *European Journal of Personality*, 12(5): 307–320.

5. Arvey, R., Rotundo, M., Johnson, W., Zhang, Z., and McGue, M. 2006. The determinants of leadership role occupancy: Genetic and personality factors. *The Leadership Quarterly*, 17(1): 1–20.

6. Arvey, R., Zhang, Z., Avolio, B., and Krueger, R. 2007. Developmental and genetic determinants of leadership role occupancy among women. *Journal of Applied Psychology*, 92(3): 693–706.

7. Oakley, B. 2008. *Evil Genes*, New York: Prometheus Books.

8. http://www.mindtools.com/pages/article/newLDR_84.htm

9. Ibid.

10. Johnson, A., Vernon, P., McCarthy, J., Molson, M., Harris, J., and Jang, K. 1998. Nature vs. nurture: Are leaders born or made? A behavior genetic investigation of leadership style. *Twin Research*, 1(4): 216–223.

11. Johnson, A., Vernon, P., Harris, J., and Jang, K. 2004. A behavior genetic investigation of the relationship between leadership and personality. *Behavior Genetics*, 7(1): 27–32.

12. Ilies, R., Arvey, R., and Bouchard, T. 2006. Darwinism, behavioral genetics, and organizational behavior: A review and agenda for future research. *Journal of Organizational Behavior*, 27(2): 121–141.

13. Ilies, R., Gerhardt, M., and Le, H. 2004. Individual differences in leadership emergence: Integrating meta analytic findings and behavioral genetics estimates. *International Journal of Selection and Assessment*, 12(3): 207–219, p. 217.

14. Robbins and Judge, *Organizational Behavior*.

15. Judge, T., Ilies, R., Bono, J., and Gerhardt, M. 2002. Personality and leadership: A qualitative and quantitative review. *Journal of Applied Psychology*, 87(4): 765–780.

16. Loehlin, J., McCrae, R., Costa, P., and John, O. 1998. Heritabilities of common and measure-specific components of the big five personality factors. *Journal of Research in Personality*, 32(4): 431–453.

17. Simonton, D. 2001. Talent development as a multidimensional, multiplicative, and dynamic process. *Current Directions in Psychological Science*, 10(2): 39–43; Lesch, K. 2002. Neuroticism and serotonin: A developmental genetic perspective. 2002. Behavioral genetics, genomics, and personality. In R. Plomin, J. DeFries, I. Craig, and P. McGuffin (eds.), *Behavioral Genetics in the Postgenomic Era*, Washington, DC: American Psychological Association, 389–423.

18. Harrison, T. 2005. *Instinct*, Boston: Warner Business Books; Judge, T., Ilies, R., Bono, J., and Gerhardt, M. 2002. Personality and leadership: A qualitative and quantitative review. *Journal of Applied Psychology*, 87(4): 765–780.

19. http://freewill.typepad.com/genetics/leaders_and_followers/index.html

20. http://freewill.typepad.com/genetics/2005/03/leadership_abil.html

21. Neiss, M., Sedikides, C., and Stevenson, J. 2006. Genetic influences on level and stability of self-esteem. *Self and Identity*, 5(3): 247–266; Roberts, C., and Johansson, C. 1974. The inheritance of cognitive interest styles among twins. *Journal of Vocational Behavior*, 4(2): 237–243; Betsworth, D., Bouchard, T., Cooper, C., Grotevant, H., Hansen, J., Scarr, S., and Weinberg, R. 1994. Genetic and environmental influences on vocational interests assessed using adoptive and biological families and twins reared apart and together. *Journal of Vocational Behavior*, 44(3): 263–278; Moloney, D., Bouchard, T., and Segal, N. A genetic and environmental analysis of the vocational interests of monozygotic and dizygotic twins reared apart. *Journal of Vocational Behavior*, 39(1): 76–109.

22. Oakley, *Evil Genes*.

23. Arvey et al., Leadership role occupancy.

24. Ibid.

25. Carey, G. 2003. *Human Genetics for the Social Sciences*, Beverley Hills, CA: Sage.

26. Arvey et al., Leadership role occupancy.

27. Robbins and Judge, *Organizational Behavior*.

28. Oakley, *Evil Genes*.

29. Jang, K., Livesley, W., and Vernon, P. 1998. A twin study of genetic and environmental contributions to gender differences in traits delineating personality disorder. *European Journal of Personality*. 12(5): 331–344; Jang, K., Livesley, W., Vernon, P., and Jackson, D. 1996. Heritability of personality disorder traits: A twin study. *Acta Psychiatrica Scandinavica*, 94(6): 438–444. Livesley, W.; Jang, K.; Vernon, P. 1988. Phenotypic and genetic structure of traits delineating personality disorder. *Archives of General Psychiatry*. 55(10): 941–948.

30. Bouchard, T., McGue, T., Hur, Y., and Horn, J. 1998. A genetic and environmental analysis of the California Psychological Inventory using adult twins reared apart and together. *European Journal of Personality*, 12(5): 307–329.

31. Noble, E., Ozkaragoz, T., Ritchie, T., Zhang, X, Belin, T., and Sparkes, R. 1998. D_2 and D_4 dopamine receptor polymorphisms and personality. *American Journal of Medical Genetics*, 81(3): 257–267; Ebstein, R., Segman, R., Benjamin, J., Osher, Y., Nemanov, L., and Belmaker, R. 1997. $5HT_{2C}$ serotonin receptor gene polymorphism associated with the human personality trait of reward dependence: Interaction with dopamine D4 receptor (D4DR) and dopamine D3 Receptor (D3DR) polymorphisms. *American Journal of Medical Genetics*, 74(1): 65–72; Benjamin, J., Li, L., Patterson, C., Greenberg, B., Murphy, D., and Hamer, D. 1996. Population and familial association between the D4 dopamine receptor gene and measures of sensation seeking. *Nature Genetics*, 12(1): 81–84; Comings, D., Gade-Andavolu, R., Gonzalez, N., Wu, S., Muhleman, D., Blake, H., Mann, M, Dietz, G., Saucier, G., and MacMurray, J. 2000. A multivariate analysis of 59 candidate genes in personality traits: The temperament and character inventory. *Clinical Genetics*, 58(5): 375–385; Hamer, D., Greenberg, B., Sabol, S., and Murphy, D. 1999. Role of the serotonin transporter gene in temperament and character. *Journal of Personality Disorders*, 13(4): 312–328; Ebstein, R., Benjamin, J., and Belmaker, R. 2002. Behavioral genetics, genomics, and personality. In R. Plomin et al., *Behavioral Genetics*, 265–388; Plomin, R., and Caspi, A. 1998. DNA and Personality. *European Journal of Personality*, 12(5): 387–407; Reif, A., and Lesch, K. 2003. Towards a molecular architecture of personality. *Behavioral Brain Research*, 139(1): 1–20; Hamer, D. 2004. *The God Gene*, New York: Doubleday.

32. Benjamin et al., Population and familial association; Strobel; A, Wehr, A, Michel, A, and Brocke, B. 1999. Association between the dopamine D4 receptor (DRD4) exon III polymorphism and measures of novelty seeking in a German population. *Molecular Psychiatry*, 4(4): 378–384.

33. Zuckerman, M. 1983. A summing up with special sensitivity to the signals of reward in future research. In M. Zuckerman (ed.), *Biological Bases of Sensation Seeking, Impulsivity, and Anxiety*, Hillsdale, NJ: Lawrence Erlbaum, 249–260.

34. Comings et al., 59 candidate genes; Comings, D., Gonzalez, N., Wu, S., Gade, R., Muhleman, D., Saucier, G., Johnson, P., Verde, R., Rosenthal, R., Lesieur, H., Rugle, L., Miller, W., and MacMurray, J. 1999. Studies of the 48 bp repeat polymorphism of the DRD4 gene in impulsive, compulsive, and addictive behaviors: Tourette syndrome, ADHD, pathological gambling, and substance abuse. *American Journal of Medical Genetics*, 88(4): 358–368; Lesch, K., Bengel, D., Heils, A., Sabol, S., Greenberg, B., Petri, S., Benjamin, J., Muller, C., Hamer, D., and Murphy, D. 1996. Association of anxiety related trait with a polymorphism in the serotonin transporter gene regulation region. *Science*, 274(5292): 1527–1531; Reif and Lesch, Molecular architecture; Hamer et al., Serotonin transporter gene.

35. Johnson et al., A., Vernon, P., Harris, J., and Jang, K. 2004. A behavior genetic investigation of the relationship between leadership and personality. *Twin Research,* 7(1): 27–32.

36. Ibid.

37. Martinuzzi, B. 2006. Optimism: The hidden asset. Downloaded from http://www.mindtools.com/pages/article/newLDR_72.htm

38. http://freewill.typepad.com/genetics/leaders_and_followers/index.html

39. Martinuzzi, Optimism.

40. Plomin, R. 1994. *Genetics and Experience: The Interplay between Nature and Nurture.* Thousand Oaks, CA: Sage; Hamer, D., and Copeland, P. 1999. *Living with Our Genes.* New York: Anchor Books; Plomin, R., Scheier, M., Bergeman, C., Pedersen, N., Nesselroade, J., and McClearn, G. 1992. Optimism, pessimism, and mental health: A twin/adoption analysis. *Personality and Individual Differences,* 13(8): 921–930.

41. Zuckerman, M. 1994. *Behavioral Expressions and Biosocial Bases of Sensation Seeking.* Cambridge, UK: Cambridge University Press; Schooler, C., Zahn, T., Murphy, D., and Buschbaum, M. 1978. Psychological correlates of monoamine oxidase activity in normals. *The Journal of Nervous and Mental Disease,* 166(3): 177–186; Zuckerman, M., Buschbaum, M., and Murphy, D. 1980. Sensation seeking and its biological correlates. *Psychological Bulletin,* 88(1): 187–214; Hamer and Copeland, *Living with Our Genes;* Reif and Lesch, Molecular architecture.

42. Gray, J., and Thompson, P. Neurobiology of intelligence: Science and ethics. *Neuroscience,* 5(6): 471–482; Plomin, General cognitive ability. In R. Plomin et al., *Behavioral Genetics.*

43. Deary, I., Spinath, F., and Bates, T. 2006. Genetics of intelligence. *European Journal of Human Genetics,* 14: 690–700; McGue, M., and Bouchard, T. 1989. Genetic and environmental determinants of information processing and special mental abilities: A twin analysis. In Sternberg, R. (ed.), *Advances in the Psychology of Human Intelligence,* Hillsdale, NJ: Lawrence Erlbaum, 7–45; Scarr, S. 1981. *Race, Social Class, and Individual Differences in I.Q.* Hillsdale, NJ: Lawrence Erlbaum; Bouchard, T., and McGue, M. 1981. Familial studies of intelligence: A review. *Science* 212(4498): 1055–1059; Carey, *Human Genetics;* Gray and Thompson, Neurobiology of intelligence; Wright, M., De Gues, E., Ando, J., Luciano, M., Posthuma, D., Ono, Y., Hansell, N., Baal, C., Hirashi, K., Hasegawa, T., Smith, G., Geffen, G., Geffen, L., Kanba, S., Miyake, A., Martin, N., and Boomsma, D. 2001. Genetics of cognition: Outline of a collaborative twin study. *Twin Research,* 4(1): 48–56; Rose, R., Harris, E., Christian, J., and Nance, W. 1979. Genetic variance in nonverbal intelligence: Data from the kinships of identical twins. *Science,* 205(4411): 1153–1155.

44. Kickul, J., and Neurman, G. 2000. Emergent leadership behaviors: The function of personality and cognitive ability in determining teamwork performance and KSAS. *Journal of Business and Psychology,* 15(1): 27–51; Robbins and Judge, *Organizational Behavior.*

45. Judge, T., Colbert, A., and Ilies, R. 2004. Intelligence and leadership: A quantitative review and test of theoretical propositions. *Journal of Applied Psychology,* 89(3): 542–552.

46. Arvey et al., Leadership role occupancy among women.

47. Ibid.

48. Hamer, *The God Gene.*

49. Olson et al., Heritability of attitudes.

50. http://freewill.typepad.com/genetics/motivation_memory_and_the_brain/index.html

51. Ibid.

52. Ibid.

53. Ilies, Arvey, and Bouchard, Darwinism.

54. Zhang, Z., Ilies, R., and Arvey, R. 2008. Beyond genetic explanations for leadership: The moderating effect of social environment. *Working paper*, Arizona State University.

55. Ibid.

Chapter 8

1. Robbins, S., and Judge, T. 2009. *Organizational Behavior*, 13th edition. Upper Saddle River, NJ: Prentice-Hall.

2. Bouchard, T., McGue, M., Hur, Y., and Horn, J. 1998. A genetic and environmental analysis of the California Psychological Inventory using adult twins reared apart and together. *European Journal of Personality*, 12(5): 307–320.

3. Bouchard, T., and McGue, M. 1990. Genetic and rearing environmental influences on adult personality: An analysis of twins reared apart. *Journal of Personality* 58(1): 263–282; Jang, K., McCrae, R., Angleitner, A., Riemann, R., and Livesay, W. 1998. Heritability of facet-level traits in a cross-cultural twin sample: Support for a hierarchical model of personality. *Journal of Personality*, 74 (6): 1556–1565; Jang, K., Livesay, W., and Vernon, P. 1996. Heritability of the big five personality dimensions and their facets: A twin study. *Journal of Personality*, 64(3): 577–591; Loehlin, J., and Nichols, J. 1976. *Heredity, Environment, and Personality*, Austin: University of Texas Press; Horn, J., Plomin, R., and Roseman, R. 1976. Heritability of personality traits in adult male twins. *Behavior Genetics*, 6(1):17–30; Tellegen, A., Bouchard, T.; Wilcox, K., Segal, N; Lykken, D; and Roch, S. 1988. Personality similarity in twins reared apart and together. *Journal of Personality and Social Psychology*, 54(6): 1031–1039; Beer, J., Arnold, R., Loehlin, J. 1998. Genetic and Environmental Influences on MMPI Factor Scales: Joint Model Fitting to Twin and Adoption Data. *Journal of Personality and Social Psychology*, 74(3): 818–827; Bergeman, C., Chipuer, H., Plomin, R., Pedersen, N., McClearn, G., Nesselroade, J., Costa, P., and McCrae, R. 1993. Genetic and environmental effects on openness to experience, agreeableness, and conscientiousness: An adoption/twin study. *Journal of Personality*, 61(2): 159–176.

4. Johnson, W., and Kreuger, R. 2004. Genetic and environmental structure of adjectives describing the domains of the big five model of personality: A nationwide US twin study. *Journal of Research in Personality*, 38(5): 448–472.

5. Simonton, D. 2007. Talent *and* expertise: The empirical evidence for genetic endowment. *High Ability Studies*, 18(1): 83–84.

6. Keller, L., Arvey, R., Bouchard, T., Segal, N., and Davis, R. 1992. Work values: genetic and environmental influences. *Journal of Applied Psychology*, 77(1): 79–88.

7. This gene was previously known by the symbols TPRH and TPH.

8. Reuter, M., Roth, S., Holve, K, and Hennig, J. 2006. Identification of first candidate genes for creativity: A pilot study. *Brain Research*, 1069(1): 190–197.

9. Simonton, D. 2001. Talent development as a multidimensional, multiplicative, and dynamic process. *Current Directions in Psychological Science*, 10(2): 39–43.

10. Zofkova, I., Zajickova, K., Hill, M., and Horinek, A. 2002. Apolipoprotein E gene determines serum testosterone and dehydroepiandrosterone levels in postmenopausal women. *European Journal of Endocrinology*, 147(4): 503–506.

11. Akinola, M., and Mendes, W. 2008. The dark side of creativity: Biological vulnerability and negative emotions lead to greater artistic creativity. *Personality and Social Psychology Bulletin*, 34(12): 1677–1686.

12. Krug, R., Molle, M., Dodt, C., Fehm, H., and Born, J. 2003. Acute influences of estrogen and testosterone on divergent and convergent thinking in postmenopausal women. *Neurospychopharmacology*, 28(8): 1538–1545.

13. Reuter, M., Panksepp, J., Schnabel, N., Kellerhoff, N., Kempel, P., and Hennig, J. 2005. Personality and biological markers of creativity. *European Journal of Personality*, 19(2): 83–95.

14. Oakley, B. 2008. *Evil Genes*, New York: Prometheus Books.

15. Previc, F. 1999. Dopamine and the origins of human intelligence. *Brain and Cognition*, 41(3): 299–350; Reuter, M., Peters, K., Schroeter, K., Koebke, W., Lenardon, D., Bloch, B., and Hennig, J. 2005. The influence of the dopaminergic system on cognitive function: A molecular genetic approach. *Behavioural Brain Research*, 164(1): 93–99.

16. Robbins and Judge, *Organizational Behavior*.

17. Bouchard, T. 1994. Genes, environment, personality. *Science*, 264(5166): 1700–1; Heath, A., Cloninger, C., and Martin, N. 1994. Testing a model for the genetic structure of personality: A comparison of the personality systems of Cloninger and Eysenck. *Journal of Personality and Social Psychology*, 66(4): 762–775; Loehlin, J., and Gough, H. 1990. Genetic and environmental variation on the California Psychological Inventory vector scales. *Journal of Personality Assessment*, 54(3–4): 463–468.

18. Feist, G. 1999. The influence of personality on artistic and scientific creativity. In R. Sternberg (ed.), *Handbook of Creativity*, Cambridge, UK: Cambridge University Press, 273–296.

19. Kramer, P. 2005. *Against Depression*, New York: Penguin Books.

20. Bouchard, Genes, environment, personality; Heath, A., Cloninger, C., and Martin, N. 1994. Testing a model for the genetic structure of personality: A comparison of the personality systems of Cloninger and Eysenck. *Journal of Personality and Social Psychology*, 66(4): 762–775; Loehlin, J., and Gough, H. 1990. Genetic and environmental variation on the California Psychological Inventory vector scales. *Journal of Personality Assessment*, 54(3–4): 463–468.

21. Robbins and Judge, *Organizational Behavior*.

22. Ibid.

23. Bouchard, Genes, environment, personality; Bouchard and McGue, Environmental influences on adult personality; Jang et al., Heritability of facet-level traits; Jang, Livesay, and Vernon, Heritability of big five; Loehlin and Nichols, *Heredity, Environment, and Personality*; Horn, Plomin, and Roseman, Heritability of personality traits; Tellegen et al., A., Personality similarity; Beer et al., MMPI Factor Scales; Bergeman et al., Openness to experience.

24. Zuckerman, M. 2005. *Psychobiology of Personality*, Cambridge, UK: Cambridge University Press; Hamer, D., and Copeland, P. 1999. *Living with Our Genes*, New York: Anchor Books; Zuckerman, M. 1994. *Behavioral Expressions and Biosocial Bases of Sensation Seeking*, Cambridge, UK: Cambridge University Press; Hur, Y., and Bouchard, T. 1997. The genetic correlation between impulsivity and sensation seeking traits. *Behavior Genetics*, 27(5): 455–463; Tellegen et al., Personality similarity; Saudino, K., Gagne, J., Grant, J., Ibatoulina, A., Marytuina, T.,

and Ravich-Sherbo, I. 1999. Genetic and environmental influences on personality in adult Russian twins. *International Journal of Behavioral Development*, 23(2): 375–389; Jang, K., McCrae, R., Angleitner, A., Rieman, R., and Livesley, W. 1998. Heritability of facet-level traits in a cross-cultural twin sample: Support for a hierarchical model of personality. *Journal of Personality and Social Psychology*, 74(6): 1556–1565.

25. Ebstein, R., Benjamin, J., and Belmaker, R. 2002. Behavioral genetics, genomics, and personality. In R. Plomin, J. DeFries, I. Craig, and P. McGuffin (eds.), *Behavioral Genetics in the Postgenomic Era*, Washington, DC: American Psychological Association, 265–388; Noble, E., Ozkaragoz, T., Ritchie, T., Zhang, X, Belin, T., and Sparkes, R. 1998. D_2 and D_4 dopamine receptor polymorphisms and personality. *American Journal of Medical Genetics*, 81(3): 257–267; Comings, D., Gade-Andavolu, R., Gonzalez, N., Wu, S., Muhleman, D., Blake, H., Mann, M, Dietz, G., Saucier, G., and MacMurray, J. 2000. A multivariate analysis of 59 candidate genes in personality traits: The temperament and character inventory. *Clinical Genetics*, 58(5): 375–385; Caldu, X., and Dreher, J. 2007. Hormonal and genetic influences on processing reward and social information. *Annals of New York Academy of Sciences*, 1118: 43–73.

26. Comings, D., Rosenthal, R., Lesieur, H., Rugle, L., Muhleman, D., Chiu, C., Dietz, G., and Gade, R. 1996. A study of the dopamine D2 receptor gene in pathological gambling. *Pharmacogenetics*, 6(3): 223–234.

27. Hamer and Copeland, *Living with Our Genes*.

28. Ibid.

29. Zuckerman, *Behavioral Expressions*; Okamoto, K., and Takaki, E. 1992. Structure of creativity measurements and their correlations with sensation seeking and need for uniqueness. *The Japanese Journal of Experimental Social Psychology*, 31(3): 203–210; Hamer and Copeland, *Living with Our Genes*.

30. Zuckerman, M. 1983. A biological theory of sensation seeking. In M. Zuckerman (ed.), *Biological Bases of Sensation Seeking, Impulsivity, and Anxiety*, Hillsdale, NJ: Lawrence Erlbaum, 229–248.

31. Hamer and Copeland, *Living with Our Genes*.

32. Zuckerman, *Behavioral Expressions*, p. 372.

33. A complete fatalist, for instance, has very external locus of control.

34. Robbins and Judge, *Organizational Behavior*.

35. Miller, J, Z., Rose, R. J. 1982. Familial resemblance in locus of control: a twin-family study of the internal-external scale, *Journal of Personality and Social Psychology*, 42(3): 535–540.

36. http://www.personalityresearch.org/papers/porzio.html

37. Hamer, D. 2004. *The God Gene*, New York: Doubleday.

38. Reuter et al., Markers of creativity.

39. Wright, L. 1997. *Twins and What They Tell Us about Who We Are*, New York: John Wiley and Sons.

40. Eaves, L., Eysenck, H., and Martin, N. 1989. *Genes, Culture, and Personality*, London: Academic Press.

41. Feist, Influence of personality. In Sternberg, *Handbook of Creativity*.

42. Fredrickson, B. 1998. What good are positive emotions? *Review of General Psychology*, 2(3): 300–319.

43. Robbins and Judge, *Organizational Behavior*.

44. Plomin, R. 1994. *Genetics and Experience: The Interplay between Nature and Nurture*, Thousand Oaks, CA: Sage; Hamer and Copeland, *Living with Our Genes*;

Plomin, R., Scheier, M., Bergeman, C., Pedersen, N., Nesselroade, J., and McClearn, G. 1992. Optimism, pessimism, and mental health: A twin/adoption analysis. *Personality and Individual Differences*, 13(8): 921–930.

45. Zuckerman, *Behavioral Expressions;* Schooler, C., Zahn, T., Murphy, D., and Buschbaum, M. 1978. Psychological correlates of monoamine oxidase activity in normals. *The Journal of Nervous and Mental Disease*, 166(3): 177–186; Zuckerman, M., Buschbaum, M., and Murphy, D. 1980. Sensation seeking and its biological correlates. *Psychological Bulletin*, 88(1): 187–214; Hamer and Copeland, *Living with Our Genes;* Reif, A., and Lesch, K. 2003. Towards a molecular architecture of personality. *Behavioral Brain Research*, 139(1): 1–20.

Chapter 9

1. Harrison, T. 2005. *Instinct*, New York: Warner Business Books.

2. Nicolaou, N., Shane, S., Cherkas, L., Hunkin, J., and Spector, T. 2008. Is the tendency to engage in entrepreneurship genetic? *Management Science*, 54(1): 167–179.

3. Zhang, Z., Zyphur, M., Narayanan, J., Arvey, R., Chaturvedi, S., Avolio, B., Lichtenstein, B., Larsson, G. Forthcoming. The genetic basis of entrepreneurship: Effects of gender and personality. *Organizational Behavior and Human Decision Processes*.

4. Nicolaou, N., and Shane, S. 2009. Entrepreneurship and occupational choice: Genetics and environmental influences. Working Paper, University of Cyprus.

5. Nicolaou, N., Shane, S., Cherkas, L., and Spector, T. 2009. Opportunity recognition and the tendency to be an entrepreneur: A bivariate genetics perspective, Working paper, University of Cyprus.

6. Harrison, *Instinct*.

7. Willerman, L. 1973. Activity level and hyperactivity in twins. *Child Development*, 44(2): 288–293.

8. Buss, A., Plomin, R., and Willerman, L. 1972 The inheritance of temperaments. *Journal of Personality*, 41(4), 513–524; Plomin, R., Pedersen, N., McClearn, G., Nesselroade, J., and Bergeman, C. 1988. EAS temperaments during the last half of the life span: Twins reared apart and twins reared together. *Psychology and Aging*, 3(1): 43–50; Scarr, S. 1966. Genetic factors in activity motivation. *Child Development*, 37(3): 663–673.

9. Rutter, M. 2006. *Genes and Behavior*. Oxford, UK: Blackwell; Sherman, D., McGue, M., and Iacono, W. 1997. Twin concordances for attention deficit hyperactivity disorder: A comparison of teachers' and mothers' reports. *American Journal of Psychiatry*, 154(4): 532–535.

10. This gene was previously known by the symbols ADRA2, ADRA2R, and ADRAR.

11. Waldman, I., and Gizer, I. 2006. The genetics of attention deficit hyperactivity disorder. *Clinical Psychology Review*, 26(4): 396–432.

12. Maestu, J., Allik, J., Merenakk, L., Eensoo, D., Parik, J., Veidebaum, T., and Harro, J. 2008. Associations between an alpha 2A adrenergic receptor gene polymorphism and adolescent personality. *American Journal of Medical Genetics Part B: Neuropsychiatric Genetics*, 147B(4): 418–423.

13. Waldman and Gizer, Attention deficit hyperactivity disorder; Cook, E, Stein, M., Krasowski, M., Cox, N., Olkon, D., Kieffer, J., and Leventhal, B. 1995.

Association of attention-deficit disorder and the dopamine transporter gene. *American Journal of Human Genetics,* 56(4): 993–998.

14. Castellanos, F., and Tannock, R. 2002. Neuroscience of attention-deficit/hyperactivity disorder: The search for endophenotypes. *Nature Reviews,* 3: 617–629; Waldman and Gizer, Attention deficit hyperactivity disorder; Comings, D., Gonzalez, N., Wu, S., Gade, R., Muhleman, D., Saucier, G., Johnson, P., Verde, R., Rosenthal, R., Lesieur, H., Rugle, L., Miller, W., and MacMurray, J. 1999. Studies of the 48 bp repeat polymorphism of the DRD4 gene in impulsive, compulsive, and addictive behaviors: Tourette syndrome, ADHD, pathological gambling, and substance abuse. *American Journal of Medical Genetics,* 88(4): 358–368; Okuyama, Y., Ishiuro, H., Nankai, M., Shibuya, H., Watanabe, A., and Arinami, T. 2000. Identification of a polymorphism in the promoter region of DRD4 associated with the human novelty seeking personality trait. *Molecular Psychiatry,* 5(1): 64–69; Plomin, R., DeFries, J., McClearn, G., and McGuffin, P. 2001. *Behavioral Genetics,* New York: Worth Publishers; Spector, T. 2003. *Your Genes Unzipped,* London: Robson Books.

15. Blum, K., Sheridan, P., Wood, R., Braverman, E., Chen, T., Cull, J., and Comings, D. 1996. The dopamine receptor gene as a determinant of reward deficiency syndrome. *Journal of the Royal Society of Medicine,* 89(7): 396–400.

16. This gene was previously known by the symbols HTR2 and 5-HT2A.

17. Waldman, I., and Gizer, I. 2006. The genetics of attention deficit hyperactivity disorder. *Clinical Psychology Review,* 26(4): 396–432; Ebstein, R., Benjamin, J., and Belmaker, R. 2002. Behavioral genetics, genomics, and personality. In R. Plomin, J. DeFries, I. Craig, and P. McGuffin (eds.), *Behavioral Genetics in the Postgenomic Era,* Washington, DC: American Psychological Association, 265–388.

18. This gene was previously known by the symbol AADC.

19. Waldman and Gizer, Attention deficit hyperactivity disorder.

20. Mannuzzza, S., Klein, R., Bessler, A., Malloy, P. LaPadula, M. 1993. Adult outcome of hyperactive boys: Education achievement, occupational rank and psychiatric status. *Archives of General Psychiatry,* 50(7): 565–576.

21. Pinker, S. 2008. *The Sexual Paradox: Men, Women, and the Real Gender Gap,* New York: Scribner.

22. Woodyard, C. 2002. Jet Blue soars on CEO's creativity. *USA Today,* October 8. Downloaded from http://www.usatoday.com/travel/news/2002/2002-10-08-jetblue-ceo.htm.

23. McGue, M., and Bouchard, T. 1989. Genetic and environmental determinants of information processing and special mental abilities: A twin analysis. In R. Sternberg (ed.), *Advances in the Psychology of Human Intelligence,* Hillsdale, NJ: Lawrence Erlbaum, 7–45; Pedersen, N., Plomin, R., Nesselroade, J., and McClearn, G. 1992. A quantitative genetic analysis of cognitive abilities during the second half of the life span. *Psychological Science,* 3(6): 346–353; Nichols, R. 1978. Twin studies of ability, personality, and interests. *Homo,* 29:158–173; Alarcon, M., Plomin, R., Fulker, D., Corley, R., and DeFries, J. 1998. Multivariate path analysis of specific cognitive abilities data at 12 years of age in the Colorado adoption project. *Behavior Genetics,* 28(4): 255–264; Flint, J. 1999. The genetic basis of cognition. *Brain,* 122(11): 2015–2031; Ando, J., Ono, Y., and Wright, M. 2001. Genetic structure of spatial and verbal working memory. *Behavior Genetics,* 31(6): 615–624; Posthuma, D., de Geus, E., and Boomsma, D. 2002. Genetic contributions to anatomical, behavioral, and neurophysiological indices of cognition. In Plomin et al., *Behavioral Genetics,* 141–161; Wright, M., De Gues, E., Ando, J.,

Luciano, M., Posthuma, D., Ono, Y., Hansell, N., Baal, C., Hirashi, K., Hasegawa, T., Smith, G., Geffen, G., Geffen, L., Kanba, S., Miyake, A., Martin, N., and Boomsma, D. 2001. Genetics of cognition: Outline of a collaborative twin study. *Twin Research*, 4(1): 48–56; Hamer, D., and Copeland, P. 1999. *Living with Our Genes*, New York: Anchor Books; Plomin et al., *Behavioral Genetics*; Winterer, G., and Goldman, D., 2003. Genetics of human prefrontal function. *Brain Research Reviews*, 43(1): 13–163; McClearn, G., Johansson, B., Berg, S., Pedersen, N., Ahern, F. Petrill, S., and Plomin, R. 1997. Substantial genetic influence on cognitive abilities in twins 80 or more years old. *Science*, 276(5318): 1560–1563.

24. Wainwright, M., Wright, M., Geffen, G., Luciano, M., and Martin, N. 2004. Genetic and environmental sources of covariance between reading tests used in neuropsychological assessment and IQ subtests. *Behavior Genetics*, 34(4): 365–376; Finkel, D., Reynolds, C., McArdle, J., and Pedersen, N. 2005. The longitudinal relationship between processing speed and cognitive ability: Genetic and environmental influences. *Behavior Genetics*, 35(5): 535–550; Luciano, M., Wright, M., Smith, G., Geffen, G., Geffen, L., and Martin, N. 2002. Genetic covariance between processing speed and IQ. In Plomin et al., *Behavioral Genetics*, 163–181; Plomin, R., and Spinath, F. 2004. Intelligence: genetics, genes, and genomics. *Journal of Personality and Social Psychology*, 86(1): 112–129; Luciano, M., Wright, M., Geffen, G., Geffen, L., Smith, G., and Martin, N. A genetic investigation of the covariation among inspection time, choice reaction time, and IQ subtest scores. *Behavior Genetics*, 34(1): 41–50; Deary, I., Spinath, F., and Bates, T. 2006. Genetics of intelligence. *European Journal of Human Genetics*, 14: 690–700; Previc, F. 1999. Dopamine and the origins of human intelligence. *Brain and Cognition*, 41(3): 299–350; Reuter, M., Peters, K., Schroeter, K., Koebke, W., Lenardon, D., Bloch, B., and Hennig, J. 2005. The influence of the dopaminergenic system on cognitive function: A molecular genetic approach. *Behavioural Brain Research*, 164(1): 93–99.

25. Tsai, S., Tu, Y., Lin, C., Chen, T., Chen, S., and Hong, C. 2002. Dopamine D2 receptor and n-methyl- d-aspartate receptor 2B subunit genetic variants and intelligence. *Neuropsychobiology*, 45(3): 128–130; Winterer and Goldman, Prefrontal function; Reuter et al., Dopaminergic system; Plomin and Spinath, Intelligence; Dick, D., Aliev, F., Kramer, J., Wang, J., Hiinrichs, A., Bertelsen, S., Kuperman, S., Schuckit, M., Nurnburger, J., Edenberg, H., Porjesz, B., Bergleiter, H., Hesselbrock, V., Goate, A., and Bierut, L. 2007. Association of CHRM2 with IQ: Converging evidence for a gene influencing intelligence. *Behavior Genetics*, 37 (2): 265–272; Deary, Spinath, and Bates, Genetics of intelligence; Barbaux, S., Plomin, R., and Whitehead, A. 2000. Polymorphisms of genes controlling homocysteine/folate metabolism and cognitive function. *Neuroreport*, 11(5): 1133–1136.

26. De Wit, G. 1993. Models of self-employment in a competitive market. *Journal of Economic Surveys*, 7(4): 367–397; De Wit, G. and Winden, F. 1989. An empirical analysis of self-employment in the Netherlands. *Small Business Economics*, 1(4): 263–272.

27. Pinker, *The Sexual Paradox*.

28. Cass Business School. 2007. *Failures in Education System Cause UK to Produce Less Dyslexic Entrepreneurs than the US*. November 15. Downloaded from http://www.cass.city.ac.uk/press/press_release_pdfs/Dyslexia%20-%20education.pdf

29. Stromsworld, K. 2001. The heritability of language: A review and meta analysis of twin, adoption, and linkage studies. *Language*, 77(4): 647–723; Pinker, *The Sexual Paradox*.

30. This gene was previously known by the symbols DUTT1, FLJ21882, and SAX3.

31. Morley, K., and Montgomery, G. 2001. The genetics of cognitive processes: Candidate genes in humans and animals. *Behavior Genetics*, 31(6): 511–531; Galaburda, A., LoTurk, J., Ramus F., Fitch, R., and Rosen, G. 2006. From genes to behavior in developmental dyslexia. *Nature Neuroscience*, 9(10): 1213–1217.

32. Personally, I am a bit skeptical that the primary way in which our genes affect our tendency to start companies is through our personalities, a point which I have expressed in my other books. Nevertheless, this explanation should be tested and I present the evidence for it here.

33. Bouchard, T. 1994. Genes, environment, and personality. *Science*, 264 (5166): 1700–1701; Barrick, M. R., and Mount, M. K. 1991. The Big Five personality dimensions and job performance: A meta-analysis. Personnel Psychology, 44(1): 1–26; Zhao, H., and Seibert, S. 2006. The big five personality dimensions and entrepreneurial status: A meta analytic review. *Journal of Applied Psychology*, 91(2): 259–271.

34. Bouchard, T., and McGue, M. 1990. Genetic and rearing environmental influences on adult personality: An analysis of twins reared apart. *Journal of Personality* 58(1): 263–282; Jang, K., Livesay, W., and Vernon, P. 1996. Heritability of the big five personality dimensions and their facets: A twin study. *Journal of Personality*, 64(3): 577–591; Loehlin, J., and Nichols, J. 1976. *Heredity, Environment, and Personality*. Austin: University of Texas Press; Tellegen, A., Bouchard, T.; Wilcox, K., Segal, N.; Lykken, D.; and Roch, S. 1988. Personality similarity in twins reared apart and together. *Journal of Personality and Social Psychology*, 54(6): 1031–1039; Reimann, R. Angleitner, A., and Strelau, J. 1997. Sociability and positive emotionality: Genetic and environmental contributions to the covariation between different facets of extraversion. *Journal of Personality*, 65(3): 449–475; Loehlin, J. 1992. *Genes and the Environment in Personality Development*, Newbury Park, CA: Sage Publications; Loehlin, J., McCrae, R., Costa, P., and John, O. 1998. Heritabilities of common and measure-specific components of the big five per sonality factors. *Journal of Research in Personality*, 32(4): 431–453; Eaves, L., and Eysenck, H. 1975. The nature of extraversion: A genetical analysis. *Journal of Personality and Social Psychology*, 32(1): 102–112; Riemann, R., Angleitner, A, Strelau, J. 1997. Genetic and environmental influences on personality: A study of twins reared together using the self- and peer report NEO-FFI scales. *Journal of Personality*, 65(3): 449–475.

35. Benjamin, J., Li, L., Patterson, C., Greenberg, B., Murphy, D., and Hamer, D. 1996. Population and familial association between the D4 dopamine receptor gene and measures of sensation seeking. *Nature Genetics*, 12: 81–84; Strobel A., Wehr, A., Michel, A., and Brocke, B. 1999. Association between the dopamine D4 receptor (DRD4) exon III polymorphism and measures of novelty seeking in a German population. *Molecular Psychiatry*, 4(4): 378–384; Farde, L., and Gusavsson, J. 1997. D2 dopamine receptors and personality traits. *Nature*, 385(6617): 590.

36. Zhao and Seibert, S. 2006. Big five and entrepreneurial status.

37. Burke, A. E., FitzRoy, F. R., Nolan, M. A. 2000. When less is more: distinguishing between entrepreneurial choice and performance. Oxford Bulletin of Economics and Statistics, 62(5): 567–587.

38. Zhang et al., Genetic basis of entrepreneurship.

39. Nicolaou, N., Shane, S., Spector, T., and Cherkas, L. 2008. Entrepreneurship and the big five personality traits: A behavioral genetics perspective. Working paper, University of Cyprus.

40. Bouchard, T., McGue, M., Hur, Y., and Horn, J. 1998. A genetic and environmental analysis of the California Psychological Inventory using adult twins reared apart and together. *European Journal of Personality*, 12(5): 307–320; Bouchard and McGue, Environmental influences on adult personality; Jang, K., McCrae, R., Angleitner, A., Riemann, R., and Livesay, W. 1998. Heritability of facet-level traits in a cross-cultural twin sample: Support for a hierarchical model of personality. *Journal of Personality*, 74(6): 1556–1565; Jang, Livesay, and Vernon, Heritability of big five; Loehlin and Nichols, *Heredity, Environment, and Personality*; Horn, J., Plomin, R., and Roseman, R. 1976. Heritability of personality traits in adult male twins. *Behavior Genetics*, 6: 17–30; Tellegen et al., Twins reared apart and together; Beer, J., Arnold, R., Loehlin, J. 1998. Genetic and Environmental Influences on MMPI Factor Scales: Joint Model Fitting to Twin and Adoption Data. *Journal of Personality and Social Psychology*, 74(3): 818–827; Loehlin, *Genes and the Environment*; Loehlin et al., Heritabilities of big five; Carey, G. 2003. *Human Genetics for the Social Sciences*, Beverley Hills, CA: Sage; Zuckerman, M. 2005. *Psychobiology of Personality*, Cambridge, UK: Cambridge University Press.

41. Lesch, K. Bengel, D., Heils, S., Sabol, Z., Greenberg, B., Petri, J., Benjamin, C., Muller, C., Hamer, D., and Murphy, D. 1996. Association of anxiety-related traits with a polymorphism in the serotonin transporter gene regulatory region. *Science*, 274(5292): 1527–1531; Strobel, A., Gutknecht, L., Roth, C., Reif, A., Mossner, R., Zeng, Y., Brocke, B., and Lesch, K. 2003. Allelic variation in 5-HT1A receptor expression is associated with anxiety and depression-related personality traits. *Journal of Neural Transmission*, 110(12): 1445–1453; Benjamin, J., Ebstein, R., and Lesch, K. 1998. Genes for personality traits: Implications for psychopathology. *International Journal of Neuropsychopharmacology*, 1(2): 153–168; Hamer and Copeland, *Living with Our Genes*; Ebstein, Benjamin, and Belmaker, Behavioral genetics, genomics, and personality. In Plomin et al., *Behavioral Genetics*; Zuckerman, M., and Kuhlman, D. 2000. Personality and risk taking: Common biosocial factors. *Journal of Personality*, 68(6): 999–1029; Hamer, D., Greenberg, B., Sabol, S., and Murphy, D. 1999. Role of the serotonin transporter gene in temperament and character. *Journal of Personality Disorders*, 13(4): 312–328; Winterer and Goldman, Prefrontal function; Comings, D., Gade-Andavolu, R., Gonzalez, N., Wu, S., Muhleman, D., Blake, H., Mann, M, Dietz, G., Saucier, G., and MacMurray, J. 2000. A multivariate analysis of 59 candidate genes in personality traits: The temperament and character inventory. *Clinical Genetics*, 58(5): 375–385.

42. Lesch, K. 2002. Neuroticism and serotonin: A developmental genetic perspective. 2002. Behavioral genetics, genomics, and personality. In Plomin et al., *Behavioral Genetics*, 389–423; Greenberg, B., Li, Q., Lucas, F., Hu, S., Sirota, L., Benjamin, J., Lesch, K., Hamer, D., and Murphy, D. 2000. Association between the serotonin transporter promoter polymorphism and personality traits in a primarily female population sample. *American Journal of Medical Genetics*, 96(2): 202–216; Hamer et al., Serotonin transporter gene; Lesch, K., Bengel, D., Heils, A., Sabol, S., Greenberg, B., Petri, S., Benjamin, J., Muller, C., Hamer, D., and Murphy, D. 1996. Association of anxiety related trait with a polymorphism in the serotonin transporter gene regulation region. *Science*, 274 (5292): 1527–1531.

43. Rauch, A., and Frese, M. 2007. Let's put the person back into entrepreneurship research: A meta-analysis on the relationship between business owners' personality traits, business creation, and success. *European Journal of Work and Organizational Psychology*, 16(4): 353–385.

44. Zhao and Seibert. Big five and entrepreneurial status.

45. Harrison, *Instinct*, p. 108.

46. Wooten, K., Timmerman, T., Folger, R. 1999. The use of personality and the five-factor model to predict new business ventures: From outplacement to start-up. *Journal of Vocational Behavior*, 54(1): 82–101.

47. Brandstetter, H. 1997. Becoming an entrepreneur—a question of personality structure? *Journal of Economic Psychology*, 18(2–3): 157–177.

48. Zhao and Seibert. Big five and entrepreneurial status.

49. Blanchflower, D., and Oswald, A. 1998. What makes an entrepreneur? *Journal of Labor Economics*, 16(1): 26–60.

50. Barrick, M. R., and Mount, M. K., Big Five.

51. Zuckerman, *Psychobiology of Personality*; Bouchard, T., and Loehlin, J. 2001. Genes, evolution and personality. *Behavior Genetics*, 31(3): 243–273; Zuckerman, M. 1995. Good and bad humors: Biochemical bases of personality and its disorders. *Psychological Science*, 6(6): 325–332; Bergeman, C., Chipuer, H., Plomin, R., Pedersen, N., McClearn, G., Nesselroade, J., Costa, P., and McCrae, R. 1993. Genetic and environmental effects on openness to experience, agreeableness, and conscientiousness: An adoption/twin study. *Journal of Personality*, 61(2): 159–176.

52. Comings et al., 59 candidate genes; Comings et al., DRD4 gene; Lesch et al., Anxiety related trait with polymorphism; Reif, A., and Lesch, K. 2003. Towards a molecular architecture of personality. *Behavioral Brain Research*, 139(1): 1–20; Hamer et al., Serotonin transporter gene.

53. Jang, K., Livesley, W., Reimann, R., Vernon, P., Hu, S., Angleitner, A., Ando, J., Ono, Y., and Hamer, D. 2001. Covariance structure of neuroticism and agreeableness: A twin and molecular genetic analysis of the role of the serotonin transporter gene. *Journal of Personality and Social Psychology*, 81(2): 295–304.

54. Zhao and Seibert. Big five and entrepreneurial status.

55. Wooten, Timmerman, and Folger, Personality and the five-factor model

56. Zhao and Seibert. Big five and entrepreneurial status.

57. Bergeman et al., Openness to experience.

58. Bouchard et al., California Psychological Inventory; Bouchard and McGue, Environmental influences on adult personality; Jang et al., Heritability of facet-level traits; Jang, Livesay, and Vernon, Heritability of big five; Loehlin and Nichols, *Heredity, Environment, and Personality*; Horn, Plomin, and Roseman, Heritability of personality traits; Tellegen et al., Personality similarity; Beer, Arnold, and Loehlin, Influences on MMPI Factor Scales; Bergeman et al., Openness to experience.

59. Noble, E., Ozkaragoz, T., Ritchie, T., Zhang, X, Belin, T., and Sparkes, R. 1998. D_2 and D_4 dopamine receptor polymorphisms and personality. *American Journal of Medical Genetics*, 81(3): 257–267; Benjamin et al., D4 dopamine receptor gene; Comings et al., 59 candidate genes; Hamer et al., Serotonin transporter gene; Ebstein, Benjamin, and Belmaker, Behavioral genetics, genomics, and personality. In Plomin et al., *Behavioral Genetics*; Plomin, R., and Caspi, A. 1998. DNA and Personality. *European Journal of Personality*, 12(5): 387–40; Ebstein, R.,

Segman, R., Benjamin, J., Osher, Y., Nemanov, L., and Belmaker, R. 1997. 5HT$_{2C}$ serotonin receptor gene polymorphism associated with the human personality trait of reward dependence: Interaction with dopamine D4 receptor (D4DR) and dopamine D3 Receptor (D3DR) polymorphisms. *American Journal of Medical Genetics*, 74(1): 65–72; Reif and Lesch, Molecular architecture of personality; Hamer, D. 2004. *The God Gene*, New York: Doubleday.

60. Locke, E., and Baum, R. 2007. Entrepreneurial motivation. In J. Baum, M. Frese and R. Baron (eds.), *The Psychology of Entrepreneurship*, Mahwah, NJ: Lawrence Erlbaum, 41–65; Zhao and Seibert, Big five and entrepreneurial status.

61. Zhao and Seibert, Big Five and entrepreneurial status.

62. Wyly, S. 2008. *1,000 Dollars and an Idea*, New York: Newmarket Press, p. 63.

63. Zhao and Seibert, Big five and entrepreneurial status.

64. Loehlin, *Genes and the Environment*; Bouchard and Loehlin, Genes, evolution and personality.

65. Comings et al., DRD4 gene.

66. Zhao and Seibert. Big five and entrepreneurial status.

67. Nicolaou et al., Entrepreneurship.

68. Nicolaou et al., Openness to experience.

69. Nicolaou et al., Entrepreneurship.

70. Rotter, J. 1966. Generalised expectancies for internal versus external control of reinforcement, *Psychological Monographs*, 80 (Whole No. 609).

71. Miller, J., and Rose, R. 1982. Familial resemblance in locus of control: a twin-family study of the internal-external scale, *Journal of Personality and Social Psychology*, 42: 535–540; Pedersen, N. L., Gatz, M., Plomin, R., Nesselroade, J.R., and McClearn, G.E. 1989. Individual differences in locus of control during the second half of the life span for identical and fraternal twins reared apart and reared together. *Journal of Gerontology*, 44(4): 100–105.

72. Rauch and Frese, Let's put the person; Wiley; Rauch, A., and Frese, M. 2007. Born to be an entrepreneur? Revisiting the personality approach to entrepreneurship. In Baum, Frese and Baron, *Psychology of Entrepreneurship*, pp. 41–66.

73. Rauch and Frese, Let's put the person; Zhao and Seibert. Big five and entrepreneurial status.

74. Schiller, B., and Crewson, P. 1997. Entrepreneurial origins: A longitudinal inquiry. *Economic Inquiry*, 35(3): 523–531.

75. Neiss, M., Stevenson, J., Sedikides, C., Finkel, E., Kumashiro, M., and Rusbult, C. 2005. Executive self, self-esteem, and negative affectivity: Relations at the phenotypic and genotypical level. *Journal of Personality and Social Psychology*, 89(4): 593–606; Lesch et al., Anxiety-related traits.

76. Rauch and Frese, Let's put the person.

77. Baron, R., and Markman, G. 1999. Cognitive mechanisms: Potential differences between entrepreneurs and non-entrepreneurs. In P. Reynolds, W. Bygrave, S. Manigart, C. Mason, G. Meyer, H. Sapienza, and K. Shaver (eds.), *Frontiers of Entrepreneurship Research*, Babson Park: Babson College, 123–137; Robinson, P., Stimpson, D., Heufner, J., and Hunt, H. 1991. An attitude approach to the prediction of entrepreneurship. *Entrepreneurship Theory and Practice*, 15(4): 13–31; Rauch and Frese, Let's put the person.

78. Zietsma, C. 1999. Opportunity knocks—or does it hide? An examination of the role of opportunity recognition in entrepreneurship. In Reynolds et al., *Frontiers of Entrepreneurship Research*, 242–246.

79. Krueger, N., and Dickson, P. 1993. How believing ourselves increases risk-taking: Perceived self-efficacy and opportunity recognition. *Decision Sciences,* 25(3): 385–400.

80. Zuckerman, *Psychobiology of Personality;* Hamer and Copeland, *Living with Our Genes;* Zuckerman, M. 1994. *Behavioral Expressions and Biosocial Bases of Sensation Seeking.* Cambridge, UK: Cambridge University Press; Hur, Y., and Bouchard, T. 1997. The genetic correlation between impulsivity and sensation seeking traits. *Behavior Genetics,* 27(5): 455–463; Tellegen, A., Lykken, D., Bouchard, T. Wilcox, K., Segal, N., and Rich, A. 1988. Personality similarity in twins reared together and apart. *Journal of Personality and Social Psychology,* 54(6): 1031–1039; Saudino, K., Gagne, J., Grant, J., Ibatoulina, A., Marytuina, T., and Ravich-Sherbo, I. 1999. Genetic and environmental influences on personality in adult Russian twins. *International Journal of Behavioral Development,* 23(2): 375–389; Jang, K., McCrae, R., Angleitner, A., Rieman, R., and Livesley, W. 1998. Heritability of facet-level traits in a cross-cultural twin sample: Support for a hierarchical model of personality. *Journal of Personality and Social Psychology,* 74(6): 1556–1565.

81. Ebstein, R. 1997. Saga of an adventure gene: Novelty seeking, substance abuse and the dopamine D4 receptor D4DR exon III repeat polymorphism. *Molecular Psychiatry,* 2(5): 381–384; Caldu, X., and Dreher, J. 2007. Hormonal and genetic influences on processing reward and social information. *Annals of New York Academy of Sciences,* 1118: 43–73; Comings et al., 59 candidate genes; Ebstein, Benjamin, and Belmaker, Behavioral genetics, genomics, and personality. In Plomin et al., *Behavioral Genetics*

82. Hamer and Copeland, *Living with Our Genes.*

83. Zuckerman, M. 2004. The shaping of personality: Genes, environments, and chance encounters. *Journal of Personality Assessment* 82(1): 11–22.

84. Nicolaou, N., Shane, S., Cherkas, L., and Spector, T. 2008. The influence of sensation seeking in the heritability of entrepreneurship. *Strategic Entrepreneurship Journal,* 2(1): 7–21.

85. Keller, L., Arvey, R., Bouchard, T., Segal, N., and Davis, R. 1992. Work values: genetic and environmental influences. *Journal of Applied Psychology,* 77(1): 79–88; Bouchard and Loehlin, Genes, evolution and personality; Loehlin, J., Neiderhiser, J., and Reiss, J. 2003. The behavior genetics of personality and the NEAD study. *Journal of Research in Personality,* 37(5): 373–387.

86. Rauch and Frese, Born an entrepreneur? In Baum, Frese, and Baron, *Psychology of Entrepreneurship;*

Hartmann, T. 2002. *ADHD Secrets of Success.* New York: Select Books; Rauch and Frese, Let's put the person.

87. Rauch and Frese, Born an entrepreneur? In Baum, Frese, and Baron, *Psychology of Entrepreneurship;* Zhao and Seibert. Big five and entrepreneurial status; Stewart, W., and Roth, P. 2001. Risk propensity differences between entrepreneurs and managers: A meta analytic review. *Journal of Applied Psychology,* 86(1): 145–153; Rauch and Frese, Let's put the person.

88. Wyly, *1,000 Dollars and an Idea,* p. 54.

89. Anohkin, A., Golsheykin, S., Grant, J., and Health, A. 2009. Heritability of risk taking in adolescence: A longitudinal twin study. *Twin Research and Human Genetics,* 12(4): 366–371.

90. Caldu and Dreher, Influences on reward and social information.

91. Rauch and Frese, Let's put the person.

92. Ekelund, J., Johansson, E., Jarvelin, M., and Lichtermann, D. 2005. Self-employment from risk aversion-evidence from psychological test data. *Labour Economics*, 12(5): 649–659.

93. Rauch and Frese, Born an entrepreneur? In Baum, Frese, and Baron, *Psychology of Entrepreneurship;* Rauch and Frese, Let's put the person; Stewart and Roth, Risk propensity differences.

94. Uusitalo, R. 2001. Homo entreprenaurus? *Applied Economics*, 33(13): 1631–1638; Blanchflower, D. 2004. Self-employment: More may not be better. *Swedish Economic Policy Review*, 11(2): 15–74.

95. Harrison, *Instinct*, pp. 30–31.

96. Young, R., and Francis, J. 1991. Entrepreneurship and innovation in small manufacturing firms. *Social Science Quarterly*, 72(1): 149–162; Hills, G., and Singh, R. 2004. Opportunity recognition. In W. Gartner, K. Shaver, N. Carter, and P. Reynolds (eds.), *Handbook of Entrepreneurial Dynamics*, Thousand Oaks, CA: Sage, 259–272; Cooper, A., and Dunkelberg, W. 1987. Entrepreneurship research: Old questions, new answers and methodological issues. *American Journal of Small Business*, 11(3): 11–23.

97. Segal, N. 1999. *Entwined Lives*, New York: Penguin Books.

98. Le, A. 1999. Empirical studies of self-employment. *Journal of Economic Surveys*, 13(4): 381–416.

Chapter 10

1. Carey, G. 2003. *Human Genetics for the Social Sciences*, Beverley Hills, CA: Sage; Ashenfelter, O., and Krueger, A. 1994. Estimates of the economic return to schooling from a new sample of twins. *American Economic Review*, 84(5): 1157–1172; Miller, P., Mulvey, C., and Martin, N. 1995. What do twin studies reveal about the economic returns to education: A comparison of Australian and U.S. findings? *American Economic Review*, 85(3): 586–599; Rouse, C. 1999. Further estimates of the economic returns to schooling from a new sample of twins. *Economics of Education Review*, 18(2): 149–157.

2. Behrman, J., Hrubec, Z., Taubman, P., and Wales, T. 1980. *Socioeconomic Success: A Study of the Effects of Genetic Endowments, Family Environment, and Schooling*, Amsterdam: North-Holland Publishing Company.

3. Ashenfelter and Krueger, Return to schooling; Behrman, J., and Taubman, P. 1989. Is schooling 'mostly in the genes?' *Journal of Political Economy*, 97(6): 1425–1446.

4. Schnittker, J. 2008. Happiness and success: Genes, families, and the psychological effects of socioeconomic position and social support. *American Journal of Sociology*, 114(S): S233-S259.

5. Johnson, W., and Krueger, R. 2006. How money buys happiness: Genetic and environmental processes linking finances and life satisfaction. *Journal of Personality and Social Psychology*, 90(4): 680–691.

6. Lichtenstein, P., Pedersen, N., and McClearn, G. 1992. The origins of individual differences in occupational status and educational level. *Acta Sociologica*, 35(1): 13–31; Tambs, K., Sundet, M., Magnus, P., and Berg, F. 1989. Genetic and environmental contributions to the covariance between occupational status, educational attainment, and IQ: A study of twins. *Behavior Genetics*, 19(2): 209–222; Behrman et al., *Socioeconomic Success*.

7. Ilies, R., Arvey, R., and Bouchard, T. 2006. Darwinism, behavioral genetics, and organizational behavior: A review and agenda for future research. *Journal of Organizational Behavior*, 27(2): 121–141.

8. Oakley, B. 2008. *Evil Genes*, New York: Prometheus Books.

9. McCall, B., Cavanaugh, M., and Arvey, R. 1997. Genetic influences on job and occupational switching. *Journal of Vocational Behavior,* 50(1): 60–77.

10. Baker, L. 1986. Estimating genetic correlations among discontinuous phenotypes: An analysis of criminal convictions and psychiatric-hospital diagnoses in Danish adoptees. *Behavior Genetics,* 16(1): 127–142; Baker, L., Mack, A., Moffit, T., and Mednick, S. 1989. Sex differences in property crime in a Danish adoption cohort. *Behavior Genetics,* 19(3): 355–370; Mednick, S., Gabrielli, W., and Hutchings, B. 1984. Genetic influences in criminal convictions: Evidence from an adoption cohort. *Science,* 224(4651): 891–893; Segal, N. 1999. *Entwined Lives,* New York: Penguin Books; Carey, G. 1992. Twin imitation for antisocial behavior: Implications for genetic and family environment research. *Journal of Abnormal Psychology,* 101(1): 18–25; Cattell, R., 1982. *The Inheritance of Personality and Ability,* New York: Academic Press.

11. Garrett, B. 2009. *Brain and Behavior,* Los Angeles: Sage.

12. Oakley, *Evil Genes.*

13. Ibid.

14. Vernon, P., Villani, V., Vickers, L., and Harris, J. 2008. A behavioral genetic investigation of the Dark Triad and the Big 5. *Personality and Individual Differences,* 44(1): 445–452.

15. Judge, T., Hurst, C., and Simon, L. 2009. Does it pay to be smart, attractive or confident (or all three)? Relationships among general mental ability, physical attrctiveness, core self-evaluations, and income. *Journal of Applied Psychology,* 94(3): 742–755.

16. Plomin, R. 2002. General cognitive ability. In R. Plomin, J. DeFries, I. Craig, and P. McGuffin (eds.), *Behavioral Genetics in the Postgenomic Era,* Washington, DC: American Psychological Association, 141–161.

17. O'Reilly, C., and Chatman, J. 1994. Working smarter and harder: A longitudinal study of managerial success. *Administrative Science Quarterly,* 39(4): 603–627.

18. Robbins, S., and Judge, T. 2009. *Organizational Behavior,* 13th edition. Upper Saddle River, NJ: Prentice-Hall.

19. O'Reilly and Chatman, Working smarter and harder.

20. Schmidt, F., Ones, D., and Hunter, J. 1992. Personnel selection. *Annual Review of Psychology,* 43: 627–670.

21. Behling, O. 1998. Employee selection: will intelligence and conscientiouoness do the job? *Academy of Management Executive,* 12(1): 77–86; O'Reilly and Chatman, Working smarter and harder.

22. Behling, Employee selection.

23. Feinstein, L. 1999. The relative economic importance, psychological and behavioural attributes developed in childhood. Working paper, London School of Economics and Political Science.

24. Harper, B., and Haq, M. 1997. Occupational attainment of men in Britain. *Oxford Economic Papers,* 49(4): 638–650.

25. Ilies, Arvey, and Bouchard, Darwinism.

26. Granovetter, M. 1974. *Getting a Job,* Ph.D. dissertation, Harvard University.

27. Borocz, J., and Southworth, C. 1998. "Who you know": Earning effects of formal and informal social network resources under late state socialism in Hungary, 1986–87. *Journal of Socio-Economics,* 27(3): 401–425.

28. Shisshkin, P. 2009. Genes and the friends you make. *Wall Street Journal,* January 27, B2.

29. Neiss, M., Sedikides, C., and Stevenson, J. 2006. Genetic influences on level and stability of self-esteem. *Self and Identity*, 5(3): 247–266.

30. Wang, L., Kick, E., Fraser, J., and Burns, T. 1999. Status attainment in America: The roles of locus of control and self-esteem in educational and occupational outcomes. *Sociological Spectrum*, 19(3): 281–298.

31. Feinstein, Attributes developed in childhood; Goldsmith, A., Veum, J., and Darity, W. 1997. The impact of psychological and human capital on wages. *Economic Inquiry*, 35(4): 815–829.

32. Viken, R., Rose, R., Kaprio, J., and Koskenvuo, M. 1994. A developmental genetic analysis of adult personality: Extraversion and neuroticism from 18 to 59 years of age. *Journal of Personality and Social Psychology*, 66(4): 722–730; Lesch, K. Bengel, D., Heils, S., Sabol, Z., Greenberg, B., Petri, J., Benjamin, C., Muller, C., Hamer, D., and Murphy, D. 1996. Association of anxiety-related traits with a polymorphism in the serotonin transporter gene regulatory region. *Science*, 274 (5292): 1527–1531; Hamer, D., Greenberg, B., Sabol, S., and Murphy, D. 1999. Role of the serotonin transporter gene in temperament and character. *Journal of Personality Disorders*, 13(4): 312–328; Benjamin, J., Ebstein, R., and Lesch, K. 1998. Genes for personality traits: Implications for psychopathology. *International Journal of Neuropsychopharmacology*, 1(2): 153–168; Comings, D., Gade-Andavolu, R., Gonzalez, N., Wu, S., Muhleman, D., Blake, H., Mann, M, Dietz, G., Saucier, G., and MacMurray, J. 2000. A multivariate analysis of 59 candidate genes in personality traits: The temperament and character inventory. *Clinical Genetics*, 58(5): 375–385; Ebstein, R., Benjamin, J., and Belmaker, R. 2002. Behavioral genetics, genomics, and personality. In Plomin et al., *Behavioral Genetics*, 265–388; Zuckerman, M., and Kuhlman, D. 2000. Personality and risk taking: Common biosocial factors. *Journal of Personality*, 68(6): 999–1029; Reif, A., and Lesch, K. 2003. Towards a molecular architecture of personality. *Behavioral Brain Research*, 139(1): 1–20; Lesch, K. 2002. Neuroticism and serotonin: A developmental genetic perspective. 2002. Behavioral genetics, genomics, and personality. In Plomin et al., *Behavioral Genetics*, 389–423.

33. Nyhus, E., and Pons, E. 2005. The effects of personality on earnings. *Journal of Economic Psychology*, 26(3): 363–384.

34. Bouchard, T., McGue, M., Hur, Y., and Horn, J. 1998. A genetic and environmental analysis of the California Psychological Inventory using adult twins reared apart and together. *European Journal of Personality*, 12(5): 307–320; Bouchard, T., and McGue, M. 1990. Genetic and rearing environmental influences on adult personality: An analysis of twins reared apart. *Journal of Personality* 58(1): 263–282; Jang, K., McCrae, R., Angleitner, A., Riemann, R., and Livesay, W. 1998. Heritability of facet-level traits in a cross-cultural twin sample: Support for a hierarchical model of personality *Journal of Personality*, 74(6): 1556–1565; Jang, K., Livesay, W., and Vernon, P. 1996. Heritability of the big five personality dimensions and their facets: A twin study. *Journal of Personality*, 64(3): 577–591; Loehlin, J., and Nichols, J. 1976. *Heredity, Environment, and Personality*, Austin: University of Texas Press; Horn, J., Plomin, R., and Roseman, R. 1976. Heritability of personality traits in adult male twins. *Behavior Genetics*, 6(1): 17–30; Tellegen, A., Bouchard, T., Wilcox, K., Segal, N., Lykken, D., and Roch, S. 1988. Personality similarity in twins reared apart and together. *Journal of Personality and Social Psychology*, 54(6): 1031–1039; Beer, J., Arnold, R., and Loehlin, J. 1998. Genetic and Environmental Influences on MMPI Factor Scales: Joint Model Fitting to Twin and Adoption Data. *Journal of Personality and Social Psychology*, 74(3): 818–827; Bergeman, C., Chipuer,

H., Plomin, R., Pedersen, N., McClearn, G., Nesselroade, J., Costa, P., and McCrae, R. 1993. Genetic and environmental effects on openness to experience, agreeableness, and conscientiousness: An adoption/twin study. *Journal of Personality*, 61(2): 159–176; Noble, E., Ozkaragoz, T., Ritchie, T., Zhang, X, Belin, T., and Sparkes, R. 1998. D_2 and D_4 dopamine receptor polymorphisms and personality. *American Journal of Medical Genetics*, 81(3): 257–267; Benjamin, J., Li, L., Patterson, C., Greenberg, B., Murphy, D., and Hamer, D. 1996. Population and familial association between the D4 dopamine receptor gene and measures of sensation seeking. *Nature Genetics*, 12: 81–84; Comings et al., 59 candidate genes; Hamer et al., Serotonin transporter gene; Ebstein, Benjamin, and Belmaker, Behavioral genetics. In Plomin et al., *Behavioral Genetics*, 265–388; Plomin, R., and Caspi, A. 1998. DNA and Personality. *European Journal of Personality*, 12(5): 387–407; Reif and Lesch, Molecular architecture; Hamer, D. 2004. *The God Gene*, New York: Doubleday; Ebstein, R., Segman, R., Benjamin, J., Osher, Y., Nemanov, L., and Belmaker, R. 1997. $5HT_{2C}$ serotonin receptor gene polymorphism associated with the human personality trait of reward dependence: Interaction with dopamine D4 receptor (D4DR) and dopamine D3 Receptor (D3DR) polymorphisms. *American Journal of Medical Genetics*, 74(1): 65–72.

35. Nyhus and Pons, Personality on earnings; Barrick, M. R., and Mount, M. K. 1991. The Big Five personality dimensions and job performance: A meta-analysis. Personnel Psychology, 44(1): 1–26.

36. Behling, Employee selection.

37. Barrick and Mount, Big five.

38. Behling, Employee selection.

39. Comings et al., 59 candidate genes; Comings, D., Gonzalez, N., Wu, S., Gade, R., Muhleman, D., Saucier, G., Johnson, P., Verde, R., Rosenthal, R., Lesieur, H., Rugle, L., Miller, W., and MacMurray, J. 1999. Studies of the 48 bp repeat polymorphism of the DRD4 gene in impulsive, compulsive, and addictive behaviors: Tourette syndrome, ADHD, pathological gambling, and substance abuse. *American Journal of Medical Genetics*, 88(4): 358–368; Lesch et al., Association of anxiety; Reif and Lesch, Molecular architecture; Hamer et al., Serotonin transporter gene.

40. DiLalla, D., Carey, G., Gottesman, I., and Bouchard, T. 1996. Heritability of MMPI personality indicators of psychopathology. *Journal of Abnormal Psychology*, 105(4): 491–499; Bouchard et al., California Psychological Inventory; Jang et al., Heritability of facet level traits; Loehlin, and Nichols, *Heredity, Environment, and Personality*; Tellegen et al. Personality similarity; Beer and Loehlin, MMPI Factor Scales; Eid, M., Reimann, R., Angleitner, A., Borkenau, P. 2003. Sociability and positive emotionality: Genetic and environmental contributions to the covariation between different facets of extraversion. 74(3): 319–346; Loehlin, J. 1992. *Genes and the Environment in Personality Development*, Newbury Park, CA: Sage Publications. Rushton, P., Fulker, D., Neale, M., Nias, D., and Eysenk, H. 1986. Altruisim and aggression: The heritability of individual differences. *Journal of Personality and Social Psychology*, 50(6): 1192–1198; Heath, A., Cloninger, C., and Martin, N. 1994. Testing a model for the genetic structure of personality: A comparison of the personality systems of Cloninger and Eysenck. *Journal of Personality and Social Psychology*, 66(4): 762–775.

41. Robbins and Judge, *Organizational Behavior*.

42. Rowe, D., and Osgood, D. 1984. Heredity and sociological theories of delinquency: A reconsideration. *American Sociological Review*, 49(4): 526–540.

43. Carey, *Human Genetics*; Zuckerman, M. 2005. *Psychobiology of Personality,* Cambridge, UK: Cambridge University Press; Bouchard, T., and Hur, J. 1998. Genetic and environmental influences on the continuous scales of the Myers-Briggs type indicator: An analysis based on twins reared apart. *Journal of Personality,* 66(2): 135–149; Loehlin, *Genes and the Environment;* Benjamin et al., D4 dopamine receptor; Strobel; A, Wehr, A, Michel, A, and Brocke, B. 1999. Association between the dopamine D4 receptor (DRD4) exon III polymorphism and measures of novelty seeking in a German population. *Molecular Psychiatry,* 4(4): 378–384; Farde, L., and Gusavsson, J. 1997. D2 dopamine receptors and personality traits. *Nature,* 385 (6617): 590.

44. Behling, Employee selection; Feinstein, Attributes developed in childhood; Robbins and Judge, *Organizational Behavior.*

45. Loehlin, *Genes and the Environment;* Bouchard, T., and Loehlin, J. 2001. Genes, evolution and personality. *Behavior Genetics,* 31(3): 243–273; Comings et al., 48 bp repeat polymorphism.

46. Behling, Employee selection.

47. Pinker, S. 2008. *The Sexual Paradox: Men, Women, and the Real Gender Gap,* New York: Scribner.

48. Plomin, R. 1994. *Genetics and Experience: The Interplay between Nature and Nurture,* Thousand Oaks, CA: Sage; Hamer, D., and Copeland, P. 1999. *Living with Our Genes,* New York: Anchor Books; Plomin, R., Scheier, M., Bergeman, C., Pedersen, N., Nesselroade, J., and McClearn, G. 1992. Optimism, pessimism, and mental health: A twin/adoption analysis. *Personality and Individual Differences,* 13(8): 921–930.

49. Zuckerman, M. 1994. *Behavioral Expressions and Biosocial Bases of Sensation Seeking,* Cambridge, UK: Cambridge University Press; Schooler, C., Zahn, T., Murphy, D., and Buschbaum, M. 1978. Psychological correlates of monoamine oxidase activity in normals. *The Journal of Nervous and Mental Disease,* 166(3): 177–186; Zuckerman, M., Buschbaum, M., and Murphy, D. 1980. Sensation seeking and its biological correlates. *Psychological Bulletin,* 88(1): 187–214; Hamer and Copeland, *Living with Our Genes;* Reif and Lesch, Molecular architecture.

50. Schnittker, Happiness and success.

51. Staw, B., and Cohen-Charash, Y. The dispositional approach to job satisfaction: more than a mirage, but not yet an oasis. *Journal of Organizational Behavior,* 26(1): 59–78; George, J. 1992. The role of personality in organizational life: Issues and evidence. *Journal of Management,* 18(2): 185–213.

52. George, Role of personality.

53. Schnittker, Happiness and success.

54. Plomin, R., Pedersen, N., McClearn, G., Nesselroade, J., and Bergeman, C. 1988. EAS temperaments during the last half of the life span: Twins reared apart and twins reared together. *Psychology and Aging,* 3(1): 43–50; Scarr, S. 1966. Genetic factors in activity motivation. *Child Development,* 37(3): 663–673; Rutter, M. 2006. *Genes and Behavior,* Oxford, UK: Blackwell; Sherman, D., McGue, M., and Iacono, W. 1997. Twin concordances for attention deficit hyperactivity disorder: A comparison of teachers' and mothers' reports. *American Journal of Psychiatry,* 154(4): 532–535.

55. Waldman, I., and Gizer, I. 2006. The genetics of attention deficit hyperactivity disorder. *Clinical Psychology Review,* 26(4): 396–432; Cook, E, Stein, M., Krasowski, M., Cox, N., Olkon, D., Kieffer, J., and Leventhal, B. 1995. Association of attention-deficit disorder and the dopamine transporter gene. *American*

Journal of Human Genetics, 56(4): 993–998; Castellanos, F., and Tannock, R. 2002. Neuroscience of attention-deficit/hyperactivity disorder: The search for endophenotypes. *Nature Reviews,* 3(8): 617–629; Waldman and Gizer, Genetics of attention deficit; Comings et al., 48 bp repeat polymorphism; Okuyama, Y., Ishiuro, H., Nankai, M., Shibuya, H., Watanabe, A., and Arinami, T. 2000. Identification of a polymorphism in the promoter region of DRD4 associated with the human novelty seeking personality trait. *Molecular Psychiatry,* 5(1): 64–69; Plomin, R., DeFries, J., McClearn, G., and McGuffin, P. 2001. *Behavioral Genetics.* New York: Worth Publishers; Spector, T. 2003. *Your Genes Unzipped,* London: Robson Books; Blum, K., Sheridan, P., Wood, R., Braverman, E., Chen, T., Cull, J., and Comings, D. 1996. The dopamine receptor gene as a determinant of reward difficiency syndrome. *Journal of the Royal Society of Medicine,* 89(7): 396–400; Ebstein, R., Benjamin, J., and Belmaker, R. 2002. Behavioral genetics, genomics, and personality. In Plomin et al., *Behavioral Genetics,* 265–388.

56. Kessler, R., Adler, L., Ames, M., Barkley, R., Birnbaum, H., Greenberg, P., Johnston, J., Spencer, T., and Ustun, T. 2005. The prevalence and effects of adult attention deficit/hyperactivity disorder on work performance in a nationally representative sample of workers. *Journal of Occupational Medicine,* 47(6): 565–572.

57. Johnson, W., and Krueger, R. 2005. Higher perceived life control decreases genetic variance in physical health: Evidence from a national twin study. *Journal of Personality and Social Psychology,* 88(1): 165–173.

58. Carey, *Human Genetics.*

59. Guo, G., Roettger, M., and Cai, T. 2008. The integration of genetic propensities into social control models of delinquency and violence among male youths. *American Sociological Review,* 73(6): 543–568.

60. O'Reilly and Chatman, Working smarter and harder.

Chapter 11

1. Anonymous. 2009. Mysterious ways. *The Economist,* January 22. Downloaded from http://www.economist.com/science/displaystory.cfm?story_-id=12971012

2. Reuter, M., Roth, S., Holve, K., and Hennig, J. 2006. Identification of the first candidate genes for creativity. *Brain Research,* 1609(1): 190–197.

3. Noble, E., Ozkaragoz, T., Ritchie, T., Zhang, X, Belin, T., and Sparkes, R. 1998. D$_2$ and D$_4$ dopamine receptor polymorphisms and personality. *American Journal of Medical Genetics,* 81(3): 257–267; Benjamin, J., Li, L., Patterson, C., Greenberg, B., Murphy, D., and Hamer, D. 1996. Population and familial association between the D4 dopamine receptor gene and measures of sensation seeking. *Nature Genetics,* 12: 81–84; Comings, D., Gade-Andavolu, R., Gonzalez, N., Wu, S., Muhleman, D., Blake, H., Mann, M, Dietz, G., Saucier, G., and MacMurray, J. 2000. A multivariate analysis of 59 candidate genes in personality traits: The temperament and character inventory. *Clinical Genetics,* 58(5): 375–385; Hamer, D., Greenberg, B., Sabol, S., and Murphy, D. 1999. Role of the serotonin transporter gene in temperament and character. *Journal of Personality Disorders,* 13 (4): 312–328; Ebstein, R., Benjamin, J., and Belmaker, R. 2002. Behavioral genetics, genomics, and personality. In R. Plomin, J. DeFries, I. Craig, and P. McGuffin (eds.), *Behavioral Genetics in the Postgenomic Era,* Washington, DC: American

Psychological Association, 265–388; Plomin, R., and Caspi, A. 1998. DNA and Personality. *European Journal of Personality*, 12(5): 387–40; Ebstein, R., Segman, R., Benjamin, J., Osher, Y., Nemanov, L., and Belmaker, R. 1997. 5HT$_{2C}$ serotonin receptor gene polymorphism associated with the human personality trait of reward dependence: Interaction with dopamine D4 receptor (D4DR) and dopamine D3 receptor (D3DR) polymorphisms. *American Journal of Medical Genetics*, 74 (1): 65–72; Reif and Lesch, K. 2003. Towards a molecular architecture of personality. *Behavioral Brain Research*, 139(1): 1–20; Hamer, D. 2004. *The God Gene*, New York: Doubleday; Jang, K., Livesley, W., Reimann, R., Vernon, P., Hu, S., Angleitner, A., Ando, J., Ono, Y., and Hamer, D. 2001. Covariance structure of neuroticism and agreeableness: A twin and molecular genetic analysis of the role of the serotonin transporter gene. *Journal of Personality and Social Psychology*, 81(2): 295–304.

4. Robbins and Judge, *Organizational Behavior*.

5. http://www.psychologycampus.com/industrial-psychology/job-satisfaction.html

6. http://freewill.typepad.com/genetics/leaders_and_followers/index.html

7. Nuffield Council on Bioethics. 2002. *Genetics and Human Behaviour*. London: Nuffield Council on Bioethics, p. 183.

8. Zhang, J., and Wang, S, 2008. Bill on genetic bias advances. *Wall Street Journal*, April 24: A11. Downloaded from http://online.wsj.com/article/SB120905087417041813.html?mod=fox_australian

9. Robbins and Judge, *Organizational Behavior*.

10. Nuffield Council on Bioethics. *Genetics and Human Behaviours*.

11. Ibid.

12. Robbins and Judge, *Organizational Behavior*.

13. Sorcher, M., and Brant, J. 2002. Are you picking the right leaders? *Harvard Business Review*, 80(2): 78–85.

14. http://freewill.typepad.com/genetics/2005/03/leadership_abil.html

15. Robbins and Judge, *Organizational Behavior*.

16. Staw, B., Bell, N., and Clausen, J. 1986. The dispositional approach to job attitudes: A lifetime longitudinal test. *Administrative Science Quarterly*, 31(1): 56–77.

17. Segal, N. 1999. New twin studies show…The career of your dreams may be the career of your genes. *Psychology Today*, September/October, 54–70.

18. Staw, Bell, and Clausen, Dispositional approach.

19. Hamer, D., and Copeland, P. 1999. *Living with Our Genes*, New York: Anchor Books, p.47.

20. http://www.hhs.gov/myhealthcare/genetictests/genetictests.html

21. Hamer and Copeland, *Living with Our Genes*.

22. Arvey, R., Rotundo, M., Johnson, W., Zhand, Z., and McGue, M. 2006. The determinants of leadership role occupancy: Genetic and personality factors. *The Leadership Quarterly*, 17(1): 1–20.

23. Furnham, A., Forde, L., and Ferrari, K. 1999. Personality and work motivation. *Personality and Individual Differences*, 26(6): 1035–1043.

24. Connolly, J., and Viswesvaran, C. 2000. The role of affectivity in job satisfaction: A meta-analysis. *Personality and Individual Differences*, 29(2): 265–281.

25. Zuckerman, M. 1994. *Behavioral Expressions and Biosocial Bases of Sensation Seeking*. Cambridge, UK: Cambridge University Press; Schooler, C., Zahn, T.,

Murphy, D., and Buschbaum, M. 1978. Psychological correlates of monoamine oxidase activity in normals. *The Journal of Nervous and Mental Disease,* 166(3): 177–186; Zuckerman, M., Buschbaum, M., and Murphy, D. 1980. Sensation seeking and its biological correlates. *Psychological Bulletin,* 88(1): 187–214; Hamer and Copeland, *Living with Our Genes;* Reif and Lesch, Molecular architecture.

26. Judge, T., and Larsen, R. 2001. Dispositional affect and job satisfaction: A review and theoretical extension. *Organizational Behavior and Human Decision Processes,* 86(1): 67–98.

27. Hamer and Copeland, *Living with Our Genes.*

28. http://www.google.com/search?hl=en&defl=en&q=define:Hindsight + Bias&sa=X&oi=glossary_definition&ct=title

29. Zweig, J. 2009. Is your investing personality in your DNA? *Wall Street Journal,* April 4–5: B1, downloaded from http://online.wsj.com/article/SB123879381940987845.html

30. Simonton, D. 2001. Talent development as a multidimensional, multiplicative, and dynamic process, *Current Directions in Psychological Science,* 10(2): 39–43.

31. Robbins and Judge, *Organizational Behavior.*

32. Harrison, T. 2005. *Instinct,* New York: Warner Business Books, p. 13.

33. Robbins and Judge, *Organizational Behavior.*

34. Keller, L., Arvey, R., Bouchard, T., Segal, N., and Davis, R. 1992. Work values: genetic and environmental influences. *Journal of Applied Psychology,* 77(1): 79–88.

35. Robbins and Judge, *Organizational Behavior.*

36. Harrison, *Instinct.*

Index